SOUL BETWEEN
THE LINES

SOUL BETWEEN THE LINES

FREEING YOUR CREATIVE SPIRIT THROUGH WRITING

DOROTHY RANDALL GRAY

AVON BOOKS ◆ NEW YORK

The author is grateful for the permisssion to reprint from "Father and Daughter" by Sonia Sanchez. Published by The Third Press.

From *The Miracle of Metaphysical Healing* by Evelyn Monahan. Copyright © 1975. Reprinted with permisssion of Prentice Hall.

Excerpt from *Women's Rituals: A Sourcebook* by Barbara G. Walker. Copyright © 1990 by Barbara G. Walker. Reprinted by permission of HarperCollins Publishers, Inc.

Dictionary definitions from Merriam-Webster's Collegiate Dictionary, 10th Edition. Copyright 1996.

Excerpt from *Uprising* from *Milking Black Bull: 11 Gay Black Poets* by G. Winston James. Copyright © 1995 by G. Winston James. Reprinted by permission of Vega Press.

Excerpt from *At Seventy* by May Sarton. Copyright © 1984 by May Sarton. Reprinted by permission of W. W. Norton & Company, Inc.

Reprinted with permission from *Zami: A New Spelling of My Name* by Audre Lorde. Copyright © 1982. Published by The Crossing Press: Freedom, CA.

"The Dead Get By with Everything" by Bill Holm was published in *The Dead Get By with Everything* (Milkweed Editions, 1990). Copyright © 1990 by Bill Holm. Reprinted with permisssion from Milkweed Editions.

AVON BOOKS

A division of
The Hearst Corporation
1350 Avenue of the Americas
New York, New York 10019

Copyright © 1998 by Dorothy Randall Gray
Inside back cover author photograph by Ann E. Chapman
Foreword © 1998 by Luisah Teish
Interior design by Kellan Peck
Published by arrangement with the author
Visit our website at http://www.AvonBooks.com
ISBN: 0-380-79142-0

Library of Congress Cataloging in Publication Data:

Gray, Dorothy Randall.
  Soul between the lines : freeing your creative spirit through writing / Dorothy Randall Gray.
    p. cm.
  1. Authorship. 2. Conduct of life. I. Title.
PN147.G68 1998   97-36440
808'.02—dc21   CIP

First Avon Books Trade Printing: March 1998

AVON TRADEMARK REG. U.S. PAT. OFF. AND IN OTHER COUNTRIES, MARCA REGISTRADA, HECHO EN U.S.A.

Printed in the U.S.A.

OPM 10 9 8 7 6 5 4 3 2 1

This book is dedicated to Hannelore Hahn,
executive director and founder of the
International Women's Writing Guild.
She believed I could fly
before I knew I had wings.

Contents

Foreword

by Luisah Teish

Dear Reader:

Open the book, and the Seal is broken. Now the energy of your evolutionary heritage, the power of your ancestral memory, and the beauty of your personal experiences will come into the light of conscious creativity.

Soul Between the Lines was conceived by the grace of Inner Authority, born from the belly of a Black Madonna, and raised in the community of spiritual growth. Its offerings are food for the mind and medicine for the soul.

Each of these chapters connects us to nature. Reading them will help you to reach for the stars while sending your roots deep into the earth. Each exercise connects us to ourselves. We are inspired to explore our deepest recesses and encouraged to render our souls into sentence.

When that which was hidden is brought into the light, it affects all who look upon it. We get to see ourselves, each other, and the energy patterns that hold our lives in place. Once these are revealed, we can transform the trash into compost, awaken dormant seeds, and reap a bountiful harvest. These are acts of Natural Magic.

Reader, you need this book and it has come to you for a reason. Some of you will produce marketable writings as a result of working with this book. Others will reap the benefit of personal fulfillment.

I need this book for several reasons. It keeps me focused on the *privilege* of writing from a spiritual perspective. It renews the *romance* of writing and provides me with a wonderful text for all kinds of classes. We all need this book because it connects our heads to our hearts and to our powerful creativity. It is revealing, empowering, and consequently healing.

Have no fear, release your reservations. Everything in this book works, so there is no failure. This book is beautifully written. Turn the page and enjoy your journey through the Heartland.

Ache O,
Teish

Luisah Teish is an internationally acclaimed storyteller, actress, teacher of African spirituality, and priestess of Oshun. She is author of *Jambalaya: The Natural Woman's Book of Personal Charms and Practical Rituals,* Harper & Row (1986), and *Carnival of the Spirit,* HarperSanFrancisco (1994).
Heartland

Home

When you think about situations and circumstances, places and people that somehow brought major changes into your life, what you are thinking about is transformation. Whether transformation is pleasant or painful, inspiring or traumatic, one thing is certain: After it happens, you are never the same. As you begin your journey into the Heartland, take time to think about the moments of transformation that have taken place in your life.

Everyone has a story to tell, a film they could make, a scene they could paint, or a song they could sing about the changes life has handed to them. Think about the words "And I was never the same" and see what comes to mind. I will be asking you to do this throughout the book. You may as well start now. This is where I'll begin.

I was drowning. The powerful undertow at Fire Island had me in its grip. I was being pulled farther and farther out to sea. The beach was deserted. The houses along the shore were too far away to hear a cry for help. I was swallowing salt water and gasping for air. I didn't know how to swim. My limbs flailed in a desperate dog paddle. They were weak and useless against the strong arm of the ocean. And I was getting tired.

It had been a perfect beach day. The sun blossomed with warmth and promise. The breeze blew off the ocean like a lover's kiss. At eight in the morning, my housemates were still asleep. The waves called me to an early romp in their waters. I slipped past the deer nibbling nearby, toward the excitement of an entire beach to myself, smiling as if headed for a rendezvous.

I stood on the sand with my arms outstretched chanting, "Ye-maya, Yemaya. Here I am, Yemaya." I had known she was an African spirit of the ocean and thought it only right to call her name before entering her realm. I waded in waist-deep and began playing my usual game. As a wave came near, I would jump just beyond the crest of it, then ride its breaking waters back to the safety of the shore. It felt like original joy to be lifted up and carried back to the ocean's edge. I was a child once more, splashing in the cool wetness at Coney Island and digging my way to China.

I was having so much fun, I hardly noticed that my feet were returning to the sand less and less often. Soon they weren't touching it at all. The waves kept coming, each one taking me farther away. I tried pushing my way back, but the ocean had other ideas. I was fifty feet away from dry land now. My orange towel was a distant speck. I was drowning and no one was around to save me.

I struggled to keep afloat. The seagulls watched and the sky stood by. Salt water burned my throat. Each time I coughed, more of its bitterness invaded my mouth. There seemed to be no point to panic, but I knew I couldn't fight much longer. Then, the thought came to me, *I'm not ready to go yet. I'm not ready to go.* Suddenly I stopped struggling. I relaxed and surrendered my body. I stretched out my arms, looked to the sky, and cried out, "Please take me home!"

From the middle of the ocean, a huge wave rose up twenty feet in the air and came crashing down on my head. It pushed me deep into the ocean's belly. I rolled through the water like a child tumbling downhill. I thought I would never see the light of day again. When I surfaced, I was closer to shore, but still unable to touch the land. I coughed salt water and prayers.

Once more I held my arms out and calmed myself. I lifted my head and asked again, "Please, take me all the way home!" Another wave even larger than the last rose from the water like a monument, and fell on me with the force of stone. Sand and salt and sea creatures invaded every part of my body. My lungs threatened to burst. I broke through the water's skin choking and spitting. I was much closer now. I could just about feel sand touching the tip of my toes. With my last strength, I paddled and stroked against the undercurrent.

Finally I was on solid ground again. I stumbled out of the water, clinging to life and the sweet taste of the morning air. I pulled myself up as best I could, turned around to face the ocean, and whispered, "Thank you. Thank you." Then my legs left me, and I collapsed onto the bright sanctuary of my towel.

Each year, experienced swimmers drown in the waters of Fire Island, their considerable skills no match for the ancient wits of the ocean. I might have been among the countless names mentioned briefly in local papers, then forgotten. Instead, I was brought home again. Maybe the ocean mother took pity on me and threw me back like a small fish who still needed to grow. Maybe my ancestors from the Middle Passage rose up from the bones and secrets in the Atlantic Ocean to make sure I lived to tell their stories. Maybe, as the old folks say, it just wasn't my time.

Whatever the reason, I was home again, given a second chance to swim through life differently. I have learned to honor the spirit of the ocean inside me, to be thankful for the blessing of being. I have learned how to go in without going under, when to stroke and when to surrender. I have learned that I am a part of everything—the earth that holds me up, the air that breathes through me, the fire that shines in my soul, and the water that delivered me from my mother's womb and brought me home again. And I was never the same.

Acknowledgments

There is an African proverb that says, "If I stand tall, it is because I stand on the shoulders of my ancestors." I am grateful to my grandparents and parents Lizzie Kitchen, Henry Hilson, Exia Hilson Jordan, Emanuel Jordan, Adele Aneuil, Antoine Sylvestre, Rosie Randall, William Randall, Ruth Jordan Randall, Anison A. Sylvester, and John Randall for paving the path toward this incarnation.

Thank you, Angel Family Robert Jordan, Isaac Jordan, Lonnie Jordan, Christine Jordan Jackson, Mary Jordan Moye, Leroy Jordan, Yvonne Sylvester Edwards, Randy Randall, and Angel Friends Tre Johnson, Dellon Wilson, Emma Louise Cannady, Doris Kaywood, and Clarence Kaywood for sending me blessings from the other side.

Thank you, Earth Angel Family Cora Mae Jackson Brown, Annie Ruth Hawkins, Juanita Randall, Joe Hawkins, Celese Hawkins, JoJo Hawkins, Dawn Marie Loyd, Xavier Spivey, Lottie May Joiner, Ann Waller Thomas, and all my other cousins, nieces, and nephews for being family to me.

I want to give a special literary shout out to Mary Taylor, who pushed me onto the writing wagon, for which I am ever grateful; Clover Anasazi Cannady, who called me every morning for two months to make sure I stayed on the wagon; Dianne Houston, who consoled me when I fell off; John Wise, who kicked me in my literary ass when I needed to get back on; Linda Fraser and Lois Wadas, who both supported my return to the writing wagon, and even bought me a new red one.

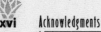

I owe a debt of gratitude to Phyllis Bretholtz and Eleanor Ott, whose financial support helped me keep the lights on; to my agent, Alice Orr, whose friendship, support, and sweet toughness helped me see my possibilities; and to my editor, Charlotte Abbott, whose unfailing enthusiasm, warmth, and support helped bring this book into the light of day.

Special thanks to Jasmine Ketcham, who patiently gave feedback on the early pages of this book; Gueniett Satyama Hyman, who fed me more than food as I wrote; and Ida Lee Watson, who kept assuring me I'd be fine.

My spirit could not possibly soar without the cherished friendship of Earth Angel Friends who have loved and tolerated me for many, many years: Dr. Shirley Elizabeth Brown Ornish, Eve Sandler, Shirley Steele, Ann Chapman, Pamela Sneed, Jamilla Johnson, Lynn Kathryn Pannell, Michelle Wright, Mavis Wiggins, Vera Boyd, Wraggs Wall, Binah Kaywood, and Nancy Cardwell.

I offer my gratitude to my spirit sisters Luisah Teish, Vivian Hester Bennerson, Suhir Black Eagle, Sister Paula Matthews, and Jane M. Howard, and to Rabbi Joseph Gelberman of The New Seminary for their spiritual wisdom.

It has truly been a blessing to have people believe in and support my Heartland workshops. My number one support has been Hannelore Hahn and the International Women's Writing Guild, whose unique blend of magic and method has transformed thousands of lives. Thank you, Bernadine Meeks of the Family Support Center, Dr. Maria Ramos of Ramos Associates, Zita Christian and the Connecticut chapter of the Romance Writers of America, Sally Booth of the Saratoga Springs chapter of the Romance Writers of America, Sandra Gould Ford of the *Shooting Star Review,* Nancy Orlen Weber of the Holistic Health Alliance, Sarah Bracey White and Emily Hanlon of the National Writer's Union, Joan Griscom of William Paterson College, and Pat Williams of the Institute for Women at Mid-Life and Beyond.

Thank you, Amanda Lichtenberg of Shades of Lavender, Susan

Hellerer of the Women's Rites Center, Ann Condon of the St. Francis Xavier Women's Circle, Myrta LeBron and Kimberly Ayoung of cable TV's *The Woman's Show,* PEN America, the Poetry Therapy Association, the Nia Collective, Gay Men of African Descent, African Ancestral Women United for Social Change, Honey Goldman, Mary Rutkovsky Ruskin, Karen Murphy, Tracy Ferdinand, Ursula Duba, Susan Hajec, and Noel Horn.

For helping me celebrate the spirit of divine madness, I thank the Five Star Egbe, my Hoochienas Bari Ellen Roberts, Chiquita Mullins Lee, Jeannetta Holiman, and Beverly Mathis, and my wild women in the woods Eleanor Ott, Tanya Russ, Jan Phillips, Cynthia Steed, Ellen Secci, and Olive Hackett Shaugnessey.

For loving help, advice, and spaces, thank you, Dr. Babette Becker, Sharifa Benepe, Jane Masi and Charlie Friedman of TRS, Kate Millett of The Farm, Bill Folkes of Randall's Ordinary Inn, Irma Quitcon, Donna Hennes, Zdena Heller, Ione, the Pauline Oliveros Foundation and my wonderful Muse Magic volunteers Eleanor Tauber, Dylan Guy, and Kmur Hardiman.

For inspiration and perspiration, thank you, Dr. Arthur Caliandro of Marble Collegiate Church, Oliver Williams and Cultural Crossroads of the Lafayette Avenue Presbyterian Church, Sonia Sanchez, Jayne Cortez, Sapphire, Laurie Carlos, Demetria Royals, Louise Diamond, Jawole Willa Jo Zollar, Edwina Lee Tyler, Elaine Pollard Lynn, Adésiña Ogunelese, June Gould, Anna Bjornsdottir, Sunneva, The Templettes, all my Heartland students, Red Hook Arts, and all the people of Red Hook, Brooklyn.

Introduction

Warning, reading this book can change your life! If you can turn these pages, you can turn on your creativity. This is a book about spirit and creation. Inside of you lives a powerful spirit. It is something you are born with, something you use every day without even thinking.

I want you to know that within this spirit is a treasure chest of unlimited creative power. Some people may think their chest is in an attic somewhere and it's too much trouble to get to. Others may know they have one but can't remember where they put it. Some already use this chest on a regular basis and might want to add some things to it.

Think of writing as the key that unlocks the chest. And as you open this chest, your spirit will bless you with greater awareness, self-discovery, and transformation.

Anyone can turn this key. *Soul Between the Lines* is about opening yourself up to your full creative entitlement and personal empowerment. If you are a painter or a poet, a sculptor or musician, a filmmaker or fiction writer, you can use this book to increase the consciousness, vision, and imagination that will make your art more powerful.

If you have been writing ten years or ten minutes or you have never written at all, you can use this book to develop emotional insight, character, and content.

If you are a spiritual seeker, these pages can help deepen your spiritual awareness and strengthen the divine connection between your inner and higher selves. If you just like reading stories, funny ones, inspirational stuff about life and the changes it puts us through, they are plenty of them in this book.

Think about it this way: When you're going on a trip, you can get there by car, take a bicycle, or board a train. You can cruise on an ocean line, hitchhike, or simply walk. No matter how you travel, the idea is to reach to your destination. Imagine that writing is your mode of transportation and the destination is your creative spirit. *Soul Between the Lines* is about taking the journey, creating the words, and arriving at the wholeness you are entitled to. I call this kind of work Writing From Your Heartland™.

Soul Between the Lines is about living and creating with your heart and soul as well as your mind and body. In it you will find dozens of provocative exercises to help you jump start your writing, meditations and affirmations to inspire you, visualizations and rituals to help you connect with your creative self. There are many fine books on the market that can tell you how to publish, find an agent, or construct stories that sell. This is not one of them.

Each chapter in this book is totally different. Each has different themes, stories, rituals, and exercises—hundreds of them, all told. You're sure to find something you can sink your teeth into. After you read all of Chapter 1, you can start with any of the other chapters. Try them on and see how they fit. Don't be afraid to let your spirit surprise you. Just walk through these pages with an open heart.

Over the seven years I have taught my Writing From Your Heartland™ workshops, I have seen my students become empowered and transformed in very deep and significant ways. These exercises, meditations, and rituals gathered from my own spirit have become powerful catalysts for others. I've seen people change jobs, lose weight, heal old hurts, launch new writing careers, connect with ancestors, close the doors on abusive relationships, and find new voices to shape their souls.

"You will never be the same!" one woman said to another

who was taking my workshop for the first time. "It's like nothing you've ever experienced," I overheard as people talked about my class at a conference. Clearly, something more than writing was happening in these workshops, something more profound than I had ever dreamed of. A rock musician credited a writing ritual of mine with helping her find a lover. An elderly man discovered his grandfather had been a Buffalo Soldier while going through a packet of old letters I had urged him not to throw away. An intimidated political speechwriter found the courage to demand a pay raise and consequently received it.

A musician whose albums had gone gold and platinum wrote, "In the safe space of Dorothy's classes, I stretched and forged ahead into uncharted territories. Found out what I could do— no limits. I received everything I needed from Dorothy's classes to successfully complete a major career transition to fiction and nonfiction writing."

A visual artist who had been blocked for years was able to reconnect with her work and paint again. After a twenty-year absence from the stage, an actor felt empowered enough to return to it at the age of 57. A video artist was able to draw powerful images from writing created in my workshop and use them for a film.

I was sitting in a restaurant one night when an African-American woman at the next table asked me about the flyer in my hands. I had just come from Sapphire's *American Dreams* book party and was reading a review of her incredible book. Bari told me her 74-year-old mother was a writer. I invited her mother to read at Muse Magic, a series I curated, and she flew in from Ohio. Afterwards, I said to Bari, "What about you? You're a writer too, you know!"

"No I'm not!" she responded. "I'm a corporate executive. My mother's the writer."

For two years, I sent her announcements about my writing workshops and urged her to come to International Women's Writing Guild conferences. I mentioned writing whenever I saw her. Nothing moved her. Later, I learned she always threw my flyers away as soon as she took them out of the mailbox.

One spring Bari injured her foot and her daughter had to bring the mail in for her. As she looked through the letters placed on her bed, she noticed yet another of my flyers. On this one there was a photo of my face. She decided to throw away that and other junk mail right after her nap. When Bari woke up, she discovered that my face had become stuck to hers. "All right, all right, Dorothy!" she yelled at the flyer. "I'll take your class!"

In the course of the workshop, she discovered she had all kinds of stories to tell—stories about her childhood in segregated Ohio, trips to church with her father, a heart-to-heart talk with her mother, and what it felt like to work in corporate America. Stories about finding the extraordinary inside the ordinary. That August, Bari finally attended IWWG at Skidmore, her first writer's conference. It was there she proudly announced, "I'm a writer!" But her biggest story was yet to be told.

In November, newspapers were filled with stories of an African-American woman executive who had filed a discrimination suit against Texaco. The case ended with a $175 million settlement, the largest amount ever awarded in a lawsuit of this nature. Now, Bari-Ellen Roberts of *Roberts v. Texaco* had an even bigger story to tell. As I write this, she is working on her first book.

Bea Sheftel, author of several short stories and novellas, wrote, "The novel I'd worked on for a few years had gone stale. My passion for it had dimmed. Dorothy's workshop restarted my emotional engine and gave me back my passion. I realized what I wanted to say in my novel and I began revising, adding more of myself. It worked!"

One woman came to a women's writing conference just to help a friend carry her equipment. She was an administrator who had never tried to write before. She ended up in my workshop because someone told her my class was lots of fun. Six months later she had completed 260 pages of a novel.

In my classes, writing has poured out as the spirit poured in. People have dared to challenge themselves and to expand their horizons. Over the years I've seen poets explore fiction and fiction writers create theater. Seasoned and beginning writers find new ways to set their words afire. My students have produced and published volumes of work, formed writing groups, and started newsletters. Potent seeds of possibility have been planted in the fertile soil of the creative spirit. Many have learned to fertilize their thoughts, tend their crops, and reap the harvests.

It took a while for me to completely accept the impact my workshops were having on people. As an African-American woman artist, performer, novelist, poet, administrator, jewelry designer, interfaith minister, and former college faculty member, I have fished in the many streams that feed my spirit. Nurturing that spirit has always been a vital part of my life. In naming my workshops, I initially hesitated to use the word *spirit,* thinking people might confuse it with religion. In time, I began to honor what I had been given, and feel blessed that a force much greater than I was working through me. I decided to own the blessing fully and let the chips fall where they may. I just prayed they would be chocolate!

As this force continued to work through me, I began to witness its impact on others. The particular combination of music and meditations, affirmations, exercises, and rituals also had the ability to awaken the healing spirit. After writing pieces for my class, a young woman reconciled with her mother after years of estrangement. A gay man found a healing outlet for his anger after the death of his lover.

In the middle of a writing journey, one woman who had felt uncomfortable being touched asked to be hugged. A writer involved in a serious car accident used the writing rituals as a balm for the grief he experienced. One definition of heal is "to feel whole." This is a book is about healing, about feeling whole again, and about using the spirit of your whole self.

In writing *Soul Between the Lines,* I have challenged myself to do what I have asked of others. I lay my soul between the lines. I pulled stories of transformation from the private pages of my own life. I left my job as executive director of an arts agency to give my writing the time and space it was demanding of me. Writing is risking. I knew if I was going to talk the talk, I had to walk the walk.

Danaan Parry says, "Work is love made visible." Teaching my Heartland workshops has truly been a labor of love. This book comes with joy from my heart and my spirit to yours. We all have a purpose in being here. Mine is to be a spiritual spur in your side and to share with you the power and inspiration of Writing From Your Heartland.™

chapter 1

·

THE HEARTLAND

·

You need only claim the events of your life to make yourself and yours. When you truly possess all you have been and done, which may take some time, you are fierce with reality.

—FLORIDA SCOTT MAXWELL

The Heartland Hotline

> Real writers store impressions, stretching them into harmonious tension. Real writers understand the elasticity of experience, and the importance of trust.
>
> —MAGGIE FOX

My grandmother used to say, "You can't see for lookin'." The older I got, the more I came to understand the wisdom of those words. We see with more than our eyes. Our vision is colored by experience and memory, by what our hearts whisper, our minds insist, our gut feelings warn us about, and history asks us not to repeat. This vision dwells within each of us in a place I call the Heartland. I define the Heartland as *the spiritual center of the creative self.*

Think of the Heartland as an axle upon which you can turn your life toward whatever kind of creativity you desire. Writing is one of the most powerful ways to access your Heartland. Writing helps your spirit unlock the door to this center of unlimited creative energy. On the other side of that door, you may find poetry and painting, memoir and music, theater, song, or just yourself. You may also find creative ways to resolve conflicts, interact with your environment, and change your life.

Writing From Your Heartland™ can help you move past any creative block you may have encountered. It ignites the creative process while empowering you as the creator. As you move your words, your words have the ability to move you. This holistic way of writing uses the spirit of who you are to help you write what you want. Meditation, music, affirmation, ritual, and visualization are all streams that help spirit to flow.

My Heartland methods are based on everything I have lived and loved—African, Eastern, Native American and Western spirituality, ethnomusicology, creative dramatics, movement, performance, channeled information, elementary-school teaching, mother nature, and mother wit. When I began to teach using these sources of inspiration, my students reported that the results were incredibly powerful and affirming. Experienced and beginning writers thrilled to find new, stimulating ways of accessing their creative spirits. In my workshops, they discovered a place of freedom from what I call the *oppression of definition:* being confined by your own definition of yourself. They began to feel at home in a space without limits.

Your Heartland will take you on a journey through different ways of seeing and will help you explore the endless ocean of your creative power. You have may have already stuck your toes into the water, skinny-dipped in that ocean, or plunged in head-first. Some of you will want to swim the English Channel, and others may just want to channel their English.

Dive in and discover the many beginnings, middles, and endings that live within these pages. Try the middles at the end and the beginnings in the middle. Whenever you want, you can define, refine, and underline. Keep your spirit open to the full spectrum of your creative self. Let the music move you and the rituals inspire you. Let the writing take you where it wants to go. Don't be afraid to let it surprise you.

Coming to Terms

As you travel through the Heartland, I will repeatedly use some basic terms. These will help you navigate your way through the rest of the book. I'd like to introduce you to these terms once over lightly, and then explain what I mean by them in greater depth in the sections that follow.

First, I have to tell you that whenever I want the lowdown on a word, I go straight to Merriam Webster's Collegiate® Dictionary, Tenth Edition. I have visited that book so many times that I feel as if we've gotten to know each other quite personally. So I'll be referring to the dictionary as Miss Webster from now on.

RITUAL

Miss Webster says a ritual is "a customarily repeated often formal act or series of acts." The Temptations might define a ritual as "the way you do the things you do." If there are certain things that you regularly do in a particular way, you can consider those things to be rituals.

From attending Super Bowl tailgate parties to sounding noisemakers at the stroke of midnight on New Year's Eve, rituals have always been a part of our everyday lives. A friend of mine spends a long, quiet time in her bathtub every Thursday night. Another calls her grandmother every Saturday morning at nine o'clock. One couple I know goes for a walk through Brooklyn's Prospect Park each New Year's Day no matter what the weather is like. I celebrate my birthday by gathering my closest friends around me and having each one give me a wish for the year.

My mother had a birthday ritual. On my birthday I would sit in the living room while she took out the good linen tablecloth and put candles on the homemade cake. Then she'd turn out the lights and call out, "Oh, Dorothy!"

"Yes, Ma, what is it?" I always replied, pretending not to know what was going on. "Come in here for a minute," she would respond. I would then go into the kitchen and act totally surprised when she and my sisters began to sing, "Happy birthday to you!" This "surprise" birthday ritual was repeated three times a year every year, once for each of her three daughters, until we left home.

Rituals help to provide an atmosphere of anticipation. They connect you with the excitement of the expected. You know what comes next, and still you look forward to it. Rituals can also set the stage for an atmosphere of creative anticipation. When you use the preparation rituals in this book, they will help your mind, body, and soul prepare for the act of creation. Words and images, awareness and feelings are all primed to flow easily onto paper or canvas and into consciousness. Rituals can help your Heartland to look forward to the excitement of transformation.

FREEWRITING

Think of this as a Heartland ATM card. It provides access to your creative self. It also helps to bypass the self-judgment and censoring that can often emerge during the writing process. To freewrite, just put your pen to the paper and write as fast as you can. Don't stop to think or worry about grammar, spelling, punctuation, or context. Also, don't lift the pen from your paper until the allotted time is up, usually about five to ten minutes.

Studies show that your inner jury can travel only 35 miles per hour, but the freewriting hand speeds along at 60. Write fast enough and that jury will never catch or convict you!

Training yourself to write by hand as fast as possible is invaluable. It also helps you pick up the pieces of life that rapidly occur around you: conversations overheard, an idea for a story, or the way the light bends around a cloud. You will want to capture as much as you can as quickly as you can.

If you can hardly read your own handwriting after writing so quickly, do what you can to make your writing legible. Just don't change, correct, or rearrange anything. You're sure to see phrases and images you'll want to expand on or add to. Just make several copies of the original freewrite. That way you will always have a clean working copy to play with.

JOURNEYS

This is the term I use instead of "writing exercises." I think it is a more accurate reflection of what actually happens during the writing process. Calling them journeys also makes it sound as if you don't have to wear tights to do them. Once you have completed a journey, you can keep it as written, use it as a journal entry, explore its visual imagery, or develop it into a story, poem, essay, screenplay, or any other creative venue your heart desires.

SEEDS

These are fragments of a whole with the ability to take on a whole life of their own. My students have told me that the *seed* process is one of the most powerful techniques they have encountered.

Collecting seeds is an active listening technique and a priceless feedback method. This act also creates a limitless supply of ideas to draw from. For example, you can read your work aloud and ask listeners to write down the words or phrases they liked or connected with. Then have them read back to you what they wrote down. These are called the *seeds* of your work.

Seeds can also be gathered from everyday situations, visual images, and personal encounters. In looking at a painting, sculpture or film, you can single out the segment of the work that most appeals to you. You might focus on the color or texture of a piece or an image in a movie that touches your heart. In a discussion, *seed* collecting can be a very effective way of getting to the heart of the matter. When you see a photograph of a refugee you might collect a seed of sadness or longing from his eyes.

One of my students successfully revised a college catalog by collecting seeds from an old version and using them to create the new catalog. Another student told me collecting seeds helps keep her awake during poetry readings. I have even gotten seeds from news broadcasts. I was struck by a midwestern farmer's personification of the devastating floods of 1992. His words were "The river just went where *she* wanted to go. There was nothing we could do to stop her."

FOOD FOR THOUGHT

These are words and phrases that may inspire additional journeys and expand on the concepts in each chapter. They also present the writer with an abundant array of writing and creative possibilities.

SEASONAL SURRENDERS

These are daily rituals that add to your spiritual and creative levels of awareness, intensify the writing experience, and strengthen your connection to the seasons inside and outside of you. Even if they seem strange to you, give them a try and have fun with them. They all have a gift to give you. Make sure you are there to receive it.

What You See Is What You Get

> Memory is revision. I have just destroyed another piece of my life to tell a story.
>
> —LYNN SHARON SCHWARTZ

There is a story about a journalist who was gathering opinions about food shortages. He decided to talk to some people from Poland, Russia, California, and New York.

When he went to the Polish person and asked, "Excuse me, what is your opinion about the food shortage?" he answered, "What is food?"

He went to the Russian asking, "Excuse me, what is your opinion about the food shortage?" The Russian replied, "What is opinion?"

He asked the Californian, "Excuse me, what is your opinion about the food shortage?" The Californian answered, "What's a shortage?"

Then he asked the New Yorker, "Excuse me, what is your

opinion about the food shortage?" and the New Yorker responded, "What's excuse me?"

That's the way it is with writing. We can all hear the same sounds and see the same objects and yet arrive at varying perceptions. Siblings growing up in the same household can have totally different recollections of actions taken by their parents, or the course of events at a particular family gathering.

In the same way, what you write can be colored by who you are and how you feel at that moment. How often have you written an angry letter, then looked at it in the light of another day? "Who wrote this?" you may have asked yourself, thankful that a calmer self decided not to mail a letter the angry self composed.

An old saying warns, "Believe half of what you see, and none of what you hear." I was sitting in a college classroom some years ago when two students suddenly burst into the room fighting with each other. After a minute or so, the professor calmly ordered, "Okay, fellows, that's enough." They immediately stopped battling and took their seats. "Now," she said turning to us, "write down exactly what you saw." She had staged the dramatic entrance for a writing exercise.

"The class was in an uproar," one student wrote, while another described the room as being "deathly still." "They kept each other locked in a bearlike grip," wrote one, while another noted, "A flurry of punches were exchanged." How could we have all been in the same classroom and yet arrive at such different conclusions about what took place? We all had to take another look at the meaning of *eyewitness*.

As you wander through the Heartland, you will be asked to look at things differently and experience them in ways you may not have tried before. For example, you will be asked to close your eyes and take a look inside—just as when you taste or smell something truly wonderful, when you are trying to remember, to listen more intently, or to concentrate, you usually find yourself closing your eyes. Removing the powerful sense of sight helps us to visualize and enhances the use of our other senses.

Inner sight is twenty-twenty. It can envision characters and scenes, help you find the words you need, help you hear dialogue, and give you all kinds of fresh perspectives. Often as I write, I close my eyes so that I can feel the words that come next or hear what the characters I'm writing about want to say. If I need to know more about what happens in a scene, I will ask, "Okay, what are you going to do now?" The character will usually tell me. Often, a character's words can come so quickly, you need shorthand to capture them all.

Tuning in to this inner terrain is also a useful way to play out new situations in your life. You can prepare for an interview, plan a confrontation, or solve all sorts of problems by letting your inner understanding whisper into the ear of your outer consciousness. Closing your eyes assists you in using your infinite spiritual senses. Taking a moment to visualize an encounter can help thoughts flow smoothly and prevent rash judgments. If you let your spirit guide you to the words and actions you need, you will approach the actual situation in a more relaxed manner.

Let the Music Muse You

> Each time we listen to beautiful music, we select an impression to weave into the harmony of our unfoldment.
>
> —F. A. NEWHOUSE

Have you ever been so moved by a piece of music that it made you cry or lifted your spirits? Have you ever listened to a song and remembered exactly where you were, who you were with, and even what you were feeling when you heard it? If the answer is yes, then you have been touched by the power of music.

"As in music, so in life," believed the ancients. They felt music became internalized by an individual, influencing the rhythm of thoughts, the melody of emotions, and the harmony of bodily health. In a current reflection of this belief, violinist Yehudi Menuhin states, "It creates order out of chaos; for rhythm imposes unanimity upon the divergent, melody imposes continuity upon the disjointed, and harmony imposes compatibility upon the incongruous."

I used to do volunteer work in a locked ward at the New York Psychiatric Hospital on Wards Island. Many of the patients were listless, nearly catatonic, and heavily medicated. Yet they suddenly came alive when I formed them into a singing group and led them in a series of doo-wop songs around an old piano. One woman who could not speak a coherent set of words burst into Broadway show tunes, and knew all the lyrics. Nietzsche put it well when he said, "Without music, life would be a mistake."

Studies have found that music can stimulate creativity, focus thinking, and expand spiritual attunement. It can affect muscular energy, influence digestion, change metabolism, and raise or lower blood pressure. Music inspires courage, instills pride, relieves stress, and speaks to every aspect of our existence.

In *The Healing Energies of Music,* Hal A. Lingerman states, "A single piece of music, carefully placed, can alter the entire atmosphere and behavior in a place." Drs. Earl W. Flosdorf and Leslie A. Chambers conducted several experiments with sound. They discovered that shrill sounds could coagulate the proteins in a liquid. In his book *The Day Music Died,* Bob Larson talks about a teenage fad that demonstrates this fact. He and his friends would go to rock concerts and put uncooked eggs at the foot of the stage. By the time the concert was over, the eggs had become hard boiled from the music.

In *The Secret Power of Music,* David Tame notes that, "Rhythms which are more harmonious and healthy have been found, depending on their tempos, to be very effective stimulants or sedatives, and they are of course much more beneficial in the long run than toxic, addictive chemicals such as Valium." Your heart usually beats at a rate of 65 to 80 beats per minute. Whether a rhythm calms or stirs you depends mainly upon how its frequency of beats relates to that heartbeat. If the tempo is about the same pace as the normal heartbeat, then the music will soothe you.

Years ago, the Columbia University School of Social Work conducted a twelve-week, highly structured relapse prevention program for methadone patients. Knowing how empowering meditation, visualization, and music had been in my workshops, I submitted a proposal to write these elements into their program. At that time, the mind, body, and spirit connection had not yet gained the level of acceptance it has today. The project directors liked the way I divided their study into three main themes and wrote guided meditation/visualizations for each. But what I think really clinched the deal with these conservative administrators was the music I selected. They agreed to my proposal.

I performed these guided meditations on three videos. In the background was music I felt would be soothing to the soul and healing for the spirit. The patients saw one videotape at the beginning of the structured sessions; another, four weeks later; and the final one, four weeks after that. The patients also received tapes of the music and were encouraged to use them to reduce stress. As a result, many of the patients reported feeling calmer, more relaxed, less angry, and more willing to face their lives without resorting to an addictive substance.

Music provides immediate access to your Heartland. I always open and close my workshops with music and use it to accompany all the writing journeys I give. Every time I sit down to do my own writing, I play music. I find it really stimulates the flow of words, thoughts, feelings, memory, and imagery. Take it along on all of your creative journeys and see what it does for you. Play music while you paint, while you are trying to make a decision, or before you leave home for the day. Use it to calm children, create an atmosphere, or change the energy in a space. Listen to a piece of music when your spirit needs nourishment and when you feel upset, wounded, or out of touch with yourself.

Be sure to select soft, meditative, or New Age music without lyrics. That way your own creativity can flow without distraction. Solo instrumentals of piano, flute, guitar, and classical adagios are all wonderful to use. I have found the following recordings wonderful for inviting and serenading the muse:

Steven Halpern, *Enhancing Creativity*. (Soundwave 200 Audio-Active)
  This tops my list. Music is recorded with subliminal (inaudible) affirmations that inspire creativity and productivity.
George Winston, *December* (Windham Hill Records)
William Ackerman, *Passages* (Windham Hill Records)
Bola Sete, *Jungle Suite* (Dancing Cat Records)
Gerald Jay Markoe, *Melodies from the Pleiades*
Paul Horn, *Inside* (Epic Records)
Michael Jones, *Sunscapes*

Start with these and then add some selections of your own. May the muse be with you.

Setting the Stage

> The writer's divine gift of 'sight' is the ability to see into the lives of the characters, and to divine meaning which propels the consciousness of the reader to a higher level of sensitivity, understanding, and humanity.
>
> —ALEXIS DeVEAUX

I have tried writing with and without meditating beforehand. There really is a difference. When I didn't meditate, I found that my thoughts flowed less freely, it was easier to become distracted, my level of concentration was lower, and I had less mental energy for developing new ideas. When I am designing a piece of jewelry or am planning to work intently on my sewing or leatherwork, meditation increases the flow of ideas and images, helps me focus, and work more effectively. Meditating and saying an affirmation before you create is like warming up the body before you exercise or take a dance class. It prepares the mind and spirit, gets the juices flowing, and loosens up those journey joints.

So before you begin writing, let your creative spirit know you will be asking it to dance. The few minutes you take to do a preparation, meditation, and affirmation ritual will reward you with many hours of creative fire. Latina writer Isabel Allende lights three candles before she begins to work—one each for her mother, grandmother, and great-grandmother, her muses. When the candles burn out, she stops writing.

PREPARATION

Set the stage for your creative sessions by sitting in a quiet space and playing meditative music. Burn incense or sage to help clear the energy of your space and alert the spirits. Begin with a preparation ritual. One such ritual is the Native American practice of calling in the four directions. Each direction has a different energy, and calling on them can stimulate your entire being.

Take three deep breaths and start with your body facing north. Hold your hands up in front of your chest, with palms turned outwards. Read the following words, turning to face the direction as you call on its spirit:

> *I call on the spirit of the north, golden spirit of earth and creation.*
> *I call upon the spirit of the east, clear spirit of air and contemplation.*
> *I call upon the spirit of the south, blue spirit of water and birth, the principle of love that sustains all things.*
> *I call upon the spirit of the west, red spirit of fire and passion, ecstasy, warmth, and joy.*

Another way of connecting is to face each direction with your arms outstretched and breathe it into your body. As you inhale, draw your hands toward your body to pull the energy of each direction into your heart. After gathering in those energies, reach up to the sky and breathe in your highest self. Then reach down to the earth to inhale your deepest self. When you end, place both hands over your heart, with the right hand of giving placed on top of the left hand of receiving.

Think about creating a preparation ritual of your own. Do something that feels right to your spirit, something that has meaning for you. I begin each day by pouring libations to my ancestors and spirit guides and asking for their blessings.

MEDITATION

Meditation accelerates the centering process, invokes the spirit, and provides immediate access to the deepest caverns of your Heartland. Each chapter's meditation is attuned to the journeys in that section. Using these meditations will intensify the level of connection between you and the spirit of the work you are about to do. Allow yourself to experience the words as you read them.

Take a deep breath. Feel the vibration of your preparation ritual as you sit in a comfortable position. Read the meditation slowly and let your mind, body and spirit receive its energy. Afterwards, close your eyes and take a moment to observe your inner landscape. Make note of the thoughts and feelings you find in the sacred space you have just created. When you open your eyes, you will be ready for your affirmation, the final step of your writing preparation. Affirmation plays a critical role in all of the things we may want to do with any of our selves.

THANKSGIVING

Morning Thanksgiving is also an important part of my day. This is when I take time to state all of the things that I am thankful for, from the use of all my senses to the ability to breathe, be joyful, think, and love. I give thanks for all the lessons that help me to grow and all the blessings that keep me glowing.

There is always something to be thankful for. Even having food, clothing, and shelter should inspire us to give thanks. There are far too many people who struggle daily to attain what we take for granted. Being mindful of that helps to put things in perspective and keeps us from focusing too much on what we *don't* have.

It had never occurred to me to be thankful for the ability to walk until an assault left me on crutches. One day I was trying to get to downtown Brooklyn to deliver a proposal before the deadline. I called a car service from my office in Red Hook, Brooklyn. I couldn't afford to waste time waiting for a bus. When the taxi came, the driver made an unusual demand. He insisted that I sit in the front with him and refused to move unless I did. When I first entered the cab, my instincts had whispered that the driver was on drugs. I thought I had caught a whiff of something ominous. I ignored it.

Time was running out to turn in the proposal. I told the driver how important it was. I knew there wasn't enough time to call and wait for another cab. I asked, then pleaded, and finally insisted that the driver take me downtown. It was a ten-minute drive away. He became agitated at my insistence. "Bitch, I don't like the way you talk!" He got out of the cab. I thought he was going to call his base. Suddenly my door was opened. The driver reached in, grabbed me by the arm, and threw me out of the cab onto the ground. I managed to get back on my feet. He was swinging and cursing at me. I was screaming and trying to duck his fists. Finally he got back into his cab and drove off.

I was in excruciating pain. I limped back into my office and called the police. What followed in the ensuing weeks felt like another assault. The police wanted me to walk outside to the patrol car so they wouldn't have to get out of their seats. My HIP doctor refused to treat me. He said he didn't want to get involved in a taxicab case because he might be called on to testify and he didn't want to take off from work. He suggested I go see a doctor.

I went to see a specialist at the HIP center, but didn't reveal the true source of my injury. He told me my leg would be fine in two weeks and I didn't have to worry. A month later my leg was still swollen and discolored and I was still in pain. I was using a folding pool cue with a dragon carved into its wood for a cane.

This time I went to a private medical doctor who billed herself as holistic. She handed me an intensive ten-page form that asked about everything except who shot JFK. I filled out medical histories of my entire family, itemized lists of my social, mental, spiritual, emotional, and physical activities, detailed descriptions of everything I ate for breakfast, lunch and dinner for a week, and more. I had even managed to smuggle X-rays of my swollen leg from the HIP clinic to show her.

"Oh, I'm no good at X-rays," she said as our session began. This was not a good sign. She went over the questionnaire with me asking questions here and there.

"I see both your parents met with tragic deaths."

"Yes, they did."

"Well, you're going to have to get over that." So much for the holistic counseling. She weighed me, checked my pulse, and gave me a Pap smear.

"What about my leg?"

"Oh, yes. How'd you hurt it again?"

My leg throbbed as I sat on the examining table. "My leg is swollen, you know. You can tell that this one is larger than the other."

"Let's see about that," she said, pulling out a tape to measure the obvious.

"You're right," she said, and handed me a bottle of vitamins.

I was billed several hundred dollars and given a referral to a chiropractor I had already planned to call. It was there that I finally got the help I had been seeking for a month and a half since the assault.

I was told that my leg was healing, but with the wrong kind of tissue. If I continued to walk on it now, it would not heal properly and I'd have a limp for the rest of my life. I had to go on crutches, have physical therapy twice a day, and make weekly chiropractic visits. I stayed on crutches for five months.

In the meantime, the police were still looking for the cabdriver who assaulted me. We did stakeouts in front of the car service headquarters where he worked. I would hide slumped down in the backseat of an unmarked police car, waiting to spot him. Finally the police did a lineup, and I picked him out. He was booked, fingerprinted, and released before I could finish filling out papers for the Victims Services Agency.

This assault happened not long after a significant relationship had come to a devastating end the week before my birthday. My 34-year-old sister Yvonne died of brain cancer the day after my birthday. I gradually realized I was no longer able to feel my joy. The physical, emotional, and spiritual wounds had taken their toll. There was a pervasive numbness that blanketed everything. It stayed for months and months until I was able to retrieve my spirit again.

Before that, I hadn't thought about being grateful for something as simple as walking without crutches. They say, "You don't miss your water till your well runs dry." Now, every day is Thanksgiving day. By the way, after eight court postponements, three district attorneys, and several attempts to get me to drop the charges, the cabdriver was finally convicted. For that, I am thankful.

After you finish sipping the sacred space of your morning ritual, take another deep breath. Your mind, body, and spirit are now thoroughly warmed up and raring to make a creative dent in the world.

WRITING ALTAR

A writing altar can be another point of focus for your creative spirit. While you are between words, as you create, the vibrations of the colors and objects around you can energize you and your work. Create a writing altar by gathering a few special objects that have meaning to you and placing them on a small cloth or in a basket near your writing area. You can use shells or rocks, flowers, candles, souvenirs, photos of relatives, artists, or writers who have inspired you. You can also use postcards from places you have visited and loved, quotations, sentences, deleted words you want to keep, things you might like to look at or dream about.

The better your altar feels to you, the more powerful it will be for you. My writing altar is a little red wagon on top of my computer, Miss Mary Mac. It has a glow-in-the dark magic wand with stars and moons inside, an angel blowing kisses at me, a picture of the Hawaiian monarch Queen Liliuokalani, and an amethyst crystal. There are also little Oshun and Quan Yin dolls, a photo of a river I drank from in Iceland, a statue of Isis with a blinking heart, a mermaid, and a few other enjoyable objects.

At one point, as I struggled to sort out my writing life after leaving my job, a wise friend sat me down and said, "Dorothy, you're a writer. It's in your blood. You're like a junkie or an alcoholic—when you're not writing, you're off the wagon!" Three days later I pushed past years of resistance and put myself on a daily writing regimen. I also put a little red wagon on top of my computer to remind me to stay on the wagon.

Affirmative Inneraction

> I am that I am, a shining being and a dweller in light who has been created from the limbs of the divine.
> —EGYPTIAN INCANTATION

On the ides of March in 1989, I handed in my resignation from a faculty position at New York University because I couldn't see the sun from my desk. For almost six years, that desk had been next to a grey-carpeted partition that did not reach the ceiling. One day it occurred to me that if I stayed there much longer, I might not reach *my* heights. I might never feel the colors of life beyond grey, or see the shining of my own light. My resignation became effective on June fifteenth. I walked away without even having looked for another job. I thought I would take two months off for good behavior and begin working again in the fall.

When September arrived, a fellow writer announced she was starting a new literary series. She asked if I could teach a writing workshop. It didn't matter that I had never taught writing before. My spirit called on me to answer with an affirmation that transformed my life: "Yes, I can!"

It was over a thousand years ago that Marcus Aurelius told us, "Our life is what our thoughts make of it." For centuries people have used affirmations to heal themselves, reduce pain, summon up courage, treat serious illness, and start new careers. For example, disco diva Gloria Gaynor gave us a universal affirmation for recovering from a broken heart when she sang, "I will survive, I will survive!"

Words have power and energy. They can kill or cure. We can all remember hurtful comments made to us, even if they were said years ago. Negative words and experiences have a way of weaving themselves into the tender fiber of our hearts. Affirmations provide a powerful, positive balance to those experiences. They have the ability to help, heal, and transform you. They strengthen the spirit, empower the will, and engage your mental, physical and emotional selves.

One day I was walking an icy street in Brooklyn when I spotted an African-American man in his sixties coming toward me with his head down. He was moving cautiously and muttering to himself, "I'm gonna fall. I'm gonna fall. I know I'm gonna fall. I fall every year."

Suddenly he looked up at me and asked, "You gonna fall?"

"No," I answered, "I never fall."

"That's right! That's the right attitude! I'm not gonna fall either," he continued to mutter as he walked past. "Nope, I'm not gonna fall. I'm not gonna fall."

We are all familiar with self-fulfilling prophecies. We constantly hear children saying, "I can't do this!" We can look into our own hearts and witness the damage done to us by diminished self-esteem and lack of faith. When you say, "I can't," you are sending out precisely the kind of energy that can prevent you from taking action. Positive statements create an energy field that magnetizes and attracts positive things to you. Think of how you feel after someone pays you a compliment. Notice how children light up when you tell them how wonderfully they are behaving.

Affirmation is also a way to free yourself from the *oppression of definition*. By that I mean being confined by your own definition. Have you ever said things like "I'm only a mother" or "I'm not an artist, I'm a just a businessperson," or even "I'm a reader, not a writer"? If you have had any of these kinds of symptoms, you may be suffering from the *oppression of definition*.

Believe it or not, I used to say, "I could never be an artist. How can they stand not having a steady paycheck? That would drive me crazy!" How many *I could never*s have you wrapped around your creative abilities? How many *I'm just*s or *I'm only*s have you put on the path of your spirit?

Oppression of definition means being stuck in style and constrained by content. It means saying, "I would never do illustration, I'm a fine artist," or "I sculpt only in stone, never in wood." It means sentencing yourself to genre prison by saying, "I don't do romance novels, I'm a technical writer," or "I'm a poet, I don't write fiction."

Even I was afflicted at one point. Years ago, I was writing poetry and had not completed any of the short stories that had gotten off to such a great start. "I could never write a novel," I said to myself. "How do people think of enough stuff to fill up a whole book? How can they work on something for years

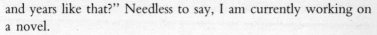

and years like that?" Needless to say, I am currently working on a novel.

What you do with your life and what you create with your art is relative to the time and space you happen to be in. As you arrive at a particular season of yourself, you may decide you need to do things in a particular way. When that season ends, you may decide to operate in an entirely different manner.

Picasso had blue period seasons and cubist seasons, Bob Dylan had acoustic and electric seasons. John Coltrane had be-bop and ballad seasons. Former Alabama governor George C. Wallace had segregationist, then integrationist seasons. In the sixties, America went through a "let it all hang out" season before it fell into the "keep it all tucked in" seasons of the seventies and eighties.

Audre Lorde talks about women who are "trapped in their seasons." Are there places in your life where you are stuck in style or constrained by content? Have you heard yourself saying, "But I've always done it this way"?

You can transform the way you create, the way you are, the way you live your life, the way you follow your dreams. And you can do it now. Because you happen to be in a season, a mindset, at a certain age or at a particular stage in life, doesn't mean you have to stay there. Seasons change and so do you. Affirmation is a way of helping you change your seasons.

CREATING AFFIRMATIONS

Affirmations have the power to transform your work and your life. They allow your spirit to try on the loose garment of other realities to see how they fit. Even if you do not fully believe in the words you are affirming, say them anyway. Repeating them creates a vibration that resonates throughout your entire being. This vibration feeds your spirit, and your spirit in turn creates the energy that brings your words into being. Affirmation is the gift that keeps on giving. It is the self-fulfilling prophecy in all of its positive splendor.

Affirmations are always phrased in the present. They speak the divine language of the Heartland. At the beginning and end of each of my workshops we always affirm ourselves—as writers, as creative creatures, as seasonal sentient beings. Think of an affirmation you can use before you begin your creative sessions. The affirmation may be about your writing, your visual images, your creative energy, your spiritual development, or any parts of your selves that need affirming. If, for example, you want your writing to be more powerful and consistent, your affirmation would then be, "My writing *is* powerful and consistent."

In one workshop a writer affirmed, "My writing is as clear as a stream in North Carolina." In another, we all shared: "I am the plentiful harvest of all my selves. I am the golden fruits of my own labor, and I have more than enough to feed my wants and needs."

One of the most powerful affirmations in existence consists of only two words, "I am." Even Popeye knew the power of this affirmation when he would say, "I am what I am, and that's all that I am." All too often, who we are is shaped by what others expect us to be or who we *think* we should be.

When we move away from the spirit of who we truly are, our inner phone gets disconnected and we can't even call ourselves for help. Affirming "I am" reconnects you with the reality that you are not your job or the title you have been given, not what your parents expect you to be, not the guilt or pain or doubt that may have shaped itself to look like you.

When you affirm "I am," you are tapping the roots of your personal power. You are reminding yourself to wear your reality like a loose garment, making sure there is room for you to breathe and expand your vision when you are feeding your spirit. You don't want your reality to get too tight around your waist when you are trying to eat a full meal.

After your meditation, the sacred space you have created is primed and waiting for your affirmation. Think about affirming whatever it is that you need for your writing, and for your life. You can use an affirmation that springs from your own spirit or find one in some of the wonderful words in books by Iyanla

Vanzant, Cecelia Williams Bryant, Shakti Gawain, or Sark. Say the affirmation in the morning to empower your day, and again at night to transform you as you sleep.

One way of using the "I am" affirmation is to cup your hands together and speak the words into your palms three times. Pause after each "I am" to breathe the words inside you and feel their warm energy. Another way is to see if a word comes to mind that might like to join in on the affirmation. You might feel guided to say, for example, "I am . . . beautiful," or "I am . . . powerful." After the affirmation is spoken, place your hands over your heart, right hand over left. Experience the power of all your *I amness*.

The August after I left my job, I attended the International Women's Writing Guild conference in Saratoga Springs. In that incredible environment where more than three hundred women had gathered, I consecrated my commitment to the written word. The two months I had originally planned to take off from a job actually turned into a year. During that year, I let writing build a nest in my heart where it could be nurtured and learn to fly again. I let life surprise me and my spirit guide me. I ate the morning sun for breakfast. It was in this precious time that I gave birth to my Writing From Your Heartland™ workshops. Seven years and hundreds of students later, I am still feasting on the joy this teaching brings and finding new ways of saying, *"Yes, I can!"*

The Journey

> To write is to taste life twice.
>
> ANAÏS NIN

One of the main points of this book is that writing can be an end, and it can also be the means to an end. A *journey* is a writing exercise. You only have to exercise your spirit in order to do one. *Journeys* are at the core of this book. They are some of the most important activities you'll find on these pages. You will find several *journeys* in each section of each chapter. Journeys put you in touch with your creative entitlement and personal empowerment.

The *journey* is the foundation on which you build story and soul searchings, art and vision, dialogue and discovery, poetry, prose, and personal transformation. You don't have to be a writer to do a *journey*. You don't have to be an artist to do a *journey*. You just have to be willing.

The definition of a journey is to travel from one place to another. During the writing process, words, thoughts, ideas and images travel from your Heartland onto paper. They travel from childhood experiences and adult encounters. They travel from family memories, night fantasies, and daydreams. They travel from paper to stage, to canvas, to film, to journal, to the seeking self. They travel from your spirit, soul, mind, and body into your every creative moment. Writing is your mode of transportation.

Heartland *journeys* help increase the imagination, build story, deepen spiritual awareness, and strengthen the divine consciousness you bring to your art and to your life. Remember, the Heartland is the spiritual center of the creative self. Your Heartland has countless gifts to give you. Writing From Your Heartland™ is a way of receiving as many of those gifts as you can use.

Okay, so how do you do a *journey*? Simple. Usually I'll give you a sentence, a thought, a situation, or a quotation that will serve as a catalyst for the writing process. You will be writing down your own take on the topic or catalyst. And each *journey* asks that you write for only a minimum of five minutes! See, I told you it was simple.

Music is always an integral part of a *journey*. It helps words and thoughts flow and provides access to your innermost spaces. Make sure there is music playing as you write. In the section "Let the Music Muse You," I talk about the importance of music in the creative process and in daily living. Be sure to select soft music without words so that yours can flow freely.

Let's talk about the kind of writing I'll be asking you to do. You are going to do something called freewriting. When you freewrite, you just put pen to paper and write as fast as you can. And you don't lift your pen from the paper until your five minutes are up. Use a kitchen timer if you'd like. As you write, don't worry about spelling, punctuation, or grammar. None of that matters in a freewrite. Whatever comes out is fine. Isn't it wonderful to have such freedom?

In fact, you might feel that having so much freedom isn't fun. Such leeway might make you downright uncomfortable. "Where are the rules?" you may say. Like Peggy Lee, you might ask, "Is that all there is?" It may take you a while to get used to the idea of a freewrite. Just keep working at it. When was the last time someone allowed you to do whatever you wanted to do and told you it would be okay?

Freewriting is a very effective way of slipping past your own internal judge and jury. When you feel yourself being called to jury duty, don't go! Just write as quickly as possible, without trying to stop and figure out what the piece should be or what should come next. Just don't *should* on yourself. Read your freewrite aloud. If your handwriting is illegible, make the writing readable, but don't change, correct, or rearrange anything. Always leave the freewriting just the way it was written.

That's a *journey*. A simple five-minute freewrite. So now you've got this page or so full of writing that you may barely be able to read. What do you do with it? If you have been able to get out of your own way successfully, you will find that this writing has come straight from the spiritual center of your creative self.

Look closely at what has just flowed through you. That *journey* may be a treasure chest of poem fragments and journal entries, ideas for essays or stories, plots for movies, images and subject matter for paintings and sculptures. There may be lines, phrases, and words you want to extract, dialogue to use, prose pieces to develop.

If you are a visual artist, you are probably always being asked to explain your work, your messages and meanings. A language for these explanations may not be so readily available to you. Do a *journey* and ask your Heartland. Just write down one sentence about your work or a few words that are important to you and your art. Then use that sentence or those words as a catalyst for a five-minute freewrite. You will be surprised at how much you will be able to extract to create a statement that is truly reflective of your artistry.

You might be at a crossroads in your life or at a spiritual standstill. Take an inspiring quotation from a spiritual source or use a meaningful question, and write it down on a piece of paper. Do a *journey* and ask your Heartland. Using that quotation or question as your five-minute freewrite topic can reflect your feelings back to you, thus connecting you with emotional insights and a clear consciousness.

Let's say you're writing a novel. You are working on the plot and are not exactly sure where you want the story to go. Do a *journey* and ask your Heartland. Write down a few of the characters' names. Then write a one-sentence description of each one's personality and appearance. Say the name of each character and ask aloud, "What will you do next?" Then do a five-minute freewrite for each. The depth of perception in your response and the quality of the character development you'll be given access to might amaze you.

These are only a few of the uses for a *journey*. You will find more in each chapter. Each one has its own theme, and the *journeys* in those chapters relate to that particular theme. You can skip around this book and sample the journeys like a smorgasbord once you have finished all of Chapter 1. You can try as many or as few as you'd like in a given day. It all depends on how much time you allot to your creative spirit on a daily basis.

Now, let's take a look at one of these *journeys* I've been

talking about. In "Rainbow of the Spirit," there is a section about red. One *journey* from that section is "paint the town red." You have already done your preparation ritual, so you're good to go. Now put on your meditative music, apply your pen to paper, and write like hell for five minutes without stopping. After the five minutes are up, take a look at your work.

"Paint the town red" might inspire thoughts about celebrations—ones that have taken place or those that have never happened. You may think about a special red dress you have always wanted or a rare night on the town you might give to someone who can really use it. Perhaps a poem or a painting might arise about a butterfly who is celebrating her transformation. Perhaps you will take a look at a transformation you have made, and plan a celebration in honor of it.

You may find yourself going back to your freewrite *journey* over and over again, each time using different segments. Make sure you keep the original freewritten pages and use only copies to work with. That way the words that came directly from your Heartland are always waiting there for you unjudged, uncensored, and unadulterated.

Seeds and Deeds

> To be of the earth is to know the restlessness of being a seed,
> the darkness of being planted, the struggle toward the light, . . .
> and the joy of bursting and bearing fruit.
>
> —JOHN SOOS

My students have told me that one of the most effective Heartland techniques they have encountered is a process I call "*collecting seeds*." It is a wonderful active listening technique and an invaluable feedback device, and it provides limitless food for your muse.

Collecting *seeds* allows you to cast new eyes at previous work and identify the power points of your work—those places where what you create makes a direct hit on the heart, mind, or spirit of another. Identifying these points gives you a solid base upon which you can build a story or focus on visual imagery. *Seeds* can also present you with opportunities for self-reflection, spiritual insights, and personal transformation.

Your name is one of the first seeds planted in your consciousness. That name carries its own special energy. Have you ever been at an airport when suddenly above the noise you were able to hear your name being paged? If asked, you probably would not be able to remember which flight had just been announced or even the words that were said before your name was called.

You connected with the energy of your name, not just the sound. Your name was a seed that you were able to single out in the midst of all the other sounds. Have you ever caught a child doing something wrong? When you called his or her name, did you notice how it made that little body jump?

Seeds are words and phrases that cause your creative spirit to jump. They can be heard above the clamor of other written or spoken words. *Seeds* are catalysts for new ideas. They may be planted in your own writings or in those of others, in conversations, billboards, advertisements, movies, speeches, catalogs, or comic books.

Collecting *seeds* is a simple process. In writing, just read your journeys or other work to a person or a group. As you read, ask them to write down the words or phrases they like and connect with or that strike a chord somewhere. Then ask them to read back to you what they have collected. On your own sheet of paper, underline those words and phrases given back to you. These bits and pieces of your work are called *seeds*. When you collect *seeds* from the writings of others, remember to label them

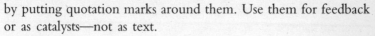

by putting quotation marks around them. Use them for feedback or as catalysts—not as text.

Here's an example of *seed* collecting in my writing workshop. A woman reads a piece describing the end of a recent relationship: "A hurricane in the heart. I felt my dreams drift out to sea like a shipwreck. The wind tore through my body and shook its foundations. The rain could not wash me enough. No shore to stand on, roof to stand under, nothing left standing. Pieces of a house that love built laying on the ground at the foot of emptiness. The eye in this storm was red and weeping."

As the other students and I listened, we quickly jotted down words and phrases that touched us or stayed with us. We then read to her the *seeds* we had collected. She in turn had to underline the words in her piece that were fed back to her. One person collected, "dreams drift out to sea like a shipwreck" and "nothing left standing." Others wrote "hurricane in the heart," "pieces of a house . . . foot of emptiness," and "the eye in this storm was red and weeping."

As the *seeds* are given back to the writer, something pretty amazing happens. Writers discover how differently each person listens to what was read. Some *seeds* were collected by everyone in the room. For other *seeds,* it was as if the words and phrases were being heard for the first time. The way in which you listen is directly related to the contents of your own Heartland. By collecting and reading the *seeds,* the listener and the writer help each other to find a deeper connection with the words themselves and the thoughts and emotions that live behind them.

If you are not in a group and a friend or associate is not available, try reading aloud to yourself or into a tape recorder. Underline the parts that make something inside of you sit up and take notice. Hearing your own words spoken aloud is invaluable. Very often your ear can pick up what your eyes fail to see. Think of hearing as another way of seeing.

These *seeds* are useful in a number of ways. Writers can identify the power points in their work by noting which of their *seeds* are mentioned over and over again. A *seed* can become a powerful catalyst for new work. Place it at the top of a page and use it for a five-minute freewrite.

I have had my students take all their underlined *seeds* and list them together. When they do this, they often find that they have created a poem, unearthed a new theme, or discovered a different slant to their writing. If you have unfinished writings or work that you are not quite satisfied with, you can extract the *seeds* from these pieces. Use them to start new ones, jump-start the old work, or add to what you have already written.

I always keep a little notebook with me to record the *seeds* I may hear on the street, in the movies, or anywhere for that matter. I never forgot a *seed* I collected from James Baldwin's play *The Amen Corner*. Diana Sands as an anguished daughter shouts at her evangelist mother, Beah Richards, "You gave your life to God—maybe I needed it more!"

Years ago, I was down south visiting my then 85-year-old grandmother. One night as she was preparing for bed, she strolled into the living room in a frilly pink chiffon nightgown. My aunt Mary was astonished. "Mama!" she exclaimed, "where are you going in *that*?" My grandmother smiled, leaned on her cane, and replied, "Honey, I want to be ready!"

Seeds are collected on more than just paper. A sculptor may carve a piece of wood into a single gnarled hand instead of the entire body. A photographer might decide to take a picture of only a particular limb of a tree, and only at a time of day when the light hits it a certain way. One composer used a single note as the basis of his song, "One Note Samba." In the classic shower scene in the movie *Psycho,* we witness Janet Leigh being killed, yet we never see the actual murder. Instead, the director chose to show us dramatic fragments: a knife-wielding hand upraised again and again, the killer's shadow, bloody water running down the drain.

Seeds from movies and television often filter into our daily usage. At one point, the whole country wanted to know,

"Where's the beef?" How many times have you heard people use these words from a now-infamous commercial: "I've fallen and I can't get up!"? Who can forget Marlon Brando's classic "I could have been a contender!" Arnold Schwarzenegger's "I'll be back!" and Cuba Gooding Jr.'s "Show me the money!"?

Seeds can also be gathered from everyday situations. When you are having a discussion, remembering the *seeds* of what is said can be a very effective way of getting to the heart of the matter. In a counseling situation or one that requires focused listening, you can use *seeds* to help you zero in on what the real need is. When you are taking an exam, the *seeds* in a question can tell you exactly what is being asked of you. Collecting *seeds* during meetings can help you figure out each person's main points.

Have you ever looked at a person and singled out a particular quality that appealed to you? Perhaps you've seen a very large woman and remarked, "She's got such a pretty face." Maybe you looked at a lovely old house in need of paint and repair and remarked, "What a lovely front porch! I can just see myself sitting there, can't you?" You might make note of a single characteristic of a person and use it to shape your opinion of them: "He's got shifty eyes, I don't trust him." Or you might place so much emphasis on one feature you don't like about yourself that you dismiss a positive comment: "You look great in that dress." "Oh, but my hips look so big in this!" In all of these instances, you were picking out *seeds*.

Think about a color or brushstroke you like in a painting, an image that appeals to you, something it reminds you of, an emotion it evokes in you—positive or negative. When you are reading or listening to something inspirational, think about the particular words that stir your spirit, touch your heart, or give you hope. When seeing a movie or play, think about the scenes that bring to mind pieces of your life, things said or unsaid, situations in need of resolution. These are all *seeds*.

Seeds are truly the gift that keeps on giving. When planted in the fertile soil of your Heartland, they can yield a whole new crop of ideas and insights. Each seed is ripe with possibility and can be harvested again and again. There is an old saying: "One can count apples, but one can never count the trees an apple will bring."

Food for Thought

If a journey is "travel from one place to another," then Food for Thought is what you eat when you get there. An infinite number of thoughts and ideas get stirred up during the writing process. Food for Thought asks you to do just that: to think about some of the other creative connections that can sprout from the theme of a chapter or from one of its sections. Think of Food for Thought as *journey* side dishes. They are an extra serving of words and phrases, associated ideas, expanded concepts, and catalysts. They can fire and inspire your imagination.

Let me show you how they can be used. For each section in this book, there are several *journeys,* or writing exercises. At the end of each section, there is a Food for Thought listing. In Chapter 2, "Rainbow of the Spirit," for example, there is a section on the color green. The Green Food for Thought lists "green with envy," "looking green around the gills," the Green Berets, *Fried Green Tomatoes,* greenhorn, "getting the green light," the Green Hornet, "green leafy vegetables," etc. All of these concepts are somehow associated with, connected to, or suggested by the color green.

You might decide to do a five-minute freewrite on "looking green around the gills," and write about being seasick during your entire honeymoon voyage. Or you can create a story on the theme. You may think about the beauty of empowering friendships in *Fried Green Tomatoes* and consider developing more supportive relationships in your life. "Green leafy vegetables" can remind you to attend to your nutritional needs. Thinking about "green with envy" might inspire you to create a painting of the Miss America competition with the faces of all the contestants colored different shades of green as they stare at the winner.

After you have tasted Food for Thought, you can decide whether what you create will be an appetizer, entree, full course meal, or dessert. By allowing other thoughts, memories, and feelings to surface, you can cook up and serve an infinite meal of possibility. Be inspired, stimulated, touched, or amused by them. Let Food for Thought feed you.

Sankofa: Looking Back and Going Forward

There is an African bird that is drawn with its body facing forward and its head looking back, symbolic of the saying "Our future is behind us." This means that in order to build our future, we have to look to our past. We've come a long way since I almost drowned in the Atlantic Ocean some pages ago. You have now been given maps that will help you travel the Heartland territories of mind, body, and spirit. You've also been given a lot to think about. Why don't we rest here for a while before we visit our last concept, Seasonal Surrenders. Let's take a moment to look back and see where we've been so far.

By now, you should be familiar with the terms we've been using in the Heartland: ritual, freewrite, *journey*, *seeds*, food for thought. You have read all about the role of music; the importance of preparation and meditation; giving thanks and setting up a writing altar. You have read about the power of affirming yourself, doing *journeys* or writing exercises, collecting *seeds* from them, then sparking the imagination further with Food for Thought. Let's see how it all works together.

1. *Start with a preparation ritual.* Whether you're getting ready

to write, draw, film, or sing, always, always, *always* do a preparation ritual first. If you are doing creative problem solving, nurturing your spirit, or connecting with yourself, always start with a
preparation ritual. It empowers the writing will and engages the
mind, body, and spirit. It primes your creative spirit to give you
just what you ask for. It is one of the most important things you
can do to enrich and expand your creative center. Why not do
a preparation ritual daily? Every day you engage in the art of
living. Every moment has the potential to be a moment of creation. Keep in mind the components of the preparation ritual.

call in the four directions—primes the spirit, enlists environmental energy
meditation—increases focus, intensifies creative process, invites
the spirit
affirmation—empowers the will, and engages the mind, body
and spirit

2. *Time for a journey*. Put on meditative music and do a five
minute freewrite on a particular idea or theme. Write without
stopping, correcting, or censoring yourself.
Next, collect seeds. These help to identify power points, areas
of connection with the heart and spirit, and much more.
Then decide and develop. What do you want to do with the
writing or with the elements in it? You can leave it as it is,
expand on it, or pull out pieces or *seeds* from it and develop
them. You can jump-start your art by looking behind the words
and seeds for montage and collage, images to string together for
poetry or a painting, photograph, or film.
You can look at the Food for Thought list and see if there is
something additional you'd like to snack on. You can use the
seeds or freewrite as the basis of a story or sonnet, screenplay,
spiritual insight, or self-reflection. You can ask, What does the
writing tell me about myself? What do the seeds reveal?
Journeying can be done as often as you have your creative

sessions, as often as you like. You may want to do several of them in one day. You may want to work with one *journey* for your entire creative session.

3. *Surrender.* You will visit with the Seasonal Surrender rituals in the next section. Rituals have power, and build creative anticipation. Seasonal Surrenders are special rituals that intensify your connection to the seasons inside and around you. They increase your level of awareness, your intuitiveness, and your spiritual consciousness. They are also powerful tools for personal transformation and healing. Take a Seasonal Surrender at least once a day like a vitamin for your spirit.

There you have the three steps: *prepare*, *journey*, and *surrender*. If you want or need to, go back and review the information in each of these sections. Then go forward into the Heartland.

Surrender

> There is a trickling of time in my life, a cascading mountain stream of moments that connect each spring and fall, each blossoming and harvest.
>
> —DANAAN PARRY

Creating can be a ritual act. If you remember, Miss Webster defines a ritual as "a customarily repeated often formal act or series of acts." If you have particular things that you regularly do in a particular way, then you might call those your rituals. On television's *Showtime at the Apollo,* for example, performers appearing on the Amateur Night segment always rub a special wooden tree stump for luck before coming onto the stage.

At Puerto Rico's festival of San Juan Baptiste, hundreds of people line up on the beach, join hands, then walk backward into the ocean seven times without looking back. Some Italian families observe Christmas Eve by serving twelve different kinds of seafood dishes. On New Year's Day, many African-Americans cook and eat hoppin' John, black-eyed peas and rice, for luck throughout the year. All of these are rituals.

Seasonal Surrenders are special rituals that intensify the writing experience, add to your spiritual and creative levels of awareness, and strengthen your connection to the seasons within and without.

Each day all kinds of earthly and cosmic energies affect your physical, mental, and spiritual selves. Rainy days may make you want to stay home and watch movies or cuddle. Lying down on sand and listening to the ocean can comfort, soothe, and heal you. Walking barefoot on the earth can give you a sense of freedom and joy.

Your environment is colored by the people around you and the places you walk through. The weather and the elements of earth, air, fire, and water all have an influence on you. These elements all live inside you as well. Imagine them earthing your desires, airing the spaces that need clarity, firing your intentions, and watering the seeds of your creative being.

When you do the Seasonal Surrenders in this book, you are connecting the inner terrains of the Heartland with the outer landscape of your experiences and environment. These rituals call on you to observe your own weather patterns and dress accordingly. They remind you to create, play, love, let go, honor what you have, and ask for what you need. They also offer you a deeper connection with the art of living, the spirit of being, and the power of healing.

Each day, try one of the Seasonal Surrenders and see how it fits. Remember, the realm of possibility expands to meet your commitment to it.

A few years ago I gave a workshop series called Inner Environments. In the sessions we focused on how the four elements could inspire and influence our lives. In one session, as we explored air, I gave each person a small jar containing two milkweed seeds for their Seasonal Surrender. Attached to the tiny brown core of these seeds are dozens of feathery hairs similar to dandelion fluff. As children, when we saw dandelion wisps floating through the air, we called them *wishees*. We believed that if you caught one and made a wish on it, the wish would come true.

I asked each person to think about something she really wanted, make a wish, blow the milkweed seed away, and let the air take her wish to the place of her dreams. One of my students was sitting on a hill in a New York City park working on a manuscript when she decided to make her wish. Suddenly a gust of wind came along and blew away not only the milkpod but all 200 pages of her manuscript as well!

As she stood in shock watching her work fly into the air, she heard a voice at the bottom of the hill calling, "G'day, miss. Don't worry. I'll get the papers for you!" A handsome Australian man appeared out of nowhere and managed to gather every single page of her manuscript. Believe it or not, as of this writing, more than four years later, they are living very happily on ninety acres of land in upstate New York. She got her wish!

Let's Put It All Together

> Writing is making sense of life.
>
> —NADINE GORDIMER

Now you are ready to travel that fertile territory known as your Heartland. You have continents of consciousness to consider. You have mountains of meditation and music to scale. You have avenues of affirmation to amble through. You have scenes of spirit and surrender to sail through. So pack some clean underwear and all the creative tools you've gathered. You have quite a journey ahead of you.

Dedicate yourself to your creative spirit. Develop a regular schedule for your creative activity. Whether it's a few hours a day or three days a week, be consistent. Write your appointment with yourself down on your calendar. Don't schedule other activities or take phone calls during those hours. Dedicate that time to your Heartland and give it the sacred space it deserves.

Discover which hours are most potent for you and make them yours. I write in the mornings, five days a week. I save the afternoons for my crafts and visual art. Give your spirit that precious gift of time—time to create, to grow, to change, to heal.

Prepare, journey, and surrender. No matter what kind of writer or artist you are, no matter what kind of spirit you are seeking, no matter what kind of life you lead—prepare, journey and surrender. Make a preparation ritual and a Seasonal Surrender part of your daily routine, whether you plan to create that day or not. Try doing a *journey* at least three times a week and see how it feels. Let the spirit walk through your writing and into the landscape of your life.

Each step you take along this journey brings you closer to your spirit, your art, your transformation, your healing. As you walk, you weave the writing. As you talk, you make the songs. As you see, you paint the world. As you breathe, you fill the spirit. Right now you have all of everything you need to create and live with your whole self. Right now you have all the colors, words, songs, films, poems, novels, and consciousness woven into your creative center, your Heartland.

Which threads will you pull from the fabric of your spirit? Which seeds will you drop along the path of your soul so you can find your way back home?

chapter 2

·

RAINBOW OF THE SPIRIT

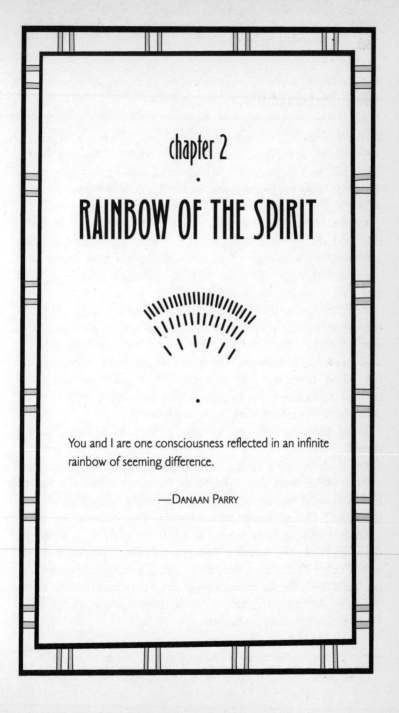

·

You and I are one consciousness reflected in an infinite rainbow of seeming difference.

—DANAAN PARRY

Coloring the Consciousness

When our spirits are down, we feel blue. When we are angry, we see red. We call a coward yellow, and someone new at a job is said to be green. We blanch at off-color jokes. We are in the pink if we're healthy and in the black if we have made a profit, and if we are broke we haven't got one red cent.

In this chapter we will take a look at the historical, the spiritual, and the metaphysical side of colors as we begin this walk on the rainbow side of town. We will explore how colors have been used through the ages, what they mean to our lives now, and how they might work for you.

Did you know that every color has its own energy? The energy in that color may attract or repel, warm or warn you. For example, take a look at how men react when a woman in a red dress walks into a room. There is a reason why stop signs are red, school buses and taxicabs are yellow, and health-food places are green. Research has been conducted on the energy of these colors and the effects they have on people.

Every color has its own vibration. Think of a tuning fork, a musical note, or the strings of a guitar vibrating when plucked. Color has a vibration similar to that, but at a different volume and a much higher frequency. Sometimes, though, it seems as if we can hear a color. I'm sure you've heard someone say, "That color is too loud!" Did you ever wonder why? The vibrations of colors connect with your body in ways you may not even be conscious of.

In her book *The Miracle of Metaphysical Healing* (Parker Publishing), Evelyn Monahan writes about being an epileptic whose arm was paralyzed. She had also suffered from blindness for nine years. She was able to overcome these disabilities using metaphysical healing through color. She writes:

Each color has its own vibratory pattern and its own special energy to offer you in bringing the miracle of metaphysical healing to yourself and loved ones. . . . Through the use of your energized mind you can surround yourself with the energies of the color that offers you the quickest road to perfect health. Aided by your highest self you can also select clothing of colors which will be of greatest benefit to you in the area of metaphysical healing.

Hospitals have studied the effect of color on patients and healing. Red has been found to increase energy, violet to endow dignity, blue to calm, and orange to promote joy. A hospital using these specific color energies might place a restless patient in a blue room and a lethargic one in a rose-colored room. The patient entrance would be painted violet, and the staff entrance would be orange in order to brighten the disposition of those caring for the patients.

Rudolf Steiner was an early-twentieth-century educator and philosopher who conducted extensive studies on the effect of color. He believed that a child's spirituality was the most critical resource for learning. His subsequent color theories were reflected in color schemes he developed for classrooms at his first school in Stuttgart. He chose colors that specifically promoted spiritual growth, enhanced the learning process, and enriched a child's development.

Ancient Egyptians used color for healing purposes as part of their temple ceremonies. Traditional Chinese doctors diagnose patients by reading what they call the color of the pulses, body organs, and complexion. Edgar Cayce, America's most prominent psychic, tells us that the vibrations we see as color originate from the spiritual realm. He says that they are merely channels for greater forces in the universe.

In a 1982 study conducted by psychic Carol Ann Liaron, she discovered that the blind could be taught to see. "They interpreted colors through feeling the density and temperature of the air that surrounds objects. They were able to distinguish colors from across the room, and shop for clothes by running their hands a few inches from the garment."

If you close your eyes and concentrate on breathing in the color blue, it has a calming effect. If you meditate on green, it can accelerate the healing process. It has been found that our organisms have the ability to emit and absorb light. Some healers have begun to use this ability to develop a variation on acupuncture. Instead of using needles to pierce certain parts of the body for healing purposes, these healers are using color to penetrate the body. They have reported success in easing specific physical complaints. Called colorpuncture, it allows access to the spirit inside by working on the physical body outside.

Scientific studies have shown that colors can improve mental abilities, increase spiritual consciousness, calm emotions, and stimulate healing influences. When an assault left me on crutches for five months, I needed color to help heal all the wounded parts of me. I wore brightly flowered dresses so I could feel as if I were receiving a bouquet of flowers every day. In the winter, I dressed myself in bright yellows, oranges, and pinks to lift my spirits again. After physical therapy and chiropractic sessions, I would hobble down the street singing some inspiring words from a South African freedom song, "Something inside so strong, I think I can make it."

Memory and experience are painted in many colors. You experience these colors every time you reach inside to create. Some of the colors are faded and some become brighter with each passing year. They change with the seasons, in different lights, with different emotions. Utilizing color as we create allows us to shape these changes and use them in ways that add depth to our sentences, souls, and situations.

Many ancient civilizations perceived the body as red, the mind as yellow, and the spirit as blue. When you access your Heartland, you engage the body, mind, and spirit in the creative process. Theo Gimbel's *Healing with Color and Light* (Fireside/Simon and Schuster) and Dan Campbell's *Edgar Cayce on the Power of*

Color, Stones, and Crystals (Warner Books) are both excellent resources for information on the holistic powers of color.

In this chapter, we will travel the terrains of red, yellow, and blue, as well as those of orange, green, and violet. Each color has its own distinct properties. Make note of these characteristics as you fully explore the infinite spectrum of the rainbow spirit.

Rainbow Meditation

Before you begin your writing, creating, or connecting sessions, remember to prepare your creative spirit with music, meditation, and affirmation. Incense or sage helps to clear energy and alert the spirits. After completing your preparation ritual, keep your hands over your heart, and read the following meditation:

The season embraces me with the rainbow spirit of her being,
and beckons the golden sun to fill my mind
with thoughts of new beginnings.

I walk in the rainbow of life every day,
breathing in the season of myself
in all of its splendor.

My words move from newness to fullness.
I am the art and the reasons for it.
I am the soul and spirit
Of everything that came before me.
I am all the future would have me be.

I am all spectrums of the spirit,
speaking my colors,
and birthing the rainbow of myself
again and again and again.

After the meditation, close your eyes and take time to observe the thoughts and feelings that color your inner landscape. Then take three deep breaths and open your eyes again. Say your affirmation, making sure it is phrased in the present, and get ready to ride the rainbow.

The Realm of Red

> I have been taught by apples
> We talked together
> On a red day
> When the sun
> Made us both shine.
>
> —DOROTHY RANDALL GRAY

Our journey starts with red, the color of fire engines, stop signs, pomegranates, and passion. We take red-eye flights and have red-letter days. We refer to a red herring as something that distracts our attention from the real issue.

Metaphysical research has found that red is associated with assertiveness, courage, passion, sexuality, and willpower. It is the color of motivation and initiative, helping us overcome feelings of limitation. It helps people cope with life and meet its challenges with enthusiasm and optimism. Red keeps us alert, enhances activity, energizes the body, and encourages self-confidence.

According to lore from the Middle Ages, a red stone or ruby was believed to hold a fiery spark from the planet Mars that "would not dim or die until the earth itself turned cold and lifeless." Rubies were used by Egyptians to warm mummies and to protect their owners from danger and misfortune.

Begin to think of red in all shades of its meanings as you walk toward your first *journey*. Take a moment to ask yourself, "What red herrings are in my creative life?"

RED JOURNEYS

Reminder: The five-minute freewrite for each journey begins with music. Write as fast as you can, keeping your pen on the paper. Let the words flow.

There is something very special about using a pen for this initial process. It just isn't the same on a computer. The initial flow from Heartland to hand allows you full access to your creative energy. Remember, you won't always have a computer, a paintbrush, or a camera with you when you need to capture an image or a thought. Train yourself to write very fast by hand.

After you write it by hand, you can always enter the freewrite into your computer and expand on it from there. Once it is on the computer, you may decide to do another freewrite based on one of the seeds. If so, just put your fingers on the keyboard and keep your eyes closed while you type. Always serenade the muse as you write.

- Pick five red items from around your house and create five sentences for each one. If you choose, for example, a tube of lipstick, a ribbon, a miniature wagon, nail polish, and an apple, you might begin: "I'm going to fix her little red wagon" or " 'They say an apple a day keeps the doctor away,' she mused as she lay in her hospital bed. 'But maybe I shouldn't have thrown it at him.' "

- Visualize a color from your childhood. Close your eyes and think of clothing you might have worn, places you visited, a toy you wanted, or perhaps an animal that was important to your life. Make note of all the sounds, smells, and memories associated with the color you have chosen. Now open your eyes and freewrite for five minutes.

- A red-letter day. Write about a special day in your life, a day that was important or significant to you in some way.

- "I saw red."
  Food for Thought: anger, embarrassment, humiliation.

- "I caught him red-handed."
  Food for Thought: fraud, embezzlement, lies of all colors, adultery, thievery, adolescent drug use.

- Paint the town red.
  Food for Thought: celebrations, hitting the lottery, *Queen for a Day*

When you have finished each of the freewrites, read them aloud to yourself. Look inside the writing and see if it tells you where it wants to go. Or see if the words just want to sit for a while and think about themselves.

RED FOOD FOR THOUGHT

Reminder: These are words or phrase associations related to or inspired by a specific theme, such as the color red. In each section, the Food for Thought list can be used like seeds to take you on countless additional writing *journeys*. Remember that the spiritual, historical, psychological, or other properties of the colors are all grounds for *journeying*. Each characteristic of any of the colors can be used to inspire your creative sessions.

- *Red envelopes on Chinese New Year*

- *Red ink*—business or financial loss

- *Red ribbon*—second-place winner

- *Red fox*—cocoa butter, stockings, comedian

- *Red light, red-light district*

- *Red neck, red wine, red tape*

- *Red pepper, red snapper, red herring*

- *Red flag, red-eye flight, red-eye* (cheap alcohol)

- *Red-blooded American, a Red* (communist)

- *Red heat, red hot, red hots* (candy or hot dogs)

- *The Red Badge of Courage*

- *The Scarlet Letter*

- *Scarlett O'Hara*

- *Bette Davis's red dress in* Jezebel

- *Red Guard,* Mao's young activists in China

- *"Red sky at dawning, sailor take warning"*

RED SEASONAL SURRENDERS

- Make a list of things about yourself that are special or significant. On red-letter days we celebrate something special. You might add to the list some ways in which you would *like* to be special.

    Consider qualities you don't usually think of as special, such as: "I am a loyal friend," "I took care of my grandmother," "I am very generous," "I am there when people need me," "I made it through a very difficult childhood," "I survived the death of (or divorce from) a loved one."

    I am sure you know people who do not have these special attributes. Much has been written about betrayals from adultery to child abuse. We read about elderly citizens who are abused and neglected, people who are emotionally and financially withholding, those who cannot be counted on, and those who could not survive a crisis. All these people made different choices about how they have needed to walk through this world. That is what makes *your* qualities special, and why these are all reasons to celebrate yourself.

Pick five things from your list and write them down on a small piece of red cloth. Place a pinch of alfalfa seeds on the side of the cloth with the writing. While thinking about those special qualities of yours, make a little bundle by twisting the edges of the cloth together and tying a length of string around the closure a few times.

This is your writing *juju* or magic bag. Keep it on your left side to receive its energy. The seeds symbolize the strengthening, growth, and empowerment of your special qualities. Alfalfa grass makes horses strong. If it can do that for horses, imagine what it can do for you.

- Wear or carry something red every day for a week—a smooth stone in your pocket, a red ribbon, an apple, underwear, socks, a scarf, or any other garment. Even if red is not a color you usually wear, do it anyway and note how it makes you feel. Don't be afraid to surprise yourself.

- Play with a red rubber ball for a while. Bounce it on the floor or throw it up against a wall and play catch with yourself. Think of it as a meditation.

- Red is associated with assertiveness, courage, willpower, motivation, and initiative. Think of three things you have been wanting to say or do that call for one or several of these qualities. Think red, wear red, and/or hold your *juju* bag, take a deep breath, then do at least one of the three things.

- Put on some soft music, and prepare for a journey to the *House Where Passion Lives*. Close your eyes and make yourself comfortable. As you listen to the music, visualize yourself walking to this house, opening the door, and going in. Think about how it is decorated, who lives there, what happens inside, and how it feels to be there. Allow yourself to fully experience any thoughts and feelings that arise. Then turn around, walk out of the house, and slowly come back to the present moment.

Orange County

In many Asian cultures, orange is a color associated with time and mystic influences. Gurus of several Eastern spiritual faiths traditionally wear orange as a symbol of their mission of selfless service and the sacrifice of their personal ego. Tantric yoga practitioners often wear orange to reflect their use of sexual energy for spiritual purposes.

Orange is an important color for combating depression and tiredness. According to Theo Gimbel in *Healing with Color and Light,* a person who has difficulty getting themselves going in the morning, can put on a pair of orange glasses and feel thoroughly awake in about fifteen minutes.

It is no accident that fast-food places like McDonald's and Howard Johnson's feature orange prominently in their restaurants. Orange assists in the assimilation of food as well as thought, and enhances dining pleasure. In an aura, orange indicates a person who is thoughtful, considerate, congenial, and eager to help.

Everyone's body has certain energy centers. In Eastern spiritual practices, these energy centers are known as *chakras*. The eight *chakras* each have a color and a specified part of the body that they radiate from, similar to rays of light. The *chakra* you might be most familiar with is the one called the *third eye*. This *chakra* is located between your eyebrows and is said to be the center of creative visualization.

The color orange is related to what is known as the *sacral chakra*. It is located in the area around the adrenal glands, which are just below your waistline. Probably because of this *chakra*'s positioning, orange is related to the womb and the procreation process. According to Legion of Light, a metaphysical research organization, one of the properties orange is said to have is the ability to channel sexual energy into outlets of creativity and accomplishment. The current practice of dressing prisoners in orange garb might just have the redirection of sexual energy as one of its motives.

We perceive light and color through our eyes. Light and color also enter the body through the skin. Color therapists use colored lights to restore the balance in or positively affect different parts of the body. They have successfully used orange to treat cholera, bronchitis, and kidney ailments.

On a metaphysical level, orange symbolizes the rising sun, awakenings, and the dawning of awareness. As it brings an openness to new perspectives, orange also helps people to access the power they need to meet life's challenges. Orange encourages the release of fears, inhibitions, and repressed emotions. It affects the warmth and goodness of the heart and is indicative of giving and letting go. The comforting energy of orange also stimulates dance and movement, joyfulness, lightness, pleasure, tolerance, and physical well-being. Self-esteem, assertiveness, and creative and harmonious interactions with others are all said to be enhanced by orange.

ORANGE JOURNEYS

- The color orange is associated with freedom and release. Write the word *freedom* and the word *release* at the top of the page, on separate pieces of paper. Do a freewrite on each one.

  Food for Thought: divorce, parole, hostages, slavery, stress reduction.

- Orange is related to concepts of time. Do a freewrite on the following question: Where do you keep the time you save?

  Years ago, some southern states did not participate in changing the clocks for daylight saving time. They had what was called *slow time* and *fast time*. You actually had to turn your watch back an hour if you were traveling from north to south.

  Food for Thought: time-saving measures that affect quality, procrastination, time shares, resistance to changing times.

- Comfort and warmth are in Orange's dominion. Do a freewrite on the phrase "All the comforts of home."

Food for Thought: "Make yourself comfortable," tight shoes, lack of physical and/or emotional warmth, Southern Comfort.

ORANGE FOOD FOR THOUGHT

- *Sunrise*

- *Sunset*

- *Warning signs*

- *Plastic protective covering at construction sites*

- *Prison uniforms*

- *Orange Bowl*

- *Agent Orange*

- *Fast-food roofs*

- *Orangeman*—In northern Ireland in 1795, a secret society was organized to support the Protestant religion as well as to defend the British sovereignty. Its members were known as orangemen.

- *Carrots, tangerines, cantaloupe, oranges*

- *Candy corn and other Halloween treats*

- *Autumn vegetables*—squash and pumpkins

ORANGE SURRENDERS

- Orange teaches us to give and let go. Make a list of five things you want to give and five things you want or need to let go of.

- Try color breathing to lift your spirits. Close your eyes and take five deep breaths. Visualize yourself breathing in orange for joy, happiness, and fun. As you exhale, breathe out the color blue.

• Use the power of the sunrise or sunset to energize you. Remember, this color encourages lightness, fun, happiness, movement, and pleasure.

Write five sentences that begin with "I feel the lightness of being when . . ." Then light a white candle in a glass and place slices of oranges, tangerines, or other sweet orange edibles around it. Burn incense and/or put on a scented oil or perfume you enjoy smelling.

Stand in the sun and read the five sentences aloud, then smile, breathe in the sun's rays, and fold the paper. Put on some lively music and let your body move freely to its energy. Hold the folded paper in your left hand or tuck it in your underwear so that it is close to the body.

After five minutes or so, read the sentences again. Place the folded paper under the saucer. Then slowly eat one or more of the sweet pieces of orange food around the white candle, allowing yourself to savor the sweetness and fullness of joy. Let the candle burn until the next sunrise or sunset.

Mellow Yellow

Like sunlight, yellow is associated with brilliance and illumination. It is the color of the mind, of intellect, joy, humor, enthusiasm, and self-esteem. Yellow is the color connected to your solar plexus, which is located just behind the stomach. It is the place inside you that harbors emotional energies. When you say, "I have a gut feeling," this is exactly where that feeling is located.

The solar plexus has also been called the soul of the individual. In his book *Healing with Color and Light,* renowned color therapist Theo Gimbel compares the solar plexus to the sun, describing it as a light that descends into the nervous system. "From here you are sensitive to situations. It is the center of human recognition and self-worth. Unresolved situations create stress here."

The ancient Hindus believed amber was a piece of the sun gone hard. A Roman healer named Pliny used amber's medicinal powers to treat headaches and stomach ailments. Egyptians cured jaundice with pulverized yellow beryl. They also believed that yellow topaz instilled wisdom and gave one power over wild animals.

Yellow stimulates the mind's reasoning qualities as well as the soul's instinctual awareness, its gut feelings. It is also the color of expressiveness, transformation, objectivity, detachment, and attention to detail. Yellow helps you to have clear thoughts and make sound judgments, permits you to see your own and other people's feelings objectively, and enables you to appreciate or criticize your creations.

The sense of hearing is associated with yellow. Closing the eyes removes the sense of sight and enhances the powers of hearing. Sound shines a different light on your experiences. Think of hearing as another way of seeing. Reading your work aloud is an important way of getting perspective on what you have written. This is one of the reasons for staged readings. The playwright needs to *hear* the script in order to *see* it. Often the ears pick up what the eyes miss: errors; words or sentences that need reworking; dialogue or scenes that looked good on paper, but don't sound right to the ear.

Yellow is the perfect color to have around your creative environment. Try keeping yellow objects in your writing area—yellow flowers in a vase, bananas, squash, grapefruit, or golden Delicious apples in a bowl. Sometimes the muse gets hungry while you write. You can always inject that delicious yellow energy directly into your body to feed her.

YELLOW JOURNEYS

Remember to do your preparation, meditation, and affirmation rituals before starting your creative sessions. You will be glad you did. Do a five-minute freewrite for each of these journeys.

- "I knew it, I just knew it." Say these words aloud, then close your eyes for a moment and give the phrase time to sink in. Now open your eyes and do a five-minute freewrite.

  Food for Thought: intuition, stockbrokers and speculations (the subject matter of several movies), betting on a sure thing, a mother's intuition, premonitions about a plane crash, psychic capacities, self-fulfilling prophecies.

- "I could feel it in the pit of my stomach."

  Food for Thought: uneasiness, meeting new people, "we have to talk," rising anger, repressed feelings, swallowing pride or fear, listening with the heart.

- "Sunshine came softly to my window today." Take a look at this line and do a freewrite.

  Food for Thought: a country retreat, winter dreams, healing, musings of a caged bird, playing hookey, a new day, hope.

YELLOW FOOD FOR THOUGHT

- *The sun, sunny disposition, Sunny Delight*

- *Songs*: "Here Comes the Sun," "Good Day Sunshine"

- *Gold, brass, topaz, yellow diamonds, chrysolite, amber*

- *Egg yolks, sunflowers, jonquils, corn, squash, bananas, lemons, grapefruit*

- *McDonald's arches, warning signs and lights*

- *Songs*: "Mellow Yellow," "Yellow Moon"

- *Yellow police tape* marking the scene of a crime

- *Yellow journalism*: sensationalist journalism featuring scandalous or distorted news items.

- *Yellow peril*: Asian laborers who were willing to work for very low wages were perceived as a threat to Western standards and civilization when they began to increase in number, power and influence.

- *Yellow jack,* a flag indicating that a ship is in quarantine

- *Yellow dog*: a person who is mean or contemptible; yellow-dog contract. In order to get a job, employers sometimes forced workers to sign an agreement vowing that they would never join a union.

- *Yellowed*—to become discolored usually through age or disease

- *Yellow*—cowardly

- *Yellow fever, yellow jaundice, yellow ocher*

- *Yellowfin tuna, yellow bird, yellow-bellied sapsucker*

- *Yellow pages, yellow jacket*

YELLOW SEASONAL SURRENDERS

- Bring fresh yellow flowers to your job or put them in an unexpected place in your house. Keep them there for at least a week. Note how the flowers make you feel and how others react to them.

- Try color breathing. Sit in a comfortable position. Place one or a few bright yellow objects in front of you. Focus on them for at least a minute as you breathe naturally, gradually allowing your body to relax more and more. Now close your eyes and visualize yourself inhaling the color yellow into your body. With each breath, feel the yellow flowing through your nostrils and right into the solar plexus in your upper abdomen. After about five minutes, slowly open your eyes.

  Breathing in yellow increases your objectivity and intellectual powers. After doing this surrender a few times, try envisioning the color in your mind, instead of using the objects as the first point of focus. This exercise is great any time you need a mental lift.

• Draw the power of the sun into your body. Stand outside or at your window. Close your eyes and let the sun kiss your face. Hold your arms out to the sun as if they were antennas and say, "I reach for the sun and my highest self." Now close your fingers around the warm rays and slowly pull the energy into your heart, placing the right hand of giving over the left hand of receiving.

• Hold a few dried peas or beans in your hand and energize them with your breath saying, "As this seed grows, so grows my _____." Think about how you would fill in the blank. Drop the peas/beans into a hole in the soil and completely cover them with earth.

Hold a glass of water in your hand and energize it with your breath, saying, "As this water feeds the soil, so am I being fed every day in every way." Pour onto the soil. Use this ritual in the spring or at any time of new beginnings.

Green Light

Green is the color of nature. In the spring, as green shoots emerge from seemingly barren branches, we are reminded of hope, renewal, and fertility. Health and healing, peace and harmony, contentment and compassion are all in the province of green.

Green dwells in the heart *chakra,* where it stimulates love, understanding, and nurturing. It is useful in helping to release fears related to intimacy and emotional involvement. The color also has a calming effect on the nervous system. Green rooms, where actors or talk-show guests wait before appearing onstage, are a manifestation of this particular effect.

The principle of balance is an important aspect of the color green. Green relates to leading a balanced life and to living in balanced relationships. This color represents the pivotal point between mind and body, ego and the higher self. Appearing at the center of the rainbow, green is also said to represent the Christ Principle as a central influence on the earth.

In ancient times breastplates created for Hebrew high priests were fitted with stones whose vibrations emitted spiritual and physical influences. By touching the emerald on his breastplate, for example, a priest was able to access its energy of wisdom and understanding, examine all facets of an issue, and arrive at a balanced judgment.

Prosperity and wealth are related to green. "Greenbacks" and "mean green" are slang references to money. Some believe that burning green candles will attract money, work, and matrimony. The beautiful goddesses of love and abundance, Het Heru in the Khametic or Egyptian tradition and Oshun in the African diaspora, both use green as one of their representative colors.

Color therapists tell us that green is associated with the sense of smell. The olfactory region of the brain is one of the first parts of that organ to evolve. This may offer a partial explanation as to why smells have the ability to evoke such vivid recollections of early experiences. In fact, each time I smell bread burning, I can still recall a comic strip from more than twenty years ago in which a husband asked his wife why she always burned his toast. She replied, "So you can scrape it to the shade you like."

GREEN JOURNEYS

- Green apples, green grapes, green eggs and ham. Do a five-minute freewrite on any green edible.

  Food for Thought: apple pie and holidays, memories of Granny Smith, being in a pickle.

- Pick out five things that have a distinct smell and place them in front of you. Try to have a mixture of smells in front of you, sweet and sour as well as bitter and pungent. Close your eyes, smell one of the items, and freewrite. Then proceed to the next ones until you have completed all five.

  Food for Thought: the carnage of war, smelling smoke, the smell of fear, perfume memories.

- Green can also represent jealousy, greed, and emotional repression. Think about an incident in your life that involved one of these three things, then do a freewrite.

  Food for Thought: *The Treasure of the Sierra Madre,* an overbearing relative or spouse, the cheerleader's mother who murdered her daughter's competitor.

- Pick out a piece of music that makes you feel loved or loving. If it has words, listen to it for a while with your eyes closed. When the selection has ended, open your eyes and freewrite. If the music has no lyrics, let it continue to play when you open your eyes to write.

GREEN FOOD FOR THOUGHT

- *Green with envy*

- *Getting the green light*

- *Looking green around the gills*

- *The green-eyed monster*—jealousy

- *Greenhorn,* a person who is unsophisticated or inexperienced

- *Green Berets*

- *Green Bay Packers*

- *Greenwich Mean Time*

- *"Greensleeves"*

- *How Green Was My Valley*

- *Fried Green Tomatoes*

- *Green Eggs and Ham,* children's book by Dr. Seuss

- *Green onions, green leafy vegetables, green tea, green beans, green salad, green apples, green pepper, watermelon, limes, pickles*

- *Greenmarket, green thumb*

- *Greenhouse, greenhouse effect*

- *Green monkey,* a West African monkey often used in medical research, for example, in the movie *Outbreak*

- *Green snake, green turtle, Green Hornet*

- *Greenback*—money

- *Putting green, greenbelt*

- *Emeralds, the Emerald City, the Emerald Isle*

GREEN SURRENDERS

- Treat yourself like a lover this week. Surprise yourself with a gift or by taking yourself somewhere you really enjoy. Make a candlelit dinner for yourself. Set the table with flowers and your favorite dinnerware. Play soft, romantic music. Take time to savor the meal and the comfort of quality solitude.

- Create a healing list. Write on a green piece of paper or use green ink to make a list of people and situations that are in need of healing. Start with yourself, then people that are close to you, the places you live, work, and play in, the environment surrounding you, and finally the planet. When you meditate or sit down to think for a while, keep this list in mind, and send green healing thoughts to the people and places on your list.

- Commit five random acts of love this week and see how it feels.

- Breathe in green and breathe out magenta to cleanse your system and feel more balanced.

- Think of all the loving things ever said to you (or loving things you *wish* had been said to you) and write them down. Put each on a separate heart-shaped piece of paper (yes, I'm asking you to cut out hearts or find a heart-shaped pad). If you must, use pink index cards. Play a love song or sweet music, read the words aloud, and stroke your cheek after each sentence. Know that you are loved.

Muse Blues

Blue is the color of the spirit. In India, deities are painted blue to show a high level of spirituality. According to an Aramaic translation of the Old Testament, lapis lazuli, a beautiful dark blue stone, was used for the tablets of the Ten Commandments Moses brought down from Sinai. The same stone was included in the wrappings of Tutankhamen's mummy. For hundreds of years, lapis lazuli was presented by priest-kings in China as an offering to the Lord of the Universe in ceremonies at the Temple of Heaven.

"Blue suggests the quiet purposefulness that should infuse our choices, our ideals," says Dan Campbell, biographer of Edgar Cayce, the "Sleeping Prophet." "The will is the fulcrum upon which choices are made because free will is the birthright that allows us to live to greater or lesser purposes." Blue is connected to the throat chakra, the center for creative self-expression located at the thyroid gland. If we think of writing as a journey of quiet purposefulness, it is no wonder that researchers often find dark blue in the auras of writers and singers.

The expression *true blue* was probably derived from some of the noted qualities associated with blue—truth and trust, loyalty and devotion. Color therapists recommend using blue in bedrooms, offices, treatment rooms, and stress areas because of its calming and relaxing qualities. They also use the color to help insomnia, nervousness, and asthmatic conditions. In times of anxiety, fear, and panic, blue soothes the mind and emotions.

The sense of taste is directly related to the color blue. In fact, when it is used to solarize water, blue acts as a taste enhancer. Water placed in a blue glass or a glass with a blue filter around it and left in the sunlight for as little as half an hour will taste sweeter than before. Some of you will probably remember those old blue seltzer bottles delivered in wooden crates.

Blue enhances contemplation and meditation and is indicative of wisdom, serenity, patience, sincerity, and reliability. All of these are qualities you will embody at various stages of your writing life.

Try doing your preparation, meditation, and affirmation rituals while sitting on, wearing, or looking at something blue. Perhaps you can keep a blue scarf or shirt, a blue hat, or special blue socks just for your writing sessions.

Since writing is a ritual act, consider dressing the part. Putting on a ritual outfit or item is another way of announcing your intentions to the creative spirit. We put on formal clothes for very special occasions, uniforms for required duties, and "dress for success" outfits to fortify your self-confidence. Each time you engage your Heartland in the writing process, it *is* a special occasion. Why not dress for writing success?

BLUE JOURNEYS

- "Blue Moon, you saw me standing alone."

    Food for thought: a one-person campaign for a just cause (Ibsen's *An Enemy of the People*), last child to be chosen for a team (Janis Ian's song "At Seventeen"), rejected lover wishing on a star, isolation and disfranchisement, loneliness—cause and effect.

- "Bluebird, bluebird on my shoulder."

    Food for Thought: pet tales, view from a prison window *(Birdman of Alcatraz),* fond or not-so-fond remembrances of childhood games.

- "Nothing but blue skies do I see."

    Food for Thought: first time in an airplane, apartment on the twenty-fifth floor, landing flat on your back, thoughts about the worst being over.

- "Dreams really do come true."

    Food for Thought: a dream prophecy, "Calgon, take me away,"; Aretha Franklin's "Daydreaming," a paralyzed person walks again, thinking the grass is greener on the other side, denial of entitlement, as in Langston Hughes' poem, "What Happens to a Dream Deferred."

- Serenity, truth, patience, and peace are one side of the coin of blue. If we look at indicators on the other side, we find fear, worry, depression, and coldness. Take a critical or traumatic situation in your life and color it blue by writing about it from both sides. First, get a clear picture of the situation in your mind. Next, ask it five questions, two from one side of blue and three from the other side.

    For example, when was there fear? Where did the peace go? Why was there coldness? Where was the honesty? What happened to the spirit? After you write the questions down, close your eyes and look at the situation again. Then put on your music and see what writing flows in the five-minute freewrite. Now, look at what you have written and see what other writing these questions evoke.

This exercise can also be used to explore other kinds of events in your life or in the lives of others, and in writing about a fictional character or about the subject of a nonfiction profile.

BLUE FOOD FOR THOUGHT

- *Talking a blue streak*
- *Talking till you're blue in the face*
- *The blues*
- *Out of the blue*
- *Once in a blue moon*
- *The boys in blue*
- *Blue ribbon* (first place)
- *Blue baby, blue blood*
- *Bluebeard, blue book*
- *Blue cheese, bluefish, blueberries*
- *Blue plate special*
- *Blue-chip stocks*
- *Bluegrass music*
- *Blue-collar workers*
- *Blue laws, blue line, blueprint*
- *Blue hair on an elderly woman*

- *Bluing for white clothing*

- *Blue bayou*

- *Blue lagoon*

- *Blue lights in the basement,* a soft, dark atmosphere with slow, soulful music

- *"Blue Christmas" "Blue Sweade Shoes"*—Elvis songs

- *The permanent frown on Taj Mahal's face because, as he sang, he "got the blues so bad one time."*

- *"The water is so blue you could dip a pen in it and write a love letter."* (A line from travel writer Kerrick Jones)

BLUE SURRENDERS

- Take a bath in your own spirit. Put a few drops of blue food coloring in your bathwater. Before you get into the water, talk to it and tell it what you would like your spirit to be bathed in. Stroke the water as you speak to it.

    Try to have at least three blue things in the water or surrounding you—cloth, flowers, fabric, grapes, etc. Have a blue candle and soft music playing. Turn out the lights and imagine that you are in the belly of the spirit and she is stroking you where you need it the most.

- Visit with the sky and stars for five minutes at least twice this week. Take the time to look up and see the world a little differently. Make note of the colors and configurations. Don't let sky deprivation strike when you're not looking. One of my favorite lines from writer Zora Neale Hurston is "We all share the same sky."

- Make a bottle of blue solarized water and drink it before your meditation or at times when you need the energy of blue to flow through your body. Just get a blue bottle, fill it with water, and leave it in the sunlight for about an hour. In addition to tasting sweeter, the water will also embody the calming and other properties of blue.

Purple Rain

When we think about transformation, prayer, or our higher power, we are looking at some of the most potent aspects of the color purple, or violet. When we think of transcendence, spiritual aspirations, or creative visualization—the art of envisioning the things we desire and empowering them to manifest—we are connecting with the inspirational elements of purple.

This direct connection to higher states of consciousness is what associates violet with the sense of touch. When a person is touched with care, a spiritual energy is emitted. Most of us have experienced the power of a healing hug, the comfort of a hand stroking our back or gently placed upon our own. This powerful energy is such an integral part of our life force that babies can die from lack of touch. Researchers have found the visualizing violet when giving a massage can actually cause the person receiving the massage to feel uplifted.

Violet is the color of that powerful center known as the third eye, located at the middle of your forehead. This center receives communications from your higher self and enhances meditation, insight, intuition, and contemplation. Color therapist Theo Gimbel states that all experiences from your past lives are stored in your third eye.

For thousands of years, violet has signified royalty, majesty, and power. Amethyst, a beautiful purple stone, has historically been a potent transmitter of violet's energy. Set into the rings of Catholic bishops, amethyst symbolized their moral victory over worldly passions. The ancient Hebrews believed amethysts had the power to summon pleasant dreams. Hunters wore the stone to assist them in capturing wild animals. Soldiers counted on amethyst for protection and to assure victory over the enemy.

The healing properties of violet can tranquilize the nerves and dissolve negativity. In color therapy, violet indicates dignity and respect in mental, emotional, and physical health. When a color therapist is conducting a diagnosis, the appearance of violet in a healthy spine means that the patient is respecting their personal mental activities, feelings, and physical body. It also means a person is behaving in a dignified way, and is treating everything in the home environment with respect.

Purple inspires meditation and forgiveness. Its vibrations can promote spiritual growth and help release old mental and emotional patterns. Traditionally, purple has also indicated devotion, service, reverence, loyalty, and grace. Purple is also the color of patience, a virtue those of us on creative and spiritual paths seek to embody.

I am sure St. Francis de Sales had us in mind when he wrote: "Be patient with everyone, but above all with yourself. Do not be disheartened by your imperfections, but always rise up with fresh courage. How are we to be patient in dealing with our neighbor's faults if we are impatient in dealing with our own? Those who are fretted by their own failings will not correct them. All profitable correction comes from a calm and peaceful mind."

In many spiritually conscious communities, there is a belief that the powerful energies of violet are growing in influence as we travel through the New Age toward the year 2000. We see the color purple appearing with a greater frequency than ever before—on advertisements, vehicles, and television weather maps and in the clothing of more and more men, women, and children. In addition, we see transformations taking place in the areas of spirituality, consciousness, and alternative medicine. We also see an increased emphasis on the importance of intuition therapy and meditation.

As violet calls us to a higher consciousness, we can allow its energies to transform our writing and our lives by keeping more of the color in our personal and professional environments. What would happen if we each followed our higher minds, if we treated each other with dignity, if we took the time to touch, to forgive? We might just heal ourselves and change the world. Give it a try.

VIOLET JOURNEYS

• It is said that violet has the ability to calm violence. Write about an incidence of violence you have been a victim of or have witnessed.

   Food for Thought: a woman who is stalked, an abused child, blaming a TV program or a movie for an act of violence.

• Many best-selling books and popular movies have been based on experiences that changed lives. Write about an experience that transformed your life.

   Food for Thought: the song "Amazing Grace" written by a repentant white slave trader, *The Shawshank Redemption,* a mother whose child suddenly disappears, near-death experiences.

• We may travel several spiritual paths before finding one that suits us. Close your eyes and ask yourself the question "When I follow my spirit, where does it take me?" Then freewrite what comes to you.

   Food for Thought: religious disputes, giving up everything to join an ashram, the lives of Buddha, Malcolm X, and Mother Teresa, movies *Gandhi* and *The Last Temptation of Christ.*

• Devotion, loyalty, and service are all indicated by violet. Write about how these words apply to an incident from your mother's life.

   Food for Thought: a twenty-five-year employee of a company, a soldier conflicted about obeying orders, health and civil service workers.

VIOLET FOOD FOR THOUGHT

- *Pansies, eggplant, grapes, blackberries, beet tops, cabbage*

- *Violets,* a traditional candied breath freshener

- *Purple,* often a color used to indicate regal or imperial power or rank

- *Christian color for Advent and Lent*

- *Purple Heart,* a military award given to armed forces members who are killed in action or wounded.

- *Purple passage.* When a particularly effective or brilliant passage occurs in an otherwise uninteresting or uninspired piece of writing, it is called a purple passage.

- *The Color Purple,* novel and movie

- *"Lavender Blue,"* song

- *"Deep Purple,"* song

- *"Purple Rain,"* song

- *The Lavender Hill Mob,* movie

- *Purple with rage*

- *Ultraviolet rays*

VIOLET SURRENDERS

- Violet can help promote forgiveness and the release and transformation of old emotional patterns. Wear or place amethyst nearby or wear something violet as you make a list of forgiveness. Using purple ink or purple paper, write down all of the people and situations that have hurt you in some way, beginning each sentence with "I forgive you for . . ."

Be sure to include things you may need to forgive yourself for. Read the list aloud each day for five days. On the fifth day, tear the list into pieces and burn it in a safe receptacle. As the paper is transformed into smoke and ash, envision the hurt being transformed as well. The next day, scatter the ashes onto the earth.

- To increase your self-respect and feeling of dignity, breathe in violet and breathe out yellow.

- Let the full moon shine its divine light on the spirit of your violet self. With a glass of grape juice in your left hand, stand in front of a window in the moonlight. Toast the moon with the juice, then speak these words into the glass: "I am patient with myself, I heal myself, and I touch the heart of all that is my self."

Slowly drink the juice and envision the power of violet flowing down your throat and into every part of your body. Bear witness to the thoughts and feelings that come up for you.

End of the Rainbow

Dolly Parton said, "If you want the rainbow, you gotta put up with the rain." You have now come to the end of the Rainbow of the Spirit. Are you looking for that pot of gold? Just look inside your Heartland. You'll find it there. Reflect on all the colors you have visited and the language landscapes they helped you paint.

You may notice that in this chapter there seemed to be two Food for Thought sections. I placed a side dish of Food alongside each journey just to give your creative spirit a jump start. You won't find this in any of the other chapters. I'm sure that by now your engines are sufficiently revved up.

Think about the colors you dress your characters in. Envision the rooms they inhabit. Notice how inanimate objects color the worlds around them. Capture these visions on canvas, paper, and film for all to see, hear, taste, touch, and smell.

Writing From Your Heartland™ calls on your patience as you travel along its many highways. We will close with the words of philosopher Edgar Cayce: "Patience is the lesson all souls must learn, not merely passiveness, but active patience. Patience allows us to learn from one experience and move on to another."

chapter 3

·

THE SACREDNESS OF SELF

Our deepest fear is not that we are inadequate. Our deepest fear is that we are powerful beyond measure. It is our light, not our darkness, that most frightens us.... As we let our own light shine, we unconsciously give other people permission to do the same.

—NELSON MANDELA, 1994 INAUGURAL SPEECH

MEDITATION FOR THE SACREDNESS OF SELF

I am passing through the gates
of the temple
of my inner sacredness,
the place where my roots dwell,
and the lifeblood of my creativity
flows like a raging river.

As the trees gather strength
from the soil beneath them,
so, too, do I draw from the fertile darkness
of my inner sanctum.

I call upon my spirit for clarity,
for sustenance,
for a warm place to keep my words
in the cool light of all my days.

I am one with the rivers,
the sap in the trees,
the blood in the veins
of the spirit of us all.

I feel the stream of life
flowing through me,
sweeping away what I no longer need,
bringing in what keeps me whole.
I am the rhythm of myself
dancing toward the core
of everything I am.

In the Beginning

There I was standing in my white vestments at the altar in the Cathedral of St. John the Divine, the world's largest gothic church. I rang a brass bell while calling on spirits, angels, and citizens of heaven, asking for blessings, and pouring libations to the ancestors. Stained-glass windows and vaulted ceilings curved around my words and the faces of hundreds who had gathered for the ordination ceremony.

I felt as if I were in the presence of an indescribably divine power. Its essence flowed through me like a tidal wave, filling every fiber of my being, every cell of a body too awestruck to tremble. This was as close to heaven as I have ever been.

Of almost a hundred students at the interfaith seminary, I had been chosen to deliver an opening incantation. After we were ordained, two of my classmates rushed over to me, one an African priestess, the other a psychic who had been helping people communicate with the dead for over thirty years.

They grabbed my arm and excitedly asked, "Did you see them? Did you see them?" They told me that as I uttered the incantation, the entire cavernous nave behind the altar had become filled with angels, ancestors, and spirits all crowding behind me, smiling and cheering me on as if to say, "You go, girl!"

When was the last time you felt as if you were in the presence of the divine? Have you ever been struck silent by the dying light of a sunset, the magnificent palette of trees in autumn, the birth of a baby, or the presence of a charismatic spiritual leader? Have you ever been moved by the beauty of someone's eyes, the thunder of organ music rumbling beneath your feet, the miracle of dawn, or the wisdom of an ancient elder?

The divine dwells in all these things. It lives around you and inside you, in every moment, with every breath you take. When difficult times walk through your life, when you are in need of peace or inspiration, you may tap into it to help you get through another day. Divine power is an energy that comes when you call it.

In this chapter, you will be going on a divine journey. It is a journey that reaches into your Heartland and puts you in touch with the presence of your creative guardian spirit. I call that divine spirit your Goddess of Creative Spirit. She helps you to connect and translate your experiences into writing, art, and transformation. The Goddess of Creative Spirit will be asking you to give her a name and to call on her for guidance whenever you create.

Next, you will erect a Temple of Creative Spirit: laying down a foundation, constructing the walls, securing the roof, and dedicating the structure. As you name and build you will be taking a look at beginnings and middles, ends and outcomes, naming explorations, physical and emotional landscapes, and the dedication process.

As you deepen the connection to the goddess and the temple energies dwelling inside you, you will also connect with the divine energy that flows through you like water down a mountainside. You will increase your awareness of it as an eternal source just waiting for you to dip your cup in and drink your fill. Prepare to quench your thirst as you journey toward the infinite bounty of the Sacredness of Self.

The Coming of the Goddess

When I was a teenager, my mother let us go through a box of old letters she had kept. I found one written by my father while he was still in the army. The line I remember most vividly is the one that read, "name the baby Dorothy." My younger sister was named after African-American actress and singer Juanita Hall, who was heavily made up to look like a Japanese woman in the movie *Flower Drum Song*.

My father wanted to name my older sister Fannie Mae after his sister, but my mother prevailed with a slightly less southern name, Annie Ruth. Think about your own name for a moment.

Where did it come from? Is there a story behind it? In one of my workshops, a woman told us her father gave her the name of an ex-girlfriend he had never forgotten. By the time her mother found out, the daughter was already a teenager.

Each name carries its own vibration, power, character, and imagery. Names of movie stars from the forties such as Hedy Lamarr, Lana Turner, Dorothy Lamour, Cary Grant, Rock Hudson, and Rita Hayworth conjure images of glamour, romance, and sensuality. Film characters with names like Stanley Kowalski, Vinnie Barbarino, Stella, and Marty evoke an everyman connection. Names of African-American musicians Count Basie, Duke Ellington, King Curtis, Queen Latifah, Lady Day, and Prince reflect a regal artistry.

"What's in a name?" a common expression goes. Patti Austin sings, "Love Me by Name," a child might complain, "He called me a name," or a couple may be married "in name only." If a person has accomplished a great deal in business or politics, we say that he "made a name for himself." If someone became notorious in a small community, you might say, "She's giving the town a bad name."

"Open up in the name of the law!" police would order, while an impatient fiancé might demand, "Name a date for the wedding!" We may shop for name brands, name people to political office, sew name tags into camp clothing, and shout, "Praise His holy name!" as we sit in church.

If you are writing a novel or short story, ask the characters what they would like to be named and see what surprising answers you get.

When you were initiated into this world you were given a name. As you walk toward your sacredness you will experience a ritual in which you name the divine energy of your sacred creative self. Let's take a closer look at the words *sacred, ritual,* and *holy.* We can pay a visit to our old friend Miss Webster, who sometimes likes to be formally addressed as Merriam-Webster's Collegiate® Dictionary, Tenth Edition. She defines *sacred* as "dedicated or set apart for the service or worship of a deity;

devoted exclusively to one service or use; entitled to reverence and respect." *Ritual,* she says, is "a customarily repeated often formal act or series of acts." *Holy* refers to something "devoted entirely to the deity or the work of the deity." A definition from a different source indicated that the word *holy* is associated with transcendence and perfection, reverence and absolute adoration.

All of these definitions have a direct application to creativity. Creating is clearly an act that is entitled to reverence and respect. When you put yourself on a regular schedule, creating then becomes ritual, a repeated act manifesting itself from the depths of your Heartland. Creating transcends and transforms reality and is deserving of absolute adoration and reverence. So when you engage in the act of creating, you are engaged in a ritual act that is sacred and holy. You are doing work that is devoted entirely to the service of your Goddess of Creative Spirit.

Remember that you are always engaged in the art of living. You may be involved in creating a more comfortable environment for your children, an elderly parent, or yourself. Maybe you're trying to create a more fulfilling lifestyle, more time and less stress for yourself. These, too, are acts of creation deserving of reverence, respect, and adoration.

INITIATION JOURNEY

Now it is time for your initiation journey, a ritual during which you will meet your Goddess of the Creative Spirit. Select a piece of meditative music and light some incense. Find a quiet, relaxed space in which to travel. Place a glass of water, a white candle, a piece of paper, and a pen in front of you.

To assist you on your journey, put a clear quartz crystal in your left hand. Close your eyes and take three deep breaths. Each time you breathe in, think, *I'm breathing in everything I need to take with me.* Each time you breathe out, think, *I'm breathing out everything I need to let go of.*

Now open your eyes. Read the following words aloud. After reading the words, let the energy visit your spirit for a while.

"I am going on a journey, traveling to a place beyond myself and inside my spirit. I can feel the energy slowly rising from my heart, moving past my throat, behind my eyes, and into the light of my mind.

The light becomes the sun, and the sun is shining upon my spirit. It warms me and guides my steps. I am outside in an open field, fertile and fragrant with all of my possibilities. The air caresses my skin as I move forward.

Ahead of me I see a temple filled with light and color, the sounds and the smells of everything that I have ever been. I study the temple carefully, carving each detail into the fibers of my heart. Its walls are thick with my every thought, what I have written, and all of the words still waiting for the light of day. It is my Temple of Creative Spirit. It feels like home, and it feels like me.

As I approach the temple, a goddess appears in the doorway. 'I have been expecting you,' she says. She takes my hand and walks me inside. She is my Goddess of Creative Spirit, a radiant reflection of all that I am entitled to be. She lives beside my spirit. Whenever I create, her hand is on mine. The goddess tells me her home is in my Heartland and that she will never leave me.

I ask what her name is. She whispers it into my ear three times, then writes it on my palm with her finger. She takes me back to the doorway of the temple. I press her name into my heart. As I walk across the field again, I look back. The goddess waves at me and says, 'I will be here whenever you need me. Just call my name.'

I journey across the sun again, through the light, past my mind, behind my eyes and into my throat. I can feel the energy flowing toward my heart, filling my spirit. I press my palm to my heart and remember."

Now close your eyes again. Let your mind and spirit take you on the journey your tongue has just told you about. Let the candle that is shining in front of you remind you of the light that always shines inside you. As you travel on your Initation Journey, make mental photographs of your surroundings and all that you pass on your walk toward your temple. Envision the details of your own temple, its colors, textures, and fixtures. Let the image of your goddess come to you—what she looks like, what she wears, how she walks.

After completing the journey, press your left palm to your heart before opening your eyes. Once your eyes are open, sit with your journey for a while. Write down everything you experienced along the way. Remember where you went and how you felt. What did your goddess say her name was? If you did not get a name during the journey, ask for it now. Put your left palm over your heart and say aloud, "Goddess, what shall I call you?" Write down the first name that comes to your mind, no matter what it is.

For the final phase of your initiation, take the glass of water in your hand. Speak the name of your goddess into the water three times. After the third time add the words "She is always with me." Slowly drink some of the water, savoring how it feels flowing down. Imagine your throat is the mountainside and the liquid is the waterfall of your creativity.

Dip the middle finger of your right hand into the glass and put a dot of water at the crown of your head, on each of your temples, between your brows (your third eye), behind each ear, and at the nape of your neck.

Congratulations! Your initiation is now complete. You are ready to begin building your temple.

Begin the Beguine

Every goddess has a temple. Miss Webster's definition of a temple is that it is "a place devoted to a special purpose." It is said that the body is the temple of the spirit. So it is that your Temple of Creative Spirit is a place devoted to the special purposes of your creativity. It houses the body of work you create. It is a treasure chest of the energy, imagination, and experiences that make up your Heartland. How do you begin building this temple? First you lay the foundation. Let's take a look at the concept of a foundation and its first steps.

A foundation is the beginning of something. It has to be solid enough to support a house or a temple, a skyscraper or a story. When I first moved to Brooklyn, my roommate and I lived in a brownstone duplex in the beautiful Clinton Hill section. The apartment included a backyard, a laundry room, two bedrooms, and a storage room, all for under $500 a month! It was the kind of New York space you dream about. We noticed that on one of the walls in the laundry room there was a space that was always damp and crumbly. But we were so grateful we didn't have to fight crowds at the neighborhood laundromat that we hardly gave the wall a thought.

After living in that wonderful space for almost three years, we received news that devastated us. We were told we would have to move out of our beloved apartment. The crumbling wall, it seems, was a foundation wall that had been extensively damaged by a slow leak on its insides. The whole building was in danger of falling down. The entire downstairs wall had to be torn apart and reconstructed. There was no telling how long that would take. My elderly Jamaican landlady said she doubted if she would ever finish paying for it in her lifetime.

"It got off to a shaky start." "It never seemed right in the first place." Have you ever heard yourself or someone else utter these words? They might be said after things went awry. They might come from an uneasy feeling you had about how something began. A feeling that was verified when that event or situation just didn't turn out right.

Why is it that something may seem too good to be true? What is at the foundation of your doubt? When you say a person got up on the wrong side of bed, you are commenting on how their entire day was affected by its beginnings. When you say, "You never get a second chance to make a first impression," you are again talking about how important it is to start off in a positive way or to "Get on the good foot," as James Brown says.

Let's say you want to establish a foundation for a piece of writing. Laying down the foundation means putting into place the pivotal point of a story, the thought, word, or deed that gave birth to all the events that followed. It is also another way of asking, How did it all begin? Ask yourself what happened and who or what it happened to. Try asking these two questions about a character or a situation you have in mind and see what answers you come up with.

If you are looking at the beginnings of an emotion, event, or experience, you might ask yourself: "When was the first time this happened? What was my first thought about it? When was the first time I felt this way?" At times you may run into people who want to begin building their lives on your foundation instead of on their own. They may want to create situations around you that do not really stem from you. Asking yourself what is really happening and who this is happening to can help you keep perspective on exactly what is yours and what is theirs.

Answers to questions about firsts give you a solid foundation for building a response to the question: What happened next? How did one person's actions create certain reactions? "For want of a nail the war was lost" is an old expression that still holds meaning today. The saying came from a war fought in colonial America during the eighteenth century. As enemy troops prepared to launch a major surprise attack, a spy sent an urgent warning to his comrades by courier.

A careless blacksmith, thinking it wouldn't make much difference, left off a nail when he was shoeing the courier's horse. As the courier raced down the road, the horseshoe with the missing nail became loosened and a sharp rock bore into the horse's hoof, causing it to stumble. As the horse fell, the courier was thrown against a tree and knocked unconscious. By the time he regained consciousness and was able to resume his journey, his troops had surrendered.

For want of a solid foundation, a story, a building, or a person might be lost. If people did not get the love they needed when they were young, they might go "looking for love in all the wrong places" as adults. African-Americans call it *home training* when children are raised with values and rules for behavior. These values may include self-respect, cleanliness, respect for your elders, and faith in God. If they are not taught properly or at all, children can spend the rest of their lives trying to recover those parts of themselves that needed these skills for growth and survival.

Often, if we see teenagers sitting down on a bus while an elderly woman stands in front of them or if they are talking to their mothers in a disrespectful way, a knowing glance will pass between me and another African-American. As we shake our heads we can almost hear ourselves thinking the same thought: "No home training!"

If you dig deeper into the concept of starts, firsts, and beginnings, the questions you ask can provide insight into physical or emotional issues that are in need of transformation: "What is the best way to start trusting again?" "What is the first sign that this relationship does not really have a solid footing?" "How do I begin to deal with my anger?" Your Goddess of Creative Spirit is always waiting to send answers and insights to you. Ask the questions, then close your eyes and let her give a name to the answers.

Also give some thought as to how bells are often used to signal beginnings. The dinner bell tells you that a meal is ready, the church bell lets you know the service is about to start. At Trinity Seaside, an Episcopal summer camp, the nuns would tap a knife against a glass of water to let us know they were about to begin an announcement. At one point on any given day or afternoon, we might hear a series of three bells ringing against the Long Island sky. It was the Angelus, a signal for us to begin silence, be still, and reflect on the presence of God.

Think about how you signal your own beginnings. And when

you hear a sound ringing from your Heartland, ask not "for whom the bell tolls; it tolls for thee."

BEGIN THE BEGUINE: JOURNEYS

Each journey in your Heartland begins with a five-minute free-write and a piece of music that helps the writing flow the way it wants and needs to. Remember, freewriting helps you bypass your internal (or infernal) censor, gives you direct access to your Heartland, and allows you to let your writing surprise you.

- Roberta Flack sings a beautiful song, "The First Time Ever I Saw Your Face." Write about what it was like the first time you met someone you either loved at first sight or eventually fell in love with.

- "I was the first one there." Say this line, close your eyes, and see yourself there. Then write about the circumstance or event that took place around these words.

- "I'm right back where I started from!" According to Greek mythology, Sisyphus had to push a huge stone up a hill in Hades, the Greek underworld. Just as the stone was nearing the top, it would roll all the way back to the bottom of the hill again. His curse was that this was destined to happen to him every single time, for eternity. Write about a time when you felt this was happening to you.

BEGIN THE BEGUINE: FOOD FOR THOUGHT

- *First in line*

- *"I should have followed my first mind"*

- *"First of all . . ."*

- *"First the tide rushes in, plants a kiss on the shore,"* from the song *"Ebb Tide"*

- *First one to speak up*

- *"The first shall be last"*

- *First light*

- *"Beginning to see the light"*

- *"Beginning to stand on my own two feet"*

- *Beginning again*

- *It's a new day*

- *New idea*

- *Newborn*

- *Firstborn*

- *"You never put me first!"*

- *"Let's start all over again"*

- *"Don't start none, won't be none!"* James Brown philosophy

- *Pavlov's bell*—salivation

- *The Hunchback of Notre Dame*

- *"When you hear the bell, come out fighting!"*

- *"Tintinnabulation . . . from the bells, bells, bells"* (Edgar Allan Poe)

- Sylvia Plath's *The Bell Jar*

- *The bell curve*

- *Doorbell*

- *School bell*

- *"Sleigh bells ring, are you listening?"*

BEGIN THE BEGUINE: SURRENDERS

- A line in an old doo-wop song goes, "I'll never hear the bells if you leave me." Think about the people you know who have left this life, people who will never hear the bells again. Take a small bell and ring it after you say each of their names aloud. Then be still and reflect on their presence in your life.

- Make a list of all the things you started in the last year and did not finish. When you have completed the list ask yourself the question "Now what?" and see what answer comes.

- If someone you care about has been wanting to start a new project, whether it be a business, a class, an exercise program, or a quilt, do something to encourage and support him or her.

And the Walls Came Tumbling Up

My sister Juanita and I loved it when the Oppenheimers had a fight. As children, we were fascinated with, even excited by the idea of listening to other children's parents argue. The Oppenheimers' apartment was right next door to ours in our Lower East Side projects.

Our older sister, Ruthie, had taught us how to put the open end of a drinking glass against the thin wall and place an ear at the other end. That way we could hear almost every word they said. Our minds would paint vivid pictures of what we thought they looked like—mouths wide open, faces in a red fury, their hands waving pointedly in the air. They never knew about the eager ears that invaded their privacy through those walls.

In one Tracy Chapman song a woman cannot get to sleep because, she sings, "Last night I heard the screaming, loud voices behind the wall." When she mentions that the police are always late or totally absent, you begin to get a picture of what is happening on the other side of that wall.

When you start to write about the heard and overheard, the seen and the suggested, you are beginning to create an environment. Since you have experienced laying your foundation by asking what happened, you can now build your walls or environments by asking where and when it happened.

As you put up walls in your Temple of Creative Spirit, you begin to paint a picture of the physical, mental, and chronological settings. These settings can be set designs for a stage production, background material for a novel, a cinematic scene from a film, or a moment of emotion in a poignant poem. You create landscapes that are defined by emotion and event. Just two lines of Tracy's song tell you the story of domestic violence taking place next door.

In Japanese Noh theater there is a saying: "When the make-believe is believed on both sides, it appears to be true." If you are writing fiction, you want to create characters that are believable. If you are writing nonfiction, you want to retell events in a way that rings true. If you are writing poetry, you want to invent images that capture the reader's belief. If you are painting a canvas, you want to engage the viewer in your vision. If you are communicating your thoughts and feelings, you want the listener to share your truths.

As you build, ask yourself what is on the other side of the walls you are creating. If you are looking at an emotional wall like anger, for example, explore what is on the other side of it. If fear is a wall, what would it take to knock it down or put a hole though it? What happens when emotions are walled in?

Whether you are looking at a character, a circumstance, a piece of life, or a piece of yourself, remember this: a wall is something you have to go over, under, around, or through, paint a different color; or pretend it's not there. Let's take some of the concepts we have talked about so far and put them to work. We will walk into the field of writing, for example, and create a character you would like to develop. Say your character is a married man, a solid kind of guy with no pretensions or major ego problems. What kind of name would you choose for him? Close your eyes and ask him what he would like to be called. Let's say he wants to be named George.

Now ask those questions: what happened and who did it happen to? When a woman he was deeply in love with three years ago reenters his life, George learns that he is the father of her 2½-year-old son. The woman is a beautiful, soft-spoken person with a backbone of steel that is not readily evident. Let's say she wants to be called Marsha. We have now established a foundation.

Where and when did it happen? They ran into each other at a New Age conference in New Mexico two days ago. What does the mental environment look like? What are the thoughts of each character? He married Marsha's former best friend six months ago, thinking it was time to move on with his life after not hearing from her for over two years. Marsha broke off the relationship abruptly when she tested positive for HIV and blamed him, only to find out later that the test was in error. What is the emotional environment; what are the feelings? They are still in love with each other.

Let's see what happens if they decide to go over, under, around, or through, paint the wall a different color, or pretend it's not there. *Over the wall:* He decides to leave his wife. *Under the wall:* They begin to have an affair. *Around the wall:* "Why don't we meet again a month from now and see how we feel about each other." *Through the wall:* "I'm going to have a talk with your wife. After all, she's the one who talked me into dumping you!" *Paint it a different color:* "My wife and I are very happy with each other. What do you want?" *Pretend it's not there:* "How do I know it's my baby?" Try this with a real-life or fictional situation of your own and see what you come up with.

Constructing an environment involves mortar made from what

I call *exquisite details,* those jewels of words and descriptions that breathe life and sparkle into your writing. "George kept twisting his wedding ring as they talked" indicates an uneasiness with his marital status. "Marsha paused, took a deep breath, then took a few uncertain steps towards his table" can signal her reluctance and discomfort at the prospect of seeing him again.

Writing "His heart jumped at the scent of jasmine in her hair" or "The way her thoughts beat beneath her belly, Marsha knew she was in trouble" paints a landscape of passion and desire. You might mention an expensive watch on his wrist or a large diamond on her finger to indicate an elevated economic status, especially if it is worn with a designer suit or dress. A frayed cuff or run-down heels convey another kind of message. Exquisite details paint pictures that are worth a thousand words.

A few well-chosen exquisite details can go a long way toward creating imagery, setting environment, and moving your work forward. I used these kinds of details in this excerpt from my poem "Southern Sonata." I wrote about some mischief my sister and I were getting into while playing on my grandfather's farm.

. . . We slipped away
From our mother
And her mother
Wrapped in red wool sweaters
In the mild southern winter . . .

Across the field
Mr. White's barn seduced us
A playground of unknown delights
That knew our names
And called them
Grandpa's corn
Lived in the barn's upper floor
An invitation surely
We folded ourselves

Around the corners of that barn
Small hands parting rough doors
That did not expect us
We moved inside like mice
Quickly
Hugging the walls
Certain of invisibility

The heady perfume
Of this rustic cathedral
The aroma of pine and hay
And the forbidden
Drugged us with excitement
Propelled our bodies

Up the ladder
And into the room
Where the corn lay in careful piles
Too neat to go untouched . . .

Robert Frost has a poem, "Mending Wall," in which he advises people to look not only at what their fences are keeping out but also at what they are keeping in. As each piece you write is a divine work in progress, so in fact is your life a work in progress, continually under divine construction. You live exquisite details each day. You face a variety of physical, mental, emotional, and chronological walls or settings every day. Whether in your life, your writing, or your other creative activities, just keep this in mind—when you run into a wall, always look for a door.

THE WALLS CAME TUMBLING UP: JOURNEYS

- Rock and roll crooner Little Anthony sang a song titled, "I'm on the Outside (Looking In)." Write about a time when you felt as if you were on the outside looking in. For a variation on this journey, write about an object or animal that might have felt like an outsider—for instance, the Ugly Duckling.

- Let's do a wall workout. Create environments for the following foundations:

    A homeless man finds a hundred-dollar bill.
    A child playing in a vacant lot comes across a dead body.
    A disgruntled secretary slips LSD into her boss's coffee.

- "I felt pushed to the wall."
    Think about a situation in which you felt as if you were being pushed to the wall. Now write about how you think it might have looked on the other side of that wall.

THE WALLS CAME TUMBLING UP: FOOD FOR THOUGHT

- *The Berlin Wall*

- *The Wailing Wall*

- *The Great Wall of China*

- *The Iron Curtain*

- *Wall Street*

- *Prison walls*

- *Uterine walls*

- *"If the walls in her bedroom could talk . . ."*

- *Walled in*

- *"He was climbing the walls"*

- *Political cry from the sixties: "Up against the wall, mother-fucker!"*

THE WALLS CAME TUMBLING UP: SURRENDERS

• They say, "Love thy neighbor as thyself, but choose your neighborhood." Do you know your neighbors on the other side of the wall either at home or at work? Whether you do or don't, bring them a flower or send them a note saying hello and wishing them a nice day.

• In a closing scene of Gloria Naylor's *Women of Brewster Place,* the community reacts to an offending wall that unfairly separated their neighborhood. "Women flung themselves against the wall, chipping away at it with knives, plastic forks, spiked shoe heels, and even bare hands."

   Make a list of the walls in your life that separate you from your dreams. Think about how you might tear them down.

• "If you can't change a situation, change your thoughts about it." Think of three situations in your life that you either need or want to change your thoughts about.

Up Above My Head

Gladys Knight and the Pips sing, "We've come to the end of our road." A line from an old gospel song goes, "I believe I'll run on and see what the end will bring." Let's run on and see what kind of endings you can bring to your stories, sketches, poems, films, plays, fiction, nonfiction, essays, grocery lists, personal dramas, family feuds, and unresolved conflicts. As we put up the roof, the final step in building the temple, we will explore closures and completion. We began with how to start. Now let's look at how to stop.

   In their song "Stop in the Name of Love," the Supremes asked us to stop before a heart was broken. Many writings and songs end with a heartbreak, a faded relationship, or the dying light of a marriage. *Stop the World I Want to Get Off* was a Broadway play. A story can end when a person or a character leaves physically, mentally, or emotionally. They may lose their minds, their hearts, or their lives. A boxer who loses his eye has had his world stopped. A young girl who is raped has had her world stopped. An old man who has had his wife of fifty years die in his arms has had his world stopped.

It was Shakespeare who said, "All good things must come to an end." Boys II Men went a step further when they sang about not being able to let go when they came to the end of their road. In the Manhattan Beach section of Brooklyn, a son continued to bathe and care for his elderly mother more than a week after she had died. People hold on to relationships, abusive situations, jobs, and even old clothing they should have left a long time ago.

How do you know when to let go of what you are creating or a situation you have created? When is a painting finished? How do you move on when your work clearly wants to? What is it you expect of yourself as a creative person, as a person who has made an art out of life?

When we read a book or watch a movie, most of us expect a happy ending, or at least one that leaves us with a sense of completion. I remember seeing Hitchcock's movie *The Birds* and having my expectations about endings completely shattered. As the main characters get into their car, birds who had previously attacked them at every opportunity just sat on the fence and watched them drive away. I was terribly disappointed at the anticlimax. I remember the audience sitting in their seats in disbelief as the credits rolled. There was an overall feeling of being cheated. We were expecting a dramatic finale or an exciting solution. Instead we were left hanging.

Perhaps we were spoiled by television programs where the killer had to be captured, the lost child found, and the mystery solved within the space of an hour. It would be great if life gave us solutions like that, tied up in a neat bundle, but it doesn't. On talk shows, happy meetings of parents, children, and siblings reunited after ten or twenty years did not always have the most pleasant outcomes once the show was over.

One couple I know had purchased a brownstone that seemed in perfect condition, only to discover water pouring down through their kitchen ceiling the first time they took a shower. A friend of mine fought like hell for a promotion from a position she had held with the city for ten years. In the final analysis, the new job turned out to have fewer benefits and less flexibility, twice as much responsibility, and only a thirty-dollar pay increase after taxes and additional deductions.

"She knows no boundaries," you may say about a person who goes beyond certain decencies and considerations, someone who does not know when to stop. In Greek tragedies, when a person tries to exceed the limits of his or her human abilities by thinking he is godlike, *hamartia,* a tragic flaw, stops them in their tracks. The stories end with the characters humbled and broken as a result of a failure to recognize their own boundaries.

Politicians, executives, celebrities, cheating spouses, and abusive babysitters have met their downfall through simple devices like a microphone left on at the wrong time, a piece of paper, a slip of the tongue, a taped conversation, or cheapness. Had Hugh Grant paid for a room instead of paying for his pleasure in the backseat of an automobile, he would never have set off the chain of events that brought tremendous embarrassment to himself and his girlfriend and tremendous profit to Divine Brown.

Whether you end at the Achilles' heel or the tennis elbow of your story, write endings you'd like to read. Take your visual imagery to a point where you can feel a sense of fulfillment and completion. Look for solutions that feel as if they had you in mind. Don't leave yourself, the reader, or the viewer hanging—unless of course, that is your intention.

In O. Henry's "The Gift of the Magi," a woman cuts her hair and sells it to buy a fob for her husband's watch while her husband sells his watch to buy combs to hold her long hair. In a classic *Twi-*

light Zone episode, Burgess Meredith survives a nuclear attack that grants him his life wish—all the books he could possibly read and all the time in which to read them. But before he can enjoy his dream come true, he accidentally steps on his reading glasses.

How do you like to have things turn out—with a twist of fate or a twist of lime? What types of endings have you enjoyed? Do you want to be left up in the air or under the floorboards? Do you like powerful poems that leave you breathless? Do you prefer happy endings that lift the spirits, pensive endings that challenge the mind, or tragic ones that touch the heart? Do you like the characters to come together and explain themselves at the end, as in a Charlie Chan movie? Do you want them to be present and accounted for, or missing and mysterious?

Create endings that feel good, strong, and complete to you— ones that leave you feeling satisfied with the outcome, whatever it may be. Don't hesitate to get a reflection from a fellow writer or interested friend about how your conclusion feels and sounds to him or her. Read your writing aloud, show rough cuts and contact sheets, have staged readings, ask, "This is what I'm think- ing about doing. What do you think?" Try out different endings the way you might try on different outfits until you find just the right one. Let the ears and minds and hearts of others see and hear and taste the work, the life you are creating.

Major motion picture studios sometimes shoot two endings for a film, then test them out on various audiences to see which one they will use. Maybe you have an incident in mind you think might make a perfect finale. Create a foundation and walls for it. Create endings for your work that you may not have had the nerve to try in real life. Rewrite ones that you did try and would like to have another shot at.

Try using some of these same thoughts in your dealings with people and situations around you. Resolve conflicts in your own life in a way that feels good and complete to you. Bring all the characters together in a family feud and have them explain them- selves and their behavior in front of the others. Think of two different ways to solve a problem and then try them out on a friend to see which one you should use. Consider solutions that will lift your spirits, challenge your mind, or touch your heart. Recognize boundaries, set your limits, and be prepared for the twists and turns of life and limes.

UP ABOVE MY HEAD: JOURNEYS

- "I wish this moment would never end." What moment was that?

- "This is the last straw!" Take a page from your life or the life of a character or object and write about how you or he, she, or it arrived at this point.

- Audre Lorde wrote, "My whole life has been an altar worth its ending." Sit with this line from her poem "Call." Close your eyes and think, *What has my life been worth?* Then open your eyes and do your freewrite.

UP ABOVE MY HEAD: FOOD FOR THOUGHT

- *"Stop it!"*

- *Stoplight*

- *"Stop, you're killing me!"* (laughter)

- *"Stop me before I kill again!"* (murder)

- *"I can't seem to stop myself"*

- *"All the stop signs were there and yet . . ."*

- *"When did the music stop?"* (musical chairs or a fading romance)

- Refrain sung by the Stylistics: *"I only stop so we can start all over again."*

- *"If I can just make it to the end of the month . . ."*

- Old saying, *"A whistling woman and a cackling hen, both will come to no good end."*

- Movie: *The Endless Summer*

- Movie: *Song Without End*

- *The end is in sight*

- *"Is that the end of the cereal?"*

- *This end up*

- *Dead end*

- *The Dead End Kids*

- *"You'll be the death of me!"*

- Exasperated mother's warning to a child engaged in reckless activity: *"One of these days you're going to end up dead, and when you do, don't come crying to me!"*

- Bible quotation: *"Many that are first shall be last; and the last shall be first."*

- *"I wouldn't marry you if you were the last man on earth!"*

- *"All right, but this is the last time"*

- *Last call for alcohol*

- *The final curtain*

- *The Final Call*, a Black Muslim newspaper

- *Limitless*

- *The sky's the limit*

- *"This time you've gone too far"*

- *"This is where I draw the line"*

- *"We've done just about all we could do"*

- Jazz great Betty Carter's song: *"Look No Further"*

- *"Aren't you finished yet?"*

- Last words of Christ: *"It is finished."*

UP ABOVE MY HEAD: SURRENDERS

- Bring some unfinished business to a close. This can be something in your personal or professional life, perhaps something you have been meaning to get back to for years. Just make sure you complete it once and for all.

- I had always dreamed of hopping on a bus in Rio de Janeiro and riding it to the end of the line, as in the movie *Black Orpheus*. Once I got to Rio, I actually did hop on a bus but didn't have enough nerve to stay on until the route ended.

  Ride a bus or train to the end of its line, drive on a side road until it ends, take a walk on a dead-end street, or go to the very end of a street or avenue you have never traveled on. Stop, look around, and see what's there.

- Take the last of something of yours and give it away: "Here, you can have the last piece of pie."

This Is Dedicated to the One I Love

By now, you have become quite familiar with that divine spirit, your Goddess of Creative Spirit. Maybe you sip herbal tea or have coffee with her on a regular basis. You started out by asking her to connect you with experiences that live inside you, deep

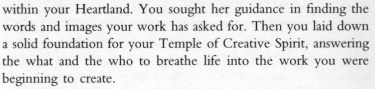

within your Heartland. You sought her guidance in finding the words and images your work has asked for. Then you laid down a solid foundation for your Temple of Creative Spirit, answering the what and the who to breathe life into the work you were beginning to create.

Next you built the walls of your temple and painted them with physical, mental, and chronological images and settings. Finally you secured the roof and explored endings, closure, and resolutions. Now that you have done all that work, it's time to get something cool to drink. It is time to dedicate that magnificent structure you have created out of your work and out of your life.

At the beginning of this chapter, I mentioned the word *dedication*. Of course, I went to the dictionary to see what Miss Webster had to say on the subject. She is truly a know-it-all. She says to dedicate is "to devote to the worship of a divine being; to set apart to a definite use; to commit to a goal or way of life." *Dedication* is defined as "an act or rite of dedication to a divine being or to a sacred use." It can call for self-sacrificing devotion.

When Carolyn McCarthy's husband was killed and her son wounded in the Long Island Railroad massacre of 1994, she decided to dedicate her life to public service. Two years later, with absolutely no political experience or connections, she ran for and successfully won a seat in the House of Representatives.

You know how to put money aside and dedicate it to a vacation fund, education, or a new house. I'm sure you have seen people who are totally dedicated to their jobs, working late into the evening and on weekends.

Parents are famous for their self-sacrificing devotion to their children. I was once talking with an attractive African-American lawyer who was a single mother. When I asked if she had ever traveled, she answered, "No, but my son has. He's been everywhere. I've given him the best of everything."

John Walsh, host of television's *America's Most Wanted,* dedicated himself to finding the killer of his son. Though he has been unsuccessful in that effort, his program has helped bring dozens of other criminals to justice.

After a ship was built, it was customary to have someone dedicate it by breaking a bottle of champagne against its hull. New buildings and roads are dedicated with ribbon cuttings. Baseball dedicates its first game by choosing a celebrity to throw out the first ball of the season. In basketball, when a player has reached a high standard of achievement and excellence, his number is retired. The player is honored by having that number dedicated solely to him.

The Shirelles sang an oldie-but-goody song in the sixties entitled, "Dedicated to the One I Love." Think of yourself as the object of that love. Keep this in mind as you perform the Dedication Ceremony for your Temple of Creative Spirit.

What do you think might happen if you dedicated yourself to that divine being that you are? What might your life be like if you became committed to your creativity as a goal or way of life? Who would you be if you gave yourself the reverence and respect that comes with all sacred territories? How would you feel if your life was characterized by transcendence and adoration? What might you achieve if you dedicated half as much time to your dreams as you do to your job, television, phone conversations, or the Sunday *Times*? Think about it.

Remember, the body is the temple of the spirit, and a temple is a place devoted to a special purpose. You have made your Temple of Creative Spirit into a splendid place devoted to the special purpose of creating your work. It is now time to dedicate that temple and all that you have built.

Dedication Ceremony

For this ritual you will need a five small shells, a glass of water, a bell, a white candle in a glass, white clothing, a white cloth or handkerchief, a piece of paper, a pen, a saucer, and incense. Shells are symbolic of infinity and prosperity. Water represents the flow of the spirit. The bell represents beginnings and endings. The candle symbolizes the flame of creativity that burns inside your Heartland. Its glass container reflects the clear vision and purpose required for your work. The color white helps to heighten awareness, dissolve limitations, and transform consciousness.

Pick a relaxed evening, preferably one with a new moon or a full moon. Carve out a peaceful piece of time for yourself so that you will not be disturbed during your ceremony. Prepare for a ritual by taking a shower. As you clean your body, empower yourself by affirming and repeating aloud, "I am washing away my limitations. I am washing away my fears." Feel free to add anything else you think needs to be washed away. Dry yourself and put on your clean white clothing.

Light the incense and put the white cloth on a table, a mantel, or an altar you may already have. Put the candle on the saucer and set them at the center of the cloth. Now light the candle. The glass of water is placed on the left side of the candle and the bell is on the right. Put the paper and pen on the table or space in front of the cloth. Take three deep breaths.

Think about a dedication you would like to make to your Temple of Creative Spirit, or your Goddess of Creative Spirit. Think about your creative work and all you bring to it. Think about your life and all it has brought to you. Take the paper and pen and write, "I dedicate myself to . . ." Now close your eyes and see what comes. When you are ready to open your eyes again, finish writing the sentence. You can have one or several sentences if you like.

Some of the dedications that have been offered are: "I dedicate myself to loving myself and the work that comes from within me." "I dedicate myself to writing my truths, living my truths, and speaking my truths, no matter what." "I dedicate myself to believing that the divine spirit will help me remove the fears that keep me from honoring my own art." "I dedicate myself to doing whatever I can to get my novel published."

Hold the shells in your left hand, the hand of receiving. Read the dedication to yourself first, allowing its energy to fill your heart and spirit. Then ring the bell and read your dedication out loud. Allow the energy of the words to fill your mind and body. After you have finished reading, ring the bell again, adding, "And so it is," and say the name of your goddess.

Take the shells and place them on the saucer surrounding the candle. Now put the fingers of your right hand into the water and sprinkle it over the shells and the glass, then on your face and your body. Sit for a while and allow yourself to absorb the smells, sights, and sensations your body is experiencing.

Let the candle burn for as long as you can. If you have a pet or children, put the candle on a high shelf. If you don't feel comfortable leaving the candle burning, put it out at night and light it again in the morning. Read your dedication each day for five days, ringing the bell at the beginning and the end and holding the shells in your left hand. After the fifth day and the final reading of your dedication, press the paper to your heart, blow out the candle, and share the water with a plant.

Keep the dedication on your writing altar or your creation altar, or tape it to your mirror so it can keep an eye on you. Keep at least one of the shells with or near you at all times. Put them in the area where you create, in your handbag, pocket, or wallet, on your desk at work, your writing altar, next to your bed, sofa, or wherever you spend a lot of time. You have blessed them with your spirit. Carrying the shells is a way of keeping that blessing with you and energizing whatever creative work you do.

Continue to celebrate the Sacredness of Self by dedicating each day to something—a beautiful flower, a song heard on the radio that you liked, an English muffin that came out just right, someone who gave you his or her seat on the subway, a skirt that fit again, a five-dollar bill found in your pocket or a friend who was there just when he or she was needed.

chapter 4

·

THE GARDEN OF ELEMENTS

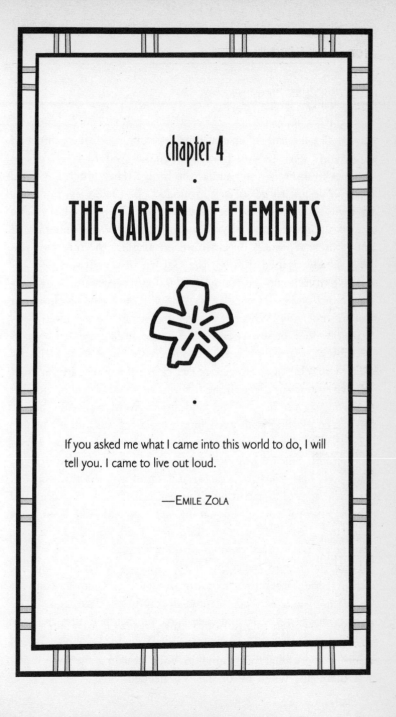

·

If you asked me what I came into this world to do, I will tell you. I came to live out loud.

—EMILE ZOLA

In the Garden

Have you ever had to air out your differences or called someone an airhead? Perhaps you have been in hot water or referred to a past encounter as water under the bridge. How often have you heard "I've got to get myself grounded" or "She's got both feet on the ground"? Ever been fired up or fired? Maybe you've danced to music played by the group Earth, Wind and Fire. If any of these sentences or situations are familiar to you, then you have already tiptoed through the Garden of the Elements.

The four elements—earth, air, fire, and water—live inside and outside of our bodies. Not a day goes by without them touching our lives in some way. When you take a shower in the morning, drink a cup of coffee or tea, cook breakfast, and walk to your car or to the subway, you have already encountered each of these elements. When you think about the air quality of a city you may live in, how polluted waters are affecting the fish you eat, the black churches that are being set on fire, or the land stolen from American Indians, you are connecting with even more aspects of the four elements.

Earth, air, fire, and water can also reflect emotional atmospheres and indicate how we perceive each other and ourselves. They can heal, destroy, create, and transform. In this chapter, you will be walking through the garden of each element, and choosing words for a bouquet of writings gathered from your Heartland. For each element there is a meditation, journeys or writing exercises, and seasonal surrender rituals.

Remember your basic gardening tools—preparation, journey, and surrender. Keep them by your side and use them to cultivate the fiery growth of seeds planted deeply in the fertilized soil of your creative spirit. Pay attention to the temperatures and the temperaments. Be sure to spend time with the blossoms as well as the weeds. Remember that a weed is just a flower in the wrong place.

MEDITATION FOR THE ELEMENT OF EARTH

Earth, mother of the past,
daughter of the future, sister of now,
I celebrate the secrets of your soil
as you open before me like a flower.

Your hands catch me when I fall.
Your skin is the caress of grass
kissing my bare feet as I dance.

Earth, you give, I take, I plant,
you receive and give again.
The sacred circle.
A woman forever pregnant with tomorrow.

I am ready to touch the earth parts of myself.
I am ready to plant thoughts in my fertile fields
and watch them blossom.

I am ready to celebrate the giving and groundedness
of the earth beneath me and within me.
I am ready to stand as one with her
and feel her heartbeat moving inside my body.
I am ready.

SOWING THE SACRED SOIL: EARTH

I am a child of the earth and so were my grandparents. They walk through my writings as if my words were the fields in Davisboro, Georgia where they lived their lives. I remember my grandmother wearing kneepads as she picked cotton from low bushes in the sweltering sun. The heady smell of burning logs filled the house as Grandma made sausages, baked cakes on the woodstove, and ran wet clothes through the ringer at the top of her washing machine. In their old wood frame house, iron beds were piled high with quilts, potbellied stoves with pipes traveled up into the ceiling, bacon was sliced from a thick slab, and biscuits were cut round with the rim of a teacup.

In a piece called "Southern Chronicles—Grandma Exia" (from *Gaptooth Girlfriends: The Third Act*), I pulled these earth words from my Heartland:

> The word rural was invented by towns like Davisboro. My roots, red clay, pecan trees, fields parted like hair, shades of green and brown. Houses painted white with red roofs, rocking chairs on front porches, dried hay rolled into huge bundles, cornstalks standing empty and yellowed, clouds mere brushstrokes on blue canvas, crumbling shacks with cinderblock steps, wood grey and rusted nails drying in the sun.
>
> I'm reminded that I was born in this town in an old wooden house. Years ago my mother pointed it out to me as we drove by in my uncle Leroy's Buick. The house had stood lonely and abandoned in an overgrown field. Now that house, my mother, and my uncle are gone, but my grandmother and those fields are still living where they've always lived. And it feels like summer.

I remember the stern face of my grandfather wearing overalls, splitting wood, slaughtering a hog, and squinting in the sun as he farmed the land. One day he let me sit next to him and hold the reins as the mules pulled his wagon through crisp dry leaves in the southern woods. Later, he and his friend Mr. Wicker walked across a soft bed of pine needles to cut down a Christmas tree. We made decorations for it while sitting by the fireplace. In an excerpt from a poem about him, "Southern Sonata: Movement in E for Emanuel," I wrote:

Whippoorwills and crickets
And owl conversations
Leaves rubbing hands together

My mind as busy
As this southern night
Thinking about Grandpa
He was silence and overalls
Plaid shirts and raw eggs
Sucked through a hole
He was burned lips
On steaming black coffee
Admitting no pain
Mumbling instead
"Too sweet, too sweet"

Emanuel who beat his sons
Before they misbehaved
In case he wasn't around
When they did
Emanuel still stooped
With the weight
Of nine children
A Capricorn son
Of the earth he tended
For fifty years
And didn't own . . .

The earth is a place of ancestors. Whenever you touch the ground, you can draw on the strength and guidance of the earth's wisdom and all those who have come before you. The earth is also the home of seasons. Their cycles remind us of our own, of how our sense of self is tied to forces outside of ourselves.

As you think about your connection with these seasons, consider how you connect with the other living beings that inhabit the earth. The shape of the mountains, the flow of water through the valleys, the animals, fruits and vegetables that offer themselves up for us to eat, all of these are reflections of our entwinement with this planet.

In 1852 letter to President Franklin Pierce, Native American chief Seattle wrote: "The earth does not belong to man, man belongs to the earth. All things are connected like the blood that unites us all. Man did not weave the web of life, he is merely a strand in it. Whatever he does to the web, he does to himself."

Years ago, in *Silent Spring,* Rachel Carson warned us about the cancer-causing potential of the pesticides we spray onto the earth. We bury toxic wastes in the ground, poisoning the water tables in Cape Cod, cities in Georgia, and countless other places.

We conducted underground nuclear testing, killing livestock and dangerously affecting the lives of hundreds of people in the adjacent areas. One television program about a movie shot near a test site detailed how many of the film's actors and crew had all contracted the same kind of cancer and died within a few years.

In a spiritual effort to raise environmental consciousness, a coalition of American Indians and many others formed the Sunbow 5: Walk for the Earth in 1995. They began a walking prayer across the United States to beg the earth's forgiveness for damages caused to it.

In some Indian communities a Sunbow is considered to be a sign from the Creator of great change or transition on the earth. As 83-year-old Algonquin chief William Commanda led the walk from Cape Cod to California, he was joined by Wampanoag, Hopi, and Santa Clara Pueblo Indian elders in offering healing messages to the earth and prayers for unity among black, brown, red, white, and yellow peoples—the five races of man.

How can the spirit of the earth or the soul of our selves be healed without an apology or acknowledgment that a wrong has been committed? An apology not only sets the stage for forgiveness and reconciliation but it begins to dissolve the anger, hatred, and disharmony.

In 1994, German President Roman Herzog made an apology to the Polish people, 200,000 of whom were killed by German Nazis in the Warsaw Uprising fifty years earlier. After wars with Germany, Japan, and Vietnam, the United States poured billions of dollars in reparations into these countries. We found homes and funds for thousands of refugees, compensated displaced Vietnamese with farmlands in Texas, and awarded money to the Japanese for property seized during World War II.

When a person is tried for committing an act of violence, it is deemed an even greater crime if he or she shows no remorse. We expect compensation if we are displaced from our homes because the government needs the land. We expect to be paid for work we have done. We even expect our children to say they are sorry if they have injured another child or adult. It is therefore understandable why some African-Americans feel they are owed an apology and reparations for the horrors of slavery that robbed an entire race of people of their lands, language, families, heritage, religion, and humanity.

The earth of America is soaked with the sweat and sadness, the bones and blood of slaves that tended a soil they never owned. Yet the United States has never offered an apology or compensation. How then can a people move toward a future untainted by the bitter seeds of past crimes for which no remorse was shown?

What were some of your earliest associations with the earth? Did you roll down a hill or go digging for earthworms? In school, did you fill a small milk container with soil, plant a bean in it, and watch it miraculously grow in a few days? Did you track muddy footprints into the house or fall down and get dirt on your clothing?

Perhaps as an adult, you have started to think about protecting planet earth and saving the rain forests as priceless medicinal herbs are destroyed to make room for more hamburger cattle. Maybe you have become concerned about the catastrophic earth changes indicated by Mary Summer Rain, Edgar Cayce, Map of New America, Nostradamus, and Sun Bear, in which they predict the destruction of the northeast and west coasts by the year 2000.

Carole King may have been thinking of San Francisco when she sang, "I feel the earth move under my feet." The Bee Gees wrote a tune about a 1940s mining accident. The Drifters thrilled us with "Under the Boardwalk." One song about New York City chants, "The people ride in a hole in the ground." As your thoughts continue beneath the earth in a political context, envision coal miner strikes, Harriet Tubman and the Underground Railroad, the Weather Underground movement of the sixties, and political activist Joanne Chesimard having to go underground to protect herself.

Basil Farrington has said that "buried deep in the earth are precious diamonds. In order to get to them, however, we must dig and dig deep. Once we get to the foundation rock, we must apply pressure to shape and mold the diamond. It is not the digging, it is the pressure that makes diamonds." There are an infinite number of places in which the earth dwells inside your Heartland. Dig deep and expand on what you have already read. Continue to search for that which is precious. Apply all the creative pressure your soul calls for, and watch the diamonds emerge from your spirit.

EARTH JOURNEYS

Prelude: As you begin this first walk into the Garden of the Elements, you should have your basic Heartland gardening tools dangling from your belt. These tools will help connect you with the unlimited source of your creative spirit. When you use them you will find that your thoughts flow more freely, your ideas are more vibrant and plentiful, and your concentration will increase.

Start with a *preparation* ritual. How about putting on a special outfit or article of clothing for this? Perhaps you can call it clothing to create in. This can be another way of telling your spirit you are not only ready to receive its energy but dressed for it as well. You might like to prepare by facing each of the four directions and bringing their energy into your body with words or breathing. Or you may simply turn out the lights, close your eyes, and focus within.

Lay the foundation for your creative landscape with a brief *meditation.* You can use the one at the beginning of the section about each element, or one of your own. Afterwards, say an *affirmation,* using positive words phrased in the present tense. Affirmations actually energize and magnetize your words so that they become true. For example, if you are trying to get past a writing block or you want your writing to be more powerful, your affirmation might be "My writing is flowing freely and fiercely." Get the picture?

As always, when you get ready to write, put on some easy, meditative music that feels good to your soul. Make sure the music doesn't have any words or jarring energies. You might try classical or New Age, Native American flute or other solo instrumentals. Choose your *journey,* then have this music playing in the background as you begin your five-minute freewrite. Put your pen to the paper and write as quickly as you can, letting words and thoughts flow without judgment, censorship, or concern about grammar and punctuation.

Go over the freewrite only to make your writing more readable. Then take a look at what you've written and decide what you'd like to do with it. Do you think you have the beginning of something and you want to keep adding to it? Is this the end of something and you want to write its beginning? Are there images you want to explore more fully? It doesn't matter if the writing that comes out leads you to a poem, journal, theater piece, fiction, fantasy, a list of things to do for your spirit, or something that doesn't yet have a name.

Remember always to always leave the freewrite intact, just as you wrote it. Copy it over, make a xerox, or just snatch pieces from it. Read it to friends or a group and have them collect seeds. To collect seeds, they listen and write down the words, lines, and phrases they liked, that touched them in some way. Then they read back to you what they have collected. As they do, you underline these words in your freewrite. Collecting seeds is a nonjudgmental way of getting feedback, of discovering which parts of your writing had an effect on the listener. You might then use these seeds as a catalyst for further exploration.

You will find yourself going back to your freewriting exercise again and again and pulling different things out. Try taking a vacation from the page for a day or two. Then come back, look at your words with new eyes, and write some more.

"What do I need all these tools for?" you may be thinking. Why do I have to go through all of this? Why can't I just sit down and create? You can. You can do anything you want to do. You can write with a pencil, a pen, an old standard typewriter, an electric one, or a computer. You will certainly get your work done, but one method may feel more effective than another.

If you already have your creative routine down pat and you are thoroughly focused and have no blocks and plenty of ideas, these tools will only add to and deepen what you are doing. If you want to get more in touch with your creative self or to explore others ways of expressing it, or if you need more motivation or stimulation in any area, these same tools will help you to provide that for yourself.

You probably know how easy it is to get distracted when you are trying to create at home. The phone rings, hunger strikes, laundry calls you from the bathroom, your children need attention, a friend is having yet another crisis. These Heartland tools can help you stay focused on the spiritual priorities of your life and your art as you move toward your creative entitlement.

EARTH JOURNEYS

- Audre Lorde wrote, "I may be a weed in the garden of women I have loved." Write about a time when you felt that someone or something was a weed in your garden.

- In ancient times, Aztecs covered their pyramids with earth to hide and protect them from the Spaniards. Think about your childhood. When did you need to hide or protect yourself?

- The United States has broken practically every land treaty they have made with the American Indians. Write about a broken promise that lodged itself in your heart.

- The earth is the inescapable past. From which earth part of your past would you like to escape?

EARTH FOOD FOR THOUGHT

- *Earth*—third planet from the sun, a sphere of mortal life, pursuits and pleasures as distinguished from those of a spiritual nature.

- *Earth mother*: the feminine principle of fertility, a divine resource of life on earth

- *Earthbound:* lacking imagination

- *Earthenware*

- *Earth science*

- *Earthshine*: the light of the sun that illuminates the dark part of the moon when it is reflected by the earth—also known as earthlight

- *"Salt of the earth"*

- *Salting the earth so nothing will ever grow there again*

- *Sprinkling ashes on the earth, "ashes to ashes, dust to dust"*

- Mahler composition, *Das Lied von der Erde* (Song of the Earth)

- *"Greetings, earthling!"*

- *"Earth to Dorothy. Come in, Dorothy!"*

- *Earthworm*

- Song: *"Earth angel, earth angel, will you be mine?"*

- *Earthshaking news*

- *"I felt my body become the earth, the richness and the rock,"* Danaan Parry

- *Unearthing secrets*

- *Archeology*

- *Robbing tombs*

- *Unearthly noise*

- *Earth Day*

- *Ecology*

- *Farming*

- *Reap what you sow*

- *"A very down-to-earth person"*

- *Underground*

- *Six feet under*

- *Buried alive*

- *Root vegetables*

- *Little girl trapped underground for three days*

- *I can't keep my feet on the ground*

- *Ground zero*

- *Land rush*

- *Living off the fat of the land*

- Millionaire H. L. Hunt's advice to *"buy land, it's the only thing they're not making any more of!"*

- Archimedes quotation: *"Give me a place to stand and I will move the world."*

- *Soil*

- *Soiled*

- *No longer a virgin*

- *Dirt*

- *Smut*

EARTH SEASONAL SURRENDERS

• Have an ancestor celebration for someone you loved. Let's say, for example, you choose your grandmother for this celebration. The celebration day you pick can be a birthday, Mother's Day, or another holiday you may want to share with her. You can also choose a time of year or a time in your life when you want to feel her energy close to yours.

Get a photo of your grandmother or something that belonged to her. Place it on a white cloth, the lovelier the cloth the better. If she had a favorite food, put that on a plate beside the photo. Now place a bouquet of flowers and a white candle in a glass on the cloth. Light the candle and call her name three times. Take a deep breath, then exhale, "I am here." Close your eyes and sit with her awhile.

It doesn't matter if you knew your grandmother well or didn't know her at all. One thing you can be certain of is that you did have a grandmother. If you didn't know her name, just say, "Grandma" three times. Allow her spirit to speak through your imagination and tell you what she might have liked.

If it's her birthday, get her a card and piece of cake and sing "Happy Birthday" to her. If you just want to have a day of connecting spirits, treat her as though she were a special house guest for the day. Say hello to her in the morning, have dinner and talk with her in the evening. Play music she might like to hear. Read to her and meditate with her. Tell her your problems and ask her wisdom to guide you.

In the evening, say good night to her and cover her food with an overturned glass bowl or plate. Next morning blow out the candle and kiss her goodbye until the next time. If you'd like, leave her picture there on the white cloth as a remembrance.

- Take time to feel the heartbeat of the earth this week. Go and stand some place where your feet are touching the earth. Take your shoes and socks off if you can. If for some reason you cannot do this outside, stand on a wooden floor or some other substance that came from the earth. Close your eyes and say to yourself, "I touch the earth, the earth touches me." Listen to her rhythm, and what she has to tell you.

- Danaan Parry says, "The earth is my home for this incarnation." Refugees, the homeless, and the Man Without a Country are all people who no longer have a land or home they can call their own. Think about the words *my home* and make a list of five things that they mean to you.

- Bring some earth into your house this week. Plant a seed in some soil, buy a new plant, or repot an old one.

MEDITATION FOR THE ELEMENT OF AIR

The breath of life
Is a song I was born singing.
Its child is the wind
Blowing change across my chosen path.
Its rhythm is the language
Of sound flying without wings.
Its tongue is the torrent of time
Seeking to know itself.

I breathe the world into my heart
And wait for words to answer to the light.
I taste the air with a thirsty mind,
Filling vision vessels with memory
And present tense.

I ride the air,
A ship on the ocean of the spirit,
My thoughts and prayers passengers
Bound for the unnamed unknown.

Let me feel my breath
Expanding to meet my needs,
And contracting to leave room for more.
Let me feel the breeze of myself
Moving through infinity at my own pace.
Let me feel the air
Touching me with tender fingers.
Let me feel life
Whispering the breath of love into my ears.

Now say your affirmation, put on your music, and let your spirit fill the air with your words.

FLYING WITH THE GREATEST OF EASE: AIR

I was director of a day-care center when I was called on to talk to a rather angry 5-year-old about his behavior. As I knelt down and spoke to him, he began blowing puffs of air directly into my face, as if putting out a match. That was his infuriating way of letting me know that he was not going to let my words affect him one way or another. He was actually trying to blow them away.

Later I had to marvel and even laugh at how effective his technique was. It has stayed with me to this day. In fact, I have since tried the same thing with friends—in a joking manner, of course—and they have been duly offended as well.

"She just blew me off," you say about person who has ignored your presence or your words. When you are faced with a shocking revelation the words that fall from your lips might be, "That just blew me away!" A police chief bemoaning the discovery of an undercover cop says, "His cover was blown."

Bob Dylan sang, "The answer, my friend, is blowing in the wind." We send our hopes, thoughts, and prayers into the air, aiming them at the god of our understanding. An African staff of authority often has a bird carved on top, reflecting a belief that the bird brings prayers to heaven, then flies back down with an answer to them. An old gospel song says, "When the prayer goes up, the blessings come down."

In one Native American practice, a wish is whispered to a butterfly, which is then released into the air. As it flies towards the Great Spirit, it bears the possibility of the wish's being granted.

How is it that you are able to feel something in the air? Did you ever walk into a room and find that you could still feel an argument that took place there before you arrived? You go to work and the sense of impending doom hanging in the air may hit you before you see the pink slip on your desk.

Air carries an energy of its own and holds on to other energies as well. It can cradle anger and sorrow, grief and pain in its arms until they are received by your senses. What is in the air can serve as a warning, a blessing, a joy, an embrace.

Your sixth sense often takes up residence in the air. It enables you to smell trouble, to see through the evidence of your eyes, to know the significance of a touch, and to hear the truth.

When I was growing up in the Smith Projects on Manhattan's Lower East Side, they incinerated garbage instead of compacting it as they do now. Ashes would often fly out of the building chimneys and land on my clothing. It was then that I decided I wanted to be cremated. That way if an ash fell on someone I knew, they might look at it and think of me.

Today, pollutants are spewed into the air from industries, toxic waste disposal units, and nuclear plants. Our air is further fouled by auto emissions, negative words, and toxic thoughts. We are still reading about the devastating effects of Chernobyl and the destruction of the ozone layer. We can see the thick air of fog in San Francisco, smog in Los Angeles, and vog in Hawaii.

Give some thoughts to things that fly through the air with the greatest of ease—balls and boomerangs, swings, swords, paper planes, and hot-air balloons. In the movie *Outbreak,* deadly germs are carried through the air by a sneeze. Radio and television programs go on the air. An insult hurled through the air can cause a wound that lasts for years.

When an affirmation is spoken into the air, it becomes energized. The same air that transmits electronic impulses from cellular phones carries the electrical impact of spoken words—words that have the power to hurt, heal, or help. Words bring a person's energy with them and can strike with a force that feels as if someone has actually laid a hand on you. That is why it is particularly important to be mindful of what is said in anger. An apology invites forgiveness but not forgetfulness.

What comes to mind when you think of someone who is a breath of fresh air, people who are full of hot air, something left up in the air, or cooking odors fill the air? I think of the airport on the island of Hawaii with landing strips carved right into solid fields of blackened lava.

I also think of my ex-husband, who was in the U.S. Air Force. When his plane landed in Brazil for refueling, just two days before Carnival, a rumor went around that some of the soldiers had disabled the plane by removing a small part. It took a month for a replacement part to arrive. In the meantime, the entire crew learned to samba, speak Portuguese, and drink *caipirinha.*

I have always wanted to fly. Bicycling down a long hill in Prospect Park is the closest I can come to it on a regular basis. And I am still waiting for one of those antigravity belts I saw in a movie to come on the market. Even as I write, I am making plans to go skydiving so that I can fulfill a lifelong dream.

Virginia Hamilton wrote a beautiful children's book called *The People Could Fly.* In one African tribe, as a special ritual is performed, the word *kulibaa* is chanted to enable the people to fly. I did not know this when I gave that name to my cockatiel.

My bird Kulibaa tap-dances back and forth against the inside of his metal cage, eager to be let out. At first when I actually open the door, he looks at it as if to ask, Is that door really open? Then he walks across his seed cup, positions himself in the doorway, and sits there smelling freedom. After a moment or two, he climbs to the top of the door and perches himself there for a while.

Once he fully realizes that there are no bars around him anymore, he makes a mad dash to the top of the door or flies through the house at breakneck speed as if possessed. Then he sits at the highest spot he can find, spreading his grey and yellow wings wide in triumph and celebration of his flight.

When he was young, he used to walk everywhere. I could hear his tiny toenails clicking against the linoleum in the kitchen or tipping across the wooden floor in the living room as he roamed the apartment looking for me. I could hear his mournful chirp as he stood at the foot of my bed looking up at a smiling face that was out of his reach.

One day as I made my usual gleeful run into the next room to get away from him, I saw a flash of grey and white and yellow and orange fly over my head and land in the middle of a flowerpot. Kulibaa stayed there, surprised as I was, trembling, trying to catch his breath and figure out what he was supposed to do next.

Your creative spirit can be a lot like that. It scrambles around in your inner cage of experience clamoring to be let out. It doesn't immediately run for freedom even when you open the door. It may wait for a while, then look around to see if the coast is clear.

If you listen closely, you might even hear it talking to itself: "I'm not ready to go out there yet," or "That door isn't really open, is it?" "I'm not going to go through that door because someone on the other side might just slam it in my face. You go first and see if it stays open. I'm right behind you."

Or it might say, "It's a trick! The door isn't really open—they just want me to think it is!" "I'm not sure if I can fly anyway. I tried it once before and it didn't work!" Think about the title of performance artist Pamela Sneed's book of poetry, *Imagine Being More Afraid of Freedom Than Slavery*.

Once you take those tentative steps through that doorway, you start to smell the scent of freedom. Your creative spirit spreads its wings and begins to fly. It decides what direction to take, how high to fly, where to land, where to rest, when to stop flying, and when to be still. Your Heartland is the force that moves you toward the door, the hand that opens it, and the air that carries your wings through it.

Writing From Your Heartland™ shows you how to open the door yourself and fly through it whenever you want to. Your job is to show the world the color of your wings, to make us stop in our tracks and marvel at your flight, to make us feel the wind of your words whizzing by the surface of our skin. Never let it be forgotten that you were born to fly.

AIR JOURNEYS

- The Fresh Air Fund sends city kids to the country to live for two weeks. Write about a particular situation that made you feel like saying, "I need to get some fresh air!"

- An old gospel song has the words "Over my head, I hear freedom in the air." Put the word *freedom* at the top of a piece of paper. Then close your eyes for a moment as you listen to your music. Write what comes to mind.

- Think about cooking odors you associate with your mother, your childhood, and your neighborhood. Pick one connected to each and write about what they mean to you and what you think about when you smell them.

- "Everything is up in the air right now." How does this describe a time in your life or the life of someone you know?

- One of my favorite songs by Tuck and Patti is called "Take My Breath Away." Write about something that took your breath away.

- When you are in the process of editing or finalizing something you have written, try putting it in the air by reading it aloud. What looks right on the paper won't always sound right to the ear.

AIR FOOD FOR THOUGHT

- *"You are a breath of fresh air"*
- *Shortness of breath, asthma*
- *"Wait and let me catch my breath"*
- The movie *Breathless*
- *Disappeared into thin air*
- *"He gave air to his opinions"*
- *"She gave me the air,"* a sudden break in a relationship
- *"The bombs bursting in air"*
- *The air quality today is "unacceptable"*—status reports given by television weatherpersons
- *"There's no air in here"*
- *Flat tire*
- *Stagnant air*
- *Open-air market*
- *Light and airy*
- *"I smell trouble in the air"*
- *"He smells like money"*

- *Air Jordan, Air France, Air Canada, Alitalia, etc.*
- *An air of dignity*
- *An air of luxury*
- *An air of mystery*
- *To put on airs:* to act in a haughty or affected manner
- *Air-conditioning*
- *Air-freshener*
- *Air-dried*
- *Air-cooled*
- *Air cushion*
- *Air mattress*
- *Air pump*
- *Airstream*
- *Air plant*
- *Air bag*
- *Air gun*
- *Airbrush*
- *Airlist*
- *Airspace*
- *Aircraft*
- *Aircraft carrier*
- *Airplane*
- *Air freight*
- *Airdrop*

- *Airmail*

- *Flying high*

- *A gust of wind*

- *Chicago, the Windy City*

- *Santa Ana winds*

- *Hurricane*

- *Tornado*

- *Monsoon*

- *Typhoon*

- *Cyclone*

- *Breeze*

- *Gale*

- The play *The First Breeze of Summer*

- *Empty space*

- The book *Being and Nothingness*

AIR SURRENDERS

- Do this outside or at an open window. Place both hands over your heart. What thought would you like to fill your heart with? Breathe in this thought. As it fills your heart and your lungs, stretch your arms out wide. As you exhale, visualize yourself breathing out whatever thoughts you want to remove from your heartspace. Return your hands to your heart as the thought is released into the air. Repeat at least three times.

- Take a walk for about fifteen minutes or longer. Make a list of all the smells you encounter along the way. Don't leave out any, even the ones that may come from your own body.

- Let the winds of change blow through your life. Is there something you've been meaning to change for a while but haven't gotten around to it? Perhaps you have been afraid, were unsure, or just didn't act on it for some reason.

   Use the energy of a new moon to give you the help you may need. Look at a calendar to see when the next new moon will arrive, then target that date for the change you need to make. Decide what you want to bring a different breeze to, then imagine the wind unfurling the sails of change within your spirit.

MEDITATION FOR THE ELEMENT OF FIRE

Fire, igniting the darkness
With the intangible unseen.
The yellow in the mouth of the night,
Telling tales of time's beginning.
The phoenix rises
Between fire's thighs,
And hope is given wings.

Ancient fire burning in the sky,
Bathing my soul in rivers of rays,
Pointing me to the where
In the light of the now.
Let my thoughts fill the darkness
With flames of feeling,
Stirring ashes of the past
With visions in flight.

My creative spirit burns as it heals,
Purifies as it transforms,

Enlightens as it explodes.
I am alchemy
Waving my magic
Over a mind swollen with image and intent.
I am ready to face the fire of my life
Shining with the power
To create what I create.
I am ready to feel the flames
Of my soul.

Try reading affirmations at night right before you go to bed, then putting them under your pillow. Let them empower your dreams.

FIRE AND DESIRE

There's an old joke about a man who worked in a candy factory. One day he had the misfortune to fall into a huge vat of chocolate. After struggling desperately, he began to shout, "Fire! Fire!" The other factory workers heard his cry and managed to lift him out to safety. One of the workers asked him, "Why were you yelling, 'Fire! Fire!' when you fell in?" He replied, "Who do you think would have come if I yelled, 'Chocolate! Chocolate!'?"

You might have witnessed raging fires burning through hundreds of miles of parched lands in the western states or a campfire surrounded by eager campers roasting hot dogs and marshmallows and telling ghost stories. You might have struck a match to a cigarette you shouldn't have been smoking, or entertained romantic fantasies of lying naked on a bearskin rug in front of a fireplace.

You may have passed by homeless men warming themselves over garbage can fires or been angered by the epidemic of church burnings that spread across this country. The element of fire shines its light into every corner of life. Look inside and see where its warm hands have touched you.

There was hardly a dry eye in the stadium at that unforgettable moment when Muhammad Ali stepped from the shadows to light the Olympic torch at the 1996 summer games in Atlanta. Is someone is still carrying a torch for you? The Supremes sang about a "burning, burning, yearning feeling inside me." Have you ever had one of those feelings? When Jose Feliciano sang, "Come on, baby, light my fire," many flames were kindled. Have you ever been "in heat," gotten "hot and bothered," or just been just "too hot to handle"?

I remember salivating in front of Tad's Flame-Broiled Steaks on 42nd Street. I would stand there watching fires leap through iron rods skewered with seared beef and crisp chunks of Italian bread. I can still see my mother holding pieces of freshly killed chicken over the stove's flame, burning away the last few feathers left embedded in the flesh.

It was midnight when my then-husband and I decided we could no longer endure the funky smell of an old steamer trunk we had purchased that day. We struggled to squeeze it through our Bronx apartment window and onto the fire escape for airing out. We didn't think about the late hour or the racket we must have made. We fell into bed exhausted. It wasn't long before we heard a loud banging on the door and a voice yelling, "Police, open up!"

Someone in the building had heard the noise and reported a burglary in progress. We actually had to prove we lived there. We showed them the fire escape and the offending trunk. "Okay, McGill!" the policeman shouted into the alley. "It's only a trunk!" When we looked down into the alleyway there were four cops with guns drawn, waiting for the perpetrator. Do you have any fire-escape memories?

Before I left my full-time job and began writing this book I was truly burning the candle at both ends. I was in seminary, burning the midnight oil at my job, curating a monthly women's reading series called Muse Magic, teaching weekly classes, traveling around the country giving workshops, struggling to maintain a relationship and trying to find time to eat, sleep, and go to the bathroom.

When I woke up in the morning, I felt just as tired as I was when I went to bed. When I tried to read the driver's manual to get my learner's permit, I wondered why I could not remember anything on page 6 by the time I got to page 7. I did not know I was experiencing something called burnout until I read it in a counseling manual.

In an East Indian tradition that continued right up into the nineteenth century, distraught wives were to supposed to throw themselves onto funeral pyres as the bodies of their departed husbands were being burned. During the Middle Ages, thousands of innocent women in Europe were falsely accused of witchcraft and burned at the stake. The African deity Chango spits fire and is said to be the initiator of trial by fire. In Hawaii, Pele, the fiery volcano goddess, is known to destroy and create at the same moment. She can be seen spewing molten lava from the volcano Kilauea.

Traditionally in Scandinavia, on one day of the year women wear crowns of lighted candles and sing songs to draw the sun closer to the earth. The February first Christian celebration of Candlemas had its orgins in an ancient Celtic tradition celebrating Saint Brigid. Bonfires were kept burning in order to invite her blessings and bring an end to winter.

Think of cooking as alchemy and fire as an agent of transformation turning liquid eggs into a solid scrambled mass and the ordinary ingredients of milk, flour, and sugar into extraordinary birthday cakes. Continue to fire your imagination with this element. How else it can spark your writing, your artwork, your spirit? From what source might you draw your inspiration and your perspiration?

Words can flow from the persistent hot flashes of menopause or the cigarette burns of an abused child's arm. Images can flow from doing a slow burn, getting a sunburn, or feeling heartburn. Your creative spirit can flow from watching a shooting star in August and realizing that as it burns it is dying. Let your burning desires spill out of you like lava from the volcano of your Heartland, creating new visions as they destroy anything in the way of your spirit.

FIRE JOURNEYS

Put your music on and start with a five-minute freewrite. But you've heard all of this before. I'm sure you remember, don't you?

- Write about the time you landed in hot water.

- "My ears are burning. Someone must be talking about me!"

- "You're fired!"

- A heated argument

- Hot and tired

- Burning the candle at both ends

- Burned-out buildings

 Write each of these on its own index card. Close your eyes, shuffle the cards, then pick one to write from.

- "Where there's smoke, there's fire!" Write about something that happened in the last year that might have caused you to think or say this.

- "That really burns me up!" Think about something a parent did to you that might have brought about this reaction.

FIRE FOOD FOR THOUGHT

These are all ready for you to fire them up. Take any one and freewrite from it, add to it, or let it shine another light on something you have already created.

- *Fire*: to fill with life, spirit or passion

- *Fire of a gem*: the brilliance of a stone

- *Fireball*: a person with a great deal of energy, a brilliant meteor with a luminous trail, a vaporous cloud created by a nuclear explosion.

- *"Fired up, can't take no more!"*—protest march chant

- *Fireman*

- *Fireman's ball*

- *Fire drill*

- *Fire department*

- *Fireboat*

- *Fire alarm*

- *Fire extinguisher*

- *Fireproof*

- *Fire truck*

- *Fire wall*

- *Firewood*

- *Fireworks*

- *Firefly*

- *Fire-breathing dragon*

- *Firebug*: pyromaniac

- *Firebird*, the ballet

- *Firearms*

- *Fire away!*

- *He fired the gun* (or "the gun went off")

- *Firing squad*

- *Firing pin*

- *"Fire when ready, Gridley!"*

- *Firepower:* a military unit's ability to effectively fire on a target

- *Under fire:* under enemy attack

- *Trial by fire*

- *Firing line*

- *Fire-eater*

- *Firecracker:* a person or an explosive device

- *Fireplace:* sitting by, waiting for Santa Claus

- *Firecured:* as in tobacco

- *Firing clay:* (to create pottery)

- *Fire in the Belly,* the book

- *"What are you so all fired up about?"*

- *Firebrand:* an instigator of strife or unrest, one who agitates

- *Firebreak:* land cleared in order to halt the advance of a forest fire

- *Fire and brimstone*

- *"Hellfire and damnation"*

- *"He had to stand by and watch his house burn down"*

- *Burned out:* worn out by improper, excessive or stressful use

- *Homeless as a result of a fire*

- *Burn:* to give off light, heat or gas

- *"Leave a light burning in the window"*
- *"Keep the home fires burning"*
- *Burning to tell my story*
- *Burning sands*
- *"My face is burning from the cold"*
- *Moses and the burning bush*
- *Book burning*
- *Wood-burning stove*
- *Burn unit*
- *Rope burn*
- *Heat exhaustion*
- *Prickly heat*
- *"It's not the heat, it's the humidity"* (or the humility)
- Rita Hayworth singing *"We're having a heat wave, a tropical heat wave"*
- *In the heat of battle*
- *"Is it hot enough for you?"*
- *Le jazz hot*: emotionally exciting rhythms characterized by ecstatic melodic improvisations
- *Hot-tempered*
- *Hot off the press*
- *A hot scent*
- *"That a hot one!"* retort to an unbelievable or absurd statement

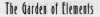

- *A hot item*

- *Hot wheels, a hot car:* a recently stolen vehicle

- *Hot:* unsafe for a fugitive from the law, or wanted by the police

- *Hot dog*

- *Hotcakes*

- *Hot sauce*

- *Hot dice:* unusually favorable

- *Hotbed:* an atmosphere that promotes rapid development or growth, as in "a hotbed of political activity"

- *Hot-blooded*

- *Hot pepper*

- *Hot rod*

- *Hotshot*

- *Hot springs*

- *"This town is too hot for you!"*

- *"I've got a hot flash for you"*

- *"I'll make it hot for you"*

- *Hotfoot:* to make a hasty retreat

- *Hothouse:* a house of prostitution, or a house of flowers and vegetables

- *In the hot seat*

- *Scorched earth policy:* Sherman going through Atlanta, Georgia

FIRE SEASONAL SURRENDER

- William Blake wrote, "Tyger! Tyger! burning bright/in the forests of the night." Make a list of at least five things you see burning brightly in yourself. Then make a list of five things you see in the dark forests inside yourself.

- Are there any bridges you may have burned behind you? If so, think about how you might begin to repair one of them; then do it.

- Get a candle in a glass and light it for someone you feel needs light in their life. Do this for yourself if you need to. As you look at the flame, think about the person, say his or her name, and add, "May the love that dwells inside you light the flame that sings within you, bringing joy that shines around you."

Water of Life

I was in Hawaii, floating on a rubber raft in the calm August ocean at the beach at Waikiki, watching the sky and listening to the waves rock me. I felt weightless, light as the air around me, peaceful and totally content. It was as if I had returned the source, to a place where my entire body, mind and soul could feel completely at ease.

We begin our lives in the water of our mother's womb. The element of water has consistently flowed through our days since that time, often bringing with it the longing to return to a primal space of nurturance, comfort, and safety.

The healing hands of water reach out to embrace and inspire us in an infinite number of ways. You may have visited a flotation tank in order to experience a return to the womb. Or you might have had your body immersed in water at a baptismal ceremony that marked the start of a new spiritual life.

Each year on Coney Island there is a special commemoration of the Middle Passage and the lost lives of our African ancestors. I had always looked forward to it with great excitement—the drums, the people, and the powerful feeling of spirit. But one year a sadness hung around my heart like an albatross. Just a year before, during that same ceremony, I had blissfully said yes to a marriage proposal. Now the unhealed wound of that lost relationship was reopened when I learned that my former fiancé would be attending the event with a new lover.

As hundreds walked into the ocean singing, dancing, drumming, saluting the ancestors, throwing flowers and fruit into the waters, I cried, tears of spirit mingled with those of pain. Then, for some reason, I began grabbing at my heart, closing my fingers around the despair, and throwing it into the water. I continued to pull the grief out of me with both hands, throwing it between the flower petals, crying and begging the ocean, "Please, Mommy, take this sadness from me. Please!"

Incredibly, after just a few minutes, something lifted. The sorrow that had so thoroughly filled my body had vanished. I stood there for a while, looking for traces, waiting for it to come back. I didn't believe those feelings could have disappeared so completely, but they had. The albatross took wing and never returned.

"Water, water everywhere nor any drop to drink." These words could have been spoken by Tallulah Bankhead and William Bendix, characters adrift at sea in the movie classic *Lifeboat*. Think of that image as a metaphor for people living in poverty in the richest country in the world, or for a lonely person surrounded by couples in love. "By the waterfall I'm calling you-u-u-u," Ruby Keeler trilled as women made their bodies into floating kaleidoscopes in Busby Berkeley's *Gold Diggers of 1933*. Utterance of the words "Niagara Falls" sparked a psychotic reaction in an Abbott and Costello comedy routine, "Slowly I turned. Step by step, inch by inch."

In the powerful drama *On the Waterfront*, Marlon Brando bemoans the failures of his life with the classic line "I could have been a contender." Are there places where that line might apply to your life? At a silent yoga retreat in the woods, we were awakened at dawn by the sweet voice of Anandi singing, "Oh, water my soul, water in the spirit of God." How often have you felt your soul needed to be watered—that it was thirsty and about to crack?

Waterloo and Watergate marked the downfall of two men in power. A watershed indicates a crucial dividing point or line. If a politician is urged to tone down the inflammatory nature of his speech, he is being asked to water it down.

If someone is crying profusely, it is said that they have "turned on the waterworks." When the sky cries, it shapes its waters into rivers, streams, lakes, ponds, brooks, and oceans. When the earth cries, it is in pain over what we have done to these waters—the dumping of industrial wastes, chemicals, or sewage; oil spills; the destruction of fish, whales, and other citizens of the deep.

In parts of the United States there are rivers so polluted that they burn when a match is tossed into them. On the North Fork of Long Island, people have to bring plastic jugs to a county station to get fresh water; the liquid flowing from their faucets is no longer drinkable.

You can use the element of water to check the way the spirit is shaping your character. You can also use this element to bring life to a character you may have written. If the character is a woman, for example, you can ask, how does she flow? What makes her stop flowing? Who or what is it that makes her waters boil over? What makes her feel like she's drowning? How does she wash away the past? Bathe in it? Drink too much of it? What makes her afraid to go near the water? What makes her afraid to come out of the water? Does she go in the deep, or does she stay in the shallow areas? Do you? How would you or the people who are close to you answer any of these questions?

When Columbus went sailing across the ocean toward the horizon, people thought for sure that he would fall off the edge of the earth. Like a stone thrown into water, his journey had a ripple effect throughout the world. It planted the seeds for a slave trade that devastated millions of African lives.

An entry in his diary also portrays his colonial attitude toward the Native Americans he claims to have "discovered." It also suggests the origin of a name they were subsequently given. He wrote, "These people are *in dios* [of God]. They give us everything so freely so it will be quick to take them over."

A skit on the old Flip Wilson comedy show had a scene in which Columbus lands in America. He sees a thriving native population already living there and insists, "Hey, y'all, I just discovered you!" A native woman retorts, "Christopher Columbus, you better go on home and discover yourself!"

As you begin to gather your thoughts about the element of water, envision your own horizons and the things that might make you fear falling off your own edges. What would happen if you journeyed past the perception of your own boundaries? Why not sail the ship of yourself across the infinite sea of your creative spirit and see what lies beyond the beyond?

WATER JOURNEYS

- "Just when you thought it was safe to go back in the water," went the advertisement for shark thriller, *Jaws 2*. Write about a time when you felt you were safe only to find out that you were not. This journey can be applied to your life, the life of someone you know, or to a character you have created.

- People say, "Go with the flow," and Toni Braxton sings "Let It Flow." Do you go with the flow or stop with the drop? Put on some flowing music, choose one of the options, and see where it takes your five-minute freewrite.

- "I touch the water, the water touches me." What are some of your earliest memories of water? Pick out one of those memories from your childhood and write about it.

WATER FOOD FOR THOUGHT

- *Water*—an odorless, tasteless liquid that falls from the clouds as rain and forms lakes, streams and rivers, a major component of all living matter.

- *"Wade in the Water,"* gospel song

- *To water*

- *Water bag*

- *Water glass*

- *Water ballet*

- *Water bed*

- *Water lily*

- *Water gap*

- *Water bearer:* Aquarius

- *Water boy:* Rudyard Kipling's poem "Gunga Din"

- *Water bird*

- *Water buffalo*

- *Water bug*

- *Water biscuit*

- *Water chestnut*

- *Water closet*

- *Water pistol*

- *Water heater*

- *Waterlogged*

- *Watermark*
- *Watermelon*
- *Water nymph or sprite*
- *Water pipe*
- *Waterproof, water-repellent, water-resistant*
- *Waterspout*
- *Water tower*
- *Waterway*
- *Water wings*
- *Water balloon*
- *Water beetle*
- *Water blister*
- *Watercolor*
- *Watercooler*
- *Watercress*
- *Waterfowl*
- *Waterless cooking*
- *Water level*
- *Water meter*
- *Water moccasin*
- *Water polo*
- *Waterpower*
- *Water rat*

- *Waterside*

- *Water ski*

- *Water snake*

- *Water spaniel*

- *Water sports*

- *Watering hole*

- *Water wave*

- *Waterwheel*

- *Water supply*

- *Watery:* weak, wishy-washy or vapid

- *Freshwater pearl*

- *Saltwater fish*

- *"My bonnie lies over the ocean / My bonnie lies over the sea."*

- *"From the mountain, to the prairie, to the ocean white with foam"* ("God Bless America")

- *Ocean's 11:* movie starring the self-named Rat Pack: Frank Sinatra, Sammy Davis, Jr., Dean Martin, and Peter Lawford

- *Ocean voyage:* getting away from it all

- *Yemaya, Olokun*: African ocean spirits

- *Sea*: a vast body of salt water covering most of the earth's surface; a great or overwhelming quantity

- *"One if by land, two if by sea"*

- *Below/above sea level*

- *Childhood chant*: "A sailor went to sea / To see what he could see / But all that he could see / Was the bottom of the deep blue sea."

- *Bobby Darin song,* "Somewhere beyond the sea"

- *"By the sea, by the sea, by the beautiful sea"*

- *Drifters song,* "Under the boardwalk, down by the sea."

- *Jonathan Livingston Seagull*

- *Georgia Sea Islands*

- *Seashore*

- *Sea horse*

- *Sea bass*

- *Sea breeze*

- *Sea legs*

- *Sea otter*

- *Sea plane*

- *Seashell*

- *Seasick*

- *Sea urchin*

- *Seaman*

- *Seamanship*

- *Sea star*

- *Sea trout*

- *Seaweed*

- *"See Dick run"* (just kidding!)

- Song lyrics to *"Ebb Tide": "First the tide rushes in, plants a kiss on the shore"*

- *High Tide Harris*

- *"The tide of public opinion turned against him"*

- *Open the floodgates*

- *Dams*

- *Dikes*

- *Rivers*

- *Lakes*

- *Ponds*

- *Brooks*

- *Beach*

- Peter Benchley's *The Deep*

- *Floating*

- *Swimming*

- *Taking a bath or shower*

- *Drowning*

- *"Drown in My Own Tears,"* Ray Charles song

- *The business went under*

- *Baptism*

- *Pouring libations*

- *Tears*

- *Urine*

- *Sap*

- *Semen*

- *Washing away the evidence after a rape*

- *Neptune*

- *Mermaids*

- *Sirens*

WATER SEASONAL SURRENDERS

- Use the element of water as an instrument of healing. This is a very special meditation called Oceans of the World Earth Mother Healing Meditation. Speak these words to an ocean, a river, or other body of water. If you cannot do this, then say the meditation as you sit in a bathtub.

> *I open my heart to the wondrous beauty that is me. I feel that beauty grow and expand beyond the confines of my physical being. I am love.*
> *I am light. I am oneness with all that is. I embrace the light within myself. I embrace the light within others, for in the light and love we create the sisterhood of healing. Light beings of all dimensions are joined with us in sisterhood, for we have called upon the power of love to heal the planet Earth.*
> *As I bring my focus to the water, I imagine it in turmoil, abused and misused, filled with pain and despair, choked and dying. I weep for it. I weep for myself and all mankind, for as we destroy the oceans, we destroy ourselves. I let my tears flow. I open my heart and my soul. I do not hold back, for my tears will replenish and cleanse the oceans of the world.*
> *And now I see the water begin to change. As I share its pain, I ease its pain. I focus my heart and soul on the water. I feel the cleansing power of love flow through me into the water. I imagine it as a pinlight flowing from deep within my being, connecting me to*

the water, radiating outwards to embrace the pink light of the people in my environment.

I see the water beginning to vibrate with a new life, a new joy, a new purpose. As the pink glow spreads farther and farther from the shore, I call out with my love to all the creatures of the sea, to the dolphins and the whales, and to the turtles, to all God's creatures. I embrace them with my pink light. I ask them to share this empowerment, to carry my message forth worldwide—that it is a New Age, an age of love and caring, an age of oneness. Together we can create a new balance, a new respect, a new healing.

My tears of pain become tears of joy as they flow into the sea, for I have accepted and joined with the divinity inside each of us. We have become a single heart, a global vibration of love. We join together to empower the ocean with loving energy that the ocean may be healed and nurtured, and that the ocean in turn may heal and nurture Mother Earth.

I allow my joy to become an overwhelming, overpowering vibration. I express it as openly as I express my pain. I fill the sea with my joy. I fill those around me with my joy. I fill myself with my joy. I dance to the vibration of that joy. I sing with the whales and the dolphins, for we have not gathered together for a funeral, but for a birth—birth of a new direction, a new spirit of oneness, a new joyful healing.

I am love. I am light. I am oneness with all that is. I embrace the light within myself. I embrace the light within each being, for in the light and love we create the sisterhood of healing. May peace, blessings, and love be with us all.

- Feed yourself with a liquid affirmation. Fill a glass with water, and say into it three times, "Water of the spirit, fill me with your life and make me whole." Then close your eyes and slowly drink the energized water. Feel the power of the words flow through your entire body. Feel the affirmation becoming an indelible part of you. Do this in the morning before you start your day, and again in the evening before going to bed.

- Go beyond your usual horizons and take a chance today. Who knows what worlds you might discover?

chapter 5

·

SPIRIT OF A WOMAN

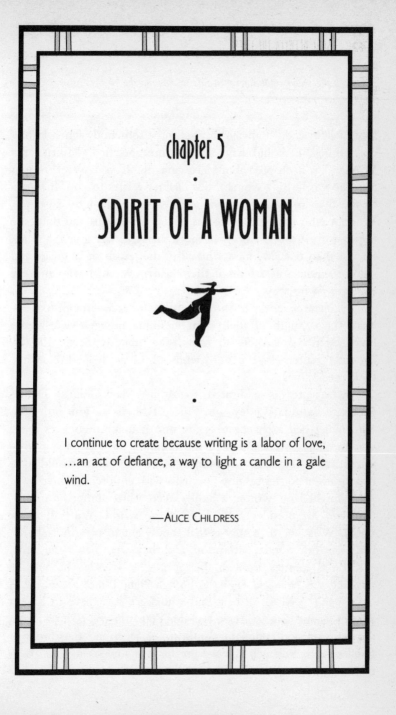

·

I continue to create because writing is a labor of love,
…an act of defiance, a way to light a candle in a gale
wind.

—ALICE CHILDRESS

Stages

Lily Tomlin said, "I always wanted to be somebody when I grew up. I guess I should have been more specific." "Spirit of a Woman" is a chapter about growing up. If you were brought into the world by a woman, this chapter relates to you. It speaks to the lives of women, who nurture the world into existence. Women who survive the storms of denied dreams and domestic oppression. Women who give more than they are given, and ask for less than that. Women who carry the jewels of language and culture in the soft armor of their hearts. Woman who make a way out of no way.

This chapter speaks to the lives of men brave enough to celebrate the strength of their own feminine power. Men whose loving spirits dare them to honor the grandmothers, mothers, daughters, sisters, lovers, and friends who have helped them live their possibilities.

This chapter is dedicated to Addie Mae Collins, Denise McNair, Cynthia Wesley, and Carole Robertson, four little girls who never had a chance to grow up, or make their lives more specific. They were killed in the bombing of a church in Birmingham, Alabama, on September 23, 1963. They would have been in their forties by now, perhaps with children of their own. They might have written a book, saved a life, climbed a mountain, run for president, or changed the world. We will never know. What we do know is that they went to play in a church basement one Sunday afternoon, and they were never the same.

On this journey through the *Spirit of a Woman* you will be traveling the *Heartland Highway* through eight *United States of Life*. You won't need a seat belt, and you don't even have to have a driver's license. Poetic license will do. Your trip will take you from the seeds of conception to the brink of birth and the throes of toddler years. You will visit the precipice of adolescence, the plains of adulthood, and the mountains of the middle ages.

Finally, your journey winds down at the sands of the senior years, the fertile desert of death, and beyond. This is a road paved with intent and experience. It is a path whose source is your Heartland.

These *United States of Life* are rich with unexplored territory, gold mines, quicksand, rain forests, and ancient caves. The first, *To Be or Not To Be,* is where conception lives. The road to the next state, *Planetary Reentry,* begins at birth. The state of *Pioneers at Play* is where toddlers and children roam. *Blood, Sweat, and Tears* takes you through adolescence, while the early adult years reside in the *Age of Consent.* In the state of the *Middle Passage,* the road takes a turn toward the middle-aged years, and on toward the state of *Silver Time* and the elder years. Your arrival at the state of *Wake-up Call* and the transformation of life signals the end of one journey and the beginning of another.

Have you ever felt ten years younger, chided a teenager for acting like a child, or commented that someone was young at heart? Have you ever watched children play dress-up, heard someone say, "I wish I'd never been born," or seen a person who was old before her time? These are all manifestations of mental, physical, and spiritual travels from one *State of Life* to another.

At any moment you may find yourself journeying from your present self to a self from your past or your future. Adult disappointments can rekindle self-esteem issues from your childhood. An elderly mother may begin to make childlike demands for care and attention. A daughter you spoon-fed can grow into either a friend feeding on a shared womanhood or an enemy swallowing a past she can't forgive.

Intersections

When you arrive at the end of each *State of Life,* you will find an Intersection marked by three major road signs: *Doubt, Reassur-*

ance, and Decision. These signs signal you to slow down, think about what to do next, and proceed accordingly. Pick a sign and begin to gather the thoughts and feelings that come with it.

One sign may strike you instantly, or two of them may seem to carry equal weight for you. Write your thoughts down. You don't have to spend any more than five minutes with these thoughts at each of the intersections. Here is an idea of some of the reflections indicated by these signs:

- Doubt Sign

  "I think I'm going the wrong way."

  "I'm not even sure where this road goes."

  "Why did I begin this trip in the first place?"

  "I hope it's not too late to turn back."

- Reassurance Sign

  "I think I'm almost there."

  "This looks familiar—I've passed this way before."

  "I'm sure this is the right way."

  "I think it's going to be okay."

- Decision Sign

  "I think I've gone far enough."

  "I like it here. I think I'll stay."

  "I'm going to go straight ahead and not make any turns."

Picture yourself pausing to think about what each sign might mean to you at various points in your life. Think about what you might say to yourself as you decide which sign to follow on your road to the next state.

Imagine, for example, that you are still in your mother's womb. You have heard a lot of yelling and screaming going on outside of your mother's belly. Before you get to the point where you are about to be born, before you reach that particular intersection, you might pause at the *Doubt Sign* and say, "I wonder if it's too late to turn back." Or you might look at the *Decision Sign* and say, "I'm not ready for this, and neither is my mother. I think I've gone far enough," then decide to stage your own miscarriage.

Each intersection allows you to chart the depth and direction of your journey. Let's say, for example, a pregnant teenager is at the Intersection between the states of *Blood, Sweat, and Tears,* and the *Age of Consent.* At the *Doubt Sign,* she might reflect, "I don't know if I'm ready for all the responsibility of having a baby." At the *Reassurance Sign* her musings may be "I'm sure I can handle this. I feel like I'm grown already." Or at the *Decision Sign,* she might reflect, "I'm going to have this baby no matter what anybody says."

Think about what your life might have been like if you had faced different sets of doubts, reassurances, or decisions at each of your own intersections. Imagine having the power to write and rewrite the course of your life. Imagine the positive transformation, the spiritual insight, the poetry, fiction, theater, biography, visual imagery, and personal essay that can come from these intersection moments.

Each visit with the *United States of Life* will bring you deeper and deeper into your Heartland. Each intersection will put you in touch with the fact that you *do* have the power to rewrite your life, both on paper and off. Each pause gifts you with an abundance of experiences to write from, grow on, and live by.

There is a saying: "If you don't know where you're going, any road will take you there." Perhaps we are all tourists on the *Heartland Highway,* equipped with cameras for taking it all in and comfortable shoes for walking through life with a minimum of pain.

Some people spend their lives looking for home, for a place of true belonging, a territory indelibly imprinted in their heart's memory. How often have we wished we could turn back the hands of time or said to ourselves, "If I had it to do all over again"? What if we could relive the precious moments in our lives and erase ones that have scarred us for life?

Writing blesses you with a literary Land Rover that can travel all terrains of speculation and imagination. You can relive and revise your experiences through fiction, poetic remembrance, theatrical performance, video biography, photo documentation, conflict resolution, heart-to-heart talks, creative confrontation, and family intervention sessions.

In some territories you may need to wait until time paves the road again. It took more than five years for me to be able to start writing a poem about the deaths of my mother and father. Keep yourself open to what your signs say as you travel through your life.

Icon Box

As you experience the richness of your passage through the United States of Life, you will accumulate a treasure chest of adventures. I will be asking you to assemble an Icon Box for this chapter, a place for storing the visible reflections of those experiences. To create your *Icon Box,* first select a nice wooden or cigar box, an old jewelry box, a gift box, a metal cookie container, or an antique tin box, or even a decorated shoe box.

At each intersection, revisit the *seeds*, *journeys*, and the *seasonal surrenders* gathered during your travels through the state. Also make note of memories that have floated to the surface. Next, choose a word and an object that reflect the writings and recollections you have encountered. Put them into your *Icon Box*. Once you have done this, you are ready to move on to the next state.

These objects you collect will be called totems. The word *totem* comes from the Ojibwa tribe, and is defined as "something that serves as an emblem or revered symbol." Your totems symbolize your passage through the *States of Life* and what you have experienced along the way.

These totems can be items such as a photo of a treasured time in your life, souvenirs from special places, a fragment or remnant of something you once wore, greeting cards, letters or articles that were significant to you, a ball you played with as a child, or a pressed flower saved from a romantic evening.

Let's visit our pregnant teenager again. Imagine what totems she would put into her *Icon Box*. Remember, she is at the intersection between *Blood, Sweat and Tears* and the *Age of Consent*. She might choose to cut out a picture of a baby and put the word *love* into the box. Or she might decide to place a condom and the word *no* in her box.

What totems would you put into the box if you were she or if she were your daughter? You will have an opportunity to visit more situations in the pages ahead.

At some of the intersections, you may want to choose more than one totem. You may also decide you need a sentence or a quotation instead of just one word. The choice is yours. Just be sure to indicate which *State of Life* the totems are for. Your *Icon Box* will grow more and more powerful as you travel through all the states of your being. It will become a priceless treasure chest of mirror and memory, a potent souvenir of your unforgettable passage through the *Spirit of a Woman*.

MEDITATION FOR SPIRIT OF A WOMAN

Before you start writing, remember that your creative spirit loves music, meditation, and affirmation. It also loves incense and sage. When the spirit smells those things, it puts its shoes on, walks right up to your door, and starts handing you things to say.

Think about your preparation ritual. Do you like what you're already doing? Do you want to add to the ritual, or change it altogether? Whether you have been calling in the directions, lighting a candle, putting on special music, or staring at a mandala, what is important is that it works best for you.

Keeping your hands over your heart, the right hand of giving over the left hand of receiving, read the following meditation:

This day showers me with light
and I am shining.
I am the intersection of words and wisdom,
sentence and story,
the co-creator of future memory.
I am the owner of my own destiny.

The journey begins with me
as I begin the journey.
I pave the road with potency and passion,
full as the harvest moon that gave itself to me.
I walk the path my words have walked before me,
when time was a thought
and I was a dream in its mind.

I walk the landscape of inner knowing
as I move through all of my seasons.
Let my passages be watered
by the spirit of all who have walked before me.
Let the path of my past,
nurture my present
as I reach toward the future of all of my selves.
And so it is.

Now close your eyes and take the time to observe the thoughts
and feelings that pass by. Take three deep breaths and open your
eyes again. Think of an affirmation phrased in the present and
prepare to visit the *Spirit of a Woman.*

To Be or Not to Be

To be or not to be, that is conception. Years ago, I got a reading
from an astrologer who told me that my parents were not truly

in love at the time of my conception. Because of their state of mind when I was conceived, she said, a particular kind of negative energy would be attracted to me throughout my lifetime. She even mentioned a specific form of energy to watch out for.

Most of her reading was incredibly accurate. Still, I could not connect with what I was told about my parents. I never forgot her words, though. In years to come, the truth of those words would become quite evident.

I once asked my grandmother how long ago a particular family event had occurred. She answered me by saying, "Oh, you wasn't originated yet!" In some societies a child is considered to be a year old when it is born, having had its origin at the time of conception. Exactly when life begins is still a subject of debate. Is conception the thought, the seed, or the breath of life? In its fullest spirit, it is all of these.

You conceive when you brainstorm, listen to people, look at the sky, walk down the street, or talk with other creative spirits. Thoughts begin to flow. The embryo of an idea develops inside the belly of your Heartland. It pushes through your spirit until finally it is born kicking and screaming onto a piece of paper. Every conscious moment is a moment of conception. You just have to open your mind and heart (and sometimes your legs) in order to receive it.

A lotus seed found inside a pyramid sprouted in a laboratory two thousand years after it had been closed in. An experience from your childhood might begin to germinate only after it lands on the potent soil of your adult years. Women may suddenly remember being abused when a seed of that situation presents itself to them. A memory might be roused by a word or piece of music or through someone's touch.

In the movie *Citizen Kane,* a powerful millionaire dies with the word *Rosebud* on his lips. No one realized that he was remembering a sled he owned in a happier time from his childhood.

I was bemoaning the Christmas madness and feeling disconnected from the spirit of the holiday when I happened to see a bag of colorfully striped hard candies in the drugstore. I was warmed by the memory they brought back to me.

On Christmas morning, brown paper bags filled with these candies, nuts, tangerines, and candy canes were always left under the tree for me and my sisters. On these bags in block letters, my mother always wrote, "To Dorothy from Santa," "To Ruthie from Santa," and "To Juanita from Santa." To this day I cannot see these candies or smell tangerines without thinking of those wonderful Christmas days of my childhood.

A woman I know of stumbled across a buried childhood trauma while she was in the middle of a novel-writing seminar. As the pain began to make itself increasingly apparent, another woman sitting nearby comforted her by saying, "God wouldn't let you remember if He didn't think you were strong enough to deal with it." I thought of Mother Teresa's words: "I know God will not give me anything I can't handle. I just wish He didn't trust me so much."

Conception can also be thought of as the union of idea and action. No matter how potent the male or fertile the female, a child cannot be conceived unless the life-giving elements of both are joined together. In her book *Reflections in the Light,* Shakti Gawain reminds us that "the union of feminine and masculine energies within the individual is the basis of all creation. Female intuition plus male action equals creativity."

Fortunately, the universe has provided many pleasurable, scientific, and ingenious ways of bringing about this union. In fact, one of the more creative fertilization techniques gave rise to my retort to an annoying man on the street who insisted on throwing his virility at me. "You can be replaced by a turkey baster," I tossed back at him.

When a woman's son was killed by a drunk driver, she transformed her grief into the conception of a support organization called MADD (Mothers Against Drunk Driving). Icarus watched the flight of birds, then conceived a method of constructing a set of wings so that he could fly. Everything that happens to us and around us inspires conception.

Sometimes that inspiration comes from thinking about things that *might* happen. What-ifs can impregnate your work with fertile imaginings. Octavia Butler's novel of speculative fiction *Parable of the Sower* envisions California in the year 2025. In the movie classic *It's a Wonderful Life,* an angel paints Jimmy Stewart a picture of how very difficult life would have been had he never been born. Dory Previn muses about immaculate conception in her song "Did Jesus Have a Baby Sister," in which the young sibling looks into her mirror and wonders if she should call herself "saviorwoman, saviorperson, or saviorette."

After its conception, a thought or an idea develops legs, arms, and vital organs during its gestation period. As it grows, it draws sustenance from the umbilical cord connected to your Heartland and from its surrounding environment.

Children are sensitive to music and outside stimuli while still in the womb. They absorb emotions and feelings stored in the body during pregnancy. They react to arguments as well as peaceful settings. They can be born angry and carry a mother's guilt or a father's reluctance. A woman I know of was born covered with acne. She connected the skin condition with her feelings of rage at being an unwanted child.

Applying some of these same concepts to the animal kingdom can bring other ideas into our consciousness. Chickens are often locked inside of cramped cages where movement is severely restricted. Livestock are routinely inseminated by artificial means and never experience the touch or companionship of another animal's body. There is a belief that an animal's feelings of discomfort and the traumatic circumstances of its life and death are ingested as its meat is taken into the body.

Before the age of sonograms people would speculate and even take bets on whether a woman was going to have a boy or a girl. There were always wise women around who swore they could tell the sex of a child just by looking at the shape of her stomach. With an all-knowing gaze they might pronounce, "You're carrying round, you got a girl in there," or "That pointy belly means a boy for sure."

Still, there was no telling how long the labor process would be or exactly what the final product would look like. There was excitement and mystery, pain and discomfort as this new creation was nurtured into being. Isn't creating pretty much the same way?

You don't have to be a woman to be pregnant with possibilities. Have you ever felt a story growing inside you or had an idea that lived with you for years or a dream that waited in your heart for the light of day? Are there projects or writings that you've started but haven't quite finished?

Have you ever held yourself back, or stopped before reaching a desired goal, saying things like "It'll never work," "I'll wait until the kids are grown," "I'll be too old once I get there," "I don't have enough time," "It might take too much out of me," "I don't have enough education." If you have ever said any of these words or had any of these experiences, you know what it is to be pregnant with possibilities.

There is a story about a successful 34-year-old businessman who had always wanted to be a doctor. He thought about it every time he looked at a physician, walked by a hospital, or even watched a medical show. But he talked himself out of his dream, saying, "I can't be a doctor. It would mean starting all over again, going back to school, doing an internship and residency. By the time I'm finished, I'll be forty years old!" And so, the story goes, he turned 40 anyway.

We all have stillborn stories and miscarried dreams. We taste them in the lives of our children and in each other. We catch the scent of them while reminiscing, looking at old photographs, or musing about hopes we may have left behind. I sometimes think about the older brother I always wanted. A year before I was born, my mother miscarried after she was punched in the stomach. The baby boy that would have been born never got a chance to meet his sisters.

A few years ago, I received a reading from an African priest in which he talked about twin spirits, one born, the other unborn. When he told me that this unborn spirit had found its way into the body of another who was close to me, a chill of recognition ran through my body. I have a very good friend named John. We are so connected that I call him my husband. Years earlier, I remembered him saying he felt as close to me as if we were born together. When I told John what the priest had said, he exclaimed, "Oh my God, that's me!" I had found my brother.

TO BE OR NOT TO BE: JOURNEYS

As always, journeys begin with music, and a five-minute freewrite, that write-as-fast-as-you-can, don't-take-your-pen-off-the-paper, uncut, uncensored, don't-look-back, something-may-be-gaining-on-you technique I keep talking about. After the freewrite, look at what has spilled out of you onto the paper. Do you want to do something with it? Would you like to complete the thoughts you still have? Perhaps you want to pick out the *seeds* and use them to do some further exploration. It's up to you.

• A child is trying to make up its mind whether or not it wants to be born. Write down what the child might be saying to itself.
   Let's say that you happen to overhear the child talking to him- or herself. What might you say to a girl child to convince her to stay in or to come out? Would you say something different to a boy child? What was the child's final decision, if one was reached?

• There is an old poem that goes:

   The saddest thing
   Of tongue and pen,
   Are these four words:
   "It might have been."

Close your eyes and say aloud three times, "It might have been," pausing between each one to let the thoughts flow from your Heartland. Now write down what came to you.

• Where do babies come from? What were you told, or what did you think when you were a child?

• A 14-year-old girl becomes pregnant as a result of a rape. What does she say to herself? What does she say to the child? What do her parents say to her? What decisions does she make?

• Take a visit back to the time before your time and write about the day you were conceived. Close your eyes and imagine what your parents might have been thinking and feeling, what they said to each other, and the place of your conception. If you happen to know any of the actual details of your origins, feel free to reinvent or embellish them.

TO BE OR NOT TO BE: SEASONAL SURRENDERS

If you have been doing the Seasonal Surrenders, you have probably noticed the effect they have on your spiritual and creative levels of awareness. If you have not yet done one of the surrenders, give some thought to your resistance. You don't have to do them all, but you will really be missing out if you don't do any. Remember, you are stretching your senses in the same way your mother had to stretch to bring you into this world.

• Make a list of five things you would like to conceive this season. You are going to use this list to make a *Conception Nest*. Write down the five items, then copy the list on another piece of paper. Take a small basket, bowl, or cup and fill it with nesting material—shredded paper, feathers, leaves, dried flowers, cotton balls, colored tissue, or fabric.

Now fold up one of your lists and tie a ribbon around it as if it were a present to yourself. Place the list in the middle of the nesting material, put a hard-boiled egg on top, and sprinkle sunflower seeds all around it. Now read your copy aloud as you hold the nest in your left hand. Allow the power of your breath to energize the *Conception Nest*.

Place the nest in a place where it won't be disturbed. Read your list at least once a day for five days, then keep the list under your pillow or by your bed to continue to energize your conception thoughts. To paraphrase a saying, "What the mind conceives, woman can achieve."

- Buy some seeds and plant them.

- Start with "If only" and see how many different ways you can complete the phrase. For example, "If only I hadn't gotten pregnant, I wouldn't have married a man I wasn't in love with."

- Talk to a pregnant woman, asking her to tell you some of the dreams she has for her child.

TO BE OR NOT TO BE INTERSECTION TIME

Congratulations! You made it through *To Be Or Not To Be!* You have now arrived at your first intersection. It's time for an intersection moment, which is not at all like a Maalox moment. Let's go over what you're supposed to do now that you're here. If you recall, each intersection is marked by the road signs *Doubt, Reassurance and Decision,* a song, and your Icon Box. You need to do only three things at this point:

1. *Choose a sign.* For example, you have just gone through conception and pregnancy, but you still haven't been born yet. Take a look at the signs below and the reflections that go with them. Then reach into your Heartland and write a line or two about your choice and your thoughts.

At Doubt's "I'm not even sure where this road goes," you might write, "I'm not sure I want to be born. My father smokes too much, my little sister wants to be an only child, and my mom keeps saying I was a mistake!"

At Reassurance's "I think it's going to be okay," you might note, "I'm not so afraid of life when my mother rubs her belly. It soothes me."

At Decision's, "I think I've gone far enough," you might record, "Today I decided not to be born. It's too cold out there."

Remember, at each intersection, you have the power to comment on and affect your future. Try on different ways of looking at life and see what happens.

- *Doubt Sign:*
    "I think I'm going the wrong way."
    "I'm not even sure where this road goes."
    "Why did I begin this trip in the first place?"
    "I hope it's not too late to turn back."
- *Reassurance Sign:*
    "I think I'm almost there."
    "This looks familiar—I've passed this way before."
    "I'm sure this is the right way."
    "I think it's going to be okay."
- *Decision Sign:*
    "I think I've gone far enough."
    "I like it here. I think I'll stay."
    "I'm going to go straight ahead, and not make any turns."

2. *Select a song.* In one African tribe, a pregnant woman sits by a tree until a song comes to her. When it does, that song is sung at her child's birth, the important occasions of that child's life, and when he or she dies. As you travel the *United States of Life,* listen for songs that sing about you.

At each intersection you will choose a song that reflects some of the emotions, events, or thoughts you have had while traveling. After exploring conception and pregnancy, for example, you may decide your song for *To Be Or Not to Be* is "I Can't Get

Started with You," "Having My Baby," "Push, Push, in the Bush," or "Papa Was a Rolling Stone."

3. *Add to your Icon Box.* What word or words, and what item could visibly reflect something you experienced as you traveled through a *State of Life*? If you conceived, were conceived, or participated in the process of conception on the night of a Luther Vandross concert, for example, you can put that ticket stub in the box.

The only thing my mother ever told me about getting pregnant is "Don't let a boy fool you." In the old days in the South, if an unmarried girl got pregnant, they referred to it by saying that the boy "fooled her." For the *To Be Or Not to Be* intersection, I would take the Joker from a deck of cards and put that into my *Icon Box* with the words "Don't let a boy fool you."

I think by now you've gotten the hang of what goes on at these intersection moments. They can be fun, insightful, and powerful. They can also be brown bags filled with all kinds of sweet, fruity, or nutty things from Santa or from your spirit. Let's see what happens for you in *Spirit of a Woman* as you're making your list and checking it twice.

TO BE OR NOT TO BE: THE INTERSECTION

Sign Time

Take another look at the pregnancy and conception writings of your journeys, seasonal surrenders and remembrances from the state of *To Be Or Not to Be*. Pick a sign, gather your words like flowers, and make a written bouquet of thoughts about the roads taken and not taken.

Name That Tune

Now that you have completed your journey through this state, what song would you play on your radio as you drive toward the next state? What about "We've Only Just Begun"? See what you can come up with.

Totem Time

This is your first opportunity to reflect on some of your encounters in a visual way. Put an object and a word or saying into your *Icon Box* and prepare to push on through to the next state.

Planetary Reentry: Birth

I was born in Davisboro, Georgia, a very small town that never made it to the map. A midwife helped my mother push me into this world. When I was eighteen months old, my family came north and settled on New York City's Lower East Side, at the edge of Chinatown.

Somewhere in the mind's heart, the place of birth is indelibly imprinted. It may live in fragments of the familiar, in dreams, or in déjà vus. It may live on a baby's tongue before that tongue finds language for it. As I work on my novel, *Tamarindo,* I continue to find the river of my writing flowing from Brooklyn to "down south" as if it were seeking its source.

The idea of something being born brings a feast of possible experiences, associations, and memories to the table. Jesus was born in a manger. Judy Garland sings of being "born in a trunk in Pocatello, Idaho," in the movie *A Star is Born.* Lions were the subject of another movie, *Born Free,* and Judy Holliday played a dumb blond in *Born Yesterday.*

In the late sixties and early seventies, the song "Born to Be Wild" blared out a rock credo for an entire group of disaffected young people in America. A frustrated mother may allude to the

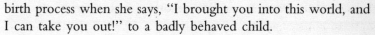

birth process when she says, "I brought you into this world, and I can take you out!" to a badly behaved child.

Almost every culture has its creation myths and stories, tales of how people came into existence. Pele, the Hawaiian goddess of the volcano, carried an egg containing her sister Hi'iaka between her breasts until the child was born. In Greek mythology, Athena was born from the head of Zeus. Yemaya, an African ocean goddess, gave birth to the most powerful orishas or deities when her stomach burst wide open. The Dogons believe their people came from the star Sirius.

I remember being told that a stork brought babies. I would see pictures of this stork flying through the air with a diaper in its beak, a helpless baby smiling innocently from inside the folds. Perhaps you shared this belief as well. Or maybe you were told babies came from a cabbage patch. This creation myth was widespread enough to give birth to the incredibly lucrative Cabbage Patch Kids, who came complete with names and birth certificates.

There is a Buddhist belief that we start out knowing everything, but our memories are erased the minute we are born. In *Birthrite* (Real Comet Press), a flip book based on Buddhist and Talmudic text, Ruth Hayes reflects these beliefs: "In the womb of the mother, the child . . . learns all the teachings and can see the whole world. As it leaves the womb . . . an angel slaps the child's mouth. It forgets everything but can regain wisdom in its lifetime." Even William Wordsworth reflects ancient Buddhist philosophy in one of his poems:

Our birth is but a sleep and a forgetting,
The soul that rises with us, our life's star,
Hath had elsewhere its setting,
And cometh from afar . . .

Some years ago, as I read Gurudas's *Gem Elixirs and Vibrational Healing* (Cassandra Press), I came across a fascinating esoteric theory about Hitler and Krishnamurti, a world religious leader of the twen-

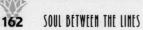

ties. His followers believed Krishnamurti was slated to be the next Christed Master or Great Teacher. In the 1930s, he was to assume the responsibility of counterbalancing negative energy and forces through his teachings. Because of Krishnamurti's decision not to take on this responsibility, the cosmic system of checks and balances was upset. Without those equally powerful positive forces to keep him in check, Hitler was thus able to come into power.

Krishnamurti's decision also had a profound impact on future generations. In an attempt to create a positive balancing force, the theory goes, thousands of people had to be pushed into birth before their time, before they had fully completed their reincarnation cycles on the spiritual plane. These people may have a deep-seated feeling that something has been wrong since birth, but have no idea what it is. They may have a sense of being ill at ease in the world and find themselves saying, "What am I doing here?" "This is not my home, I don't belong here," or even "Why was I born?"

Whether you subscribe to this theory or not, I'm sure you have met or known of people who did not seem to be from this planet or who had a sort of otherworldly nature about them. You might have even used the term *space cadet* to describe them.

One woman I know told me how as a child she used to look up at the sky all the time, waiting, she said, for her people to come and get her. A friend of mine talks about having faint memories of a time before this one, when she was happier and felt at home in her skin. She jokes about waiting for the mother ship to take her home.

Bringing someone into the world means conjuring up a name for them. Think of a name as a gift someone gives you whether you want it or not. Where did your name come from? Is it a name you like, or did you always want to be called something else? Governor Hogg of Texas named his daughter Ima, the story goes, to keep her too embarrassed to have men in her life.

New names for streets, schools, airports, and buildings are born soon after an important person dies. Actors rename themselves and begin new lives. Think of the images these names conjure up for you: Scarlett O'Hara, Mr. Deeds, Mr. Skeffington, Scrooge, Elmer Gantry, Mildred Pierce.

In traditional Africa societies, a newborn might receive a name from many sources—the circumstances surrounding its birth; in honor of its father or the day on which it was born. Among the Luo, the names of ancestors are recited while a baby is crying. If the baby stops crying when a particular name is mentioned, then he or she receives that name and is considered to be favored by that ancestor.

In festive naming ceremonies, the African family and the entire village commit themselves to the child's upbringing and general welfare. This concept has been recently promoted as the educational theory that "it takes a village to raise a child."

What is it that you call your creative work? What kind of name do you want to give it? In the Heartland we do a freewrite first to let the words have their wings so they can tell you where they want to fly. You may have wanted a girl and a boy came out. You may have wanted one child and got triplets. You may have been writing a poem and a play came out. You may have been trying to sketch and instead thought of a film you'd like to do. You may have been writing in your journal and found yourself picking up a camera. You may have been looking for answers and found yourself.

You can't just push an idea back in once it's out any more than you can push a baby back to its source. So you may as well deal with it. As your five-minute freewrite lies there on the paper, kicking and screaming for attention, you will begin to see what its face looks like, how it might grow, and what kind of noise it can really make.

With the joy of birth can come the presence of pain—labor pains that push a baby into being, inexplicable postpartum depression, the agony of being forced or obligated to give up a child at birth. Imagine your umbilical cord being connected to that child's body, remembering his birthday or wondering what she looks like and if you will ever see her again.

Have you ever gone through a painful experience without the slightest idea what the outcome might be? Have you ever reached a long-sought-after goal, then felt strangely let down or deflated? Have you ever had to give up something you really cared about? If so, then you too have experienced some of the pain of birth.

One of the most powerful exercises I have ever given in my workshop is a journey in which I use special fabrics and music to guide people through the process of giving birth to themselves. Some encountered memories of being in the womb or coming into the world. Some felt transported to another time and place beyond their conscious experience. Others cried as they felt a deep and profound connection with their mothers. After one of these journeys, a psychic from Iceland cradled the fabric as she handed it to me, saying that it had now become sacred.

Each time you create or make a new start, you are giving birth. You are deciding what kind of neighborhood you want your work to grow up in, what your spirit will be called, and how your consciousness will be raised. You might have an easy delivery or be in labor for a long time. In what setting would you like to give birth? Is there a favorite chair you like to sit in or window you like to look out of when you're calling on your creative spirit?

What time of the day or night lends itself to your creative process? Make note of where are you when you have the urge, need, or desire to do your art, write your words, paint your life. Are there patterns? Look for them. Find out what your process is, or create one that works for you. Toni Morrison wrote at night after her two children were in bed. Make time to give birth to your creative work. Just spread your spirit wide and push.

PLANETARY REENTRY: JOURNEYS

Get out your meditative music and do your five-minute freewrite so those words can slide right out of that birth canal and onto your paper. Close your eyes and let the words of each journey sink into your spirit. It will tell you what it wants to say.

Sometimes when you go back and look at the freewrite a week later, the words will look foreign to you. You might ask yourself, "Did I write this?" That's because they came straight from your Heartland without being judged by your internal jury. Just as the womb can give birth to many children, the freewrite can be the source of numerous pieces of writing. So leave it intact; copy it over several times if you like; pick out the seeds and see where they lead you.

- As a newborn baby, give your parents advice on how to raise you. Write a letter telling them what they should do to give you a proper upbringing.

- A mother has spent a lifetime having dreams, fears, or hopes about the child she gave up for adoption when she was much younger. One day her child finds her. Describe what their first meeting was like.

- Talk about a time in your life when you felt as if you were beginning again or when you felt you were being reborn.

- Write your own creation myth about how you came into being.

- In the film *Invasion of the Body Snatchers,* giant pods hatch emotionless beings that absorb a person's mind and memory when he or she falls asleep. Imagine that one of those pods is next to your bed, and this new creature is about to be born. You know that when you wake up you will be totally different. In your own version of the movie, you can decide which emotions and which parts of your being you will be reborn without. What do you decide? What are your final thoughts as you drift off to sleep?

PLANETARY REENTRY: SEASONAL SURRENDERS

- In India, an astrological chart is often done at a baby's birth so the family can identify their child's strengths and weaknesses and help guide the child toward his or her destiny. Make a list of what you think are your strengths and weaknesses.

- Pick five things you wish you had given birth to or would like to give birth to. These things can be people already on the planet, someone you think the world needs, items from nature, or inanimate objects.

- Remember, we said your name is a gift someone gives you that stays with you for the rest of your life, whether you want it or not. Perhaps you would like to give yourself the gift of another name. It can be a nickname, something you want only one person to call you, a name you *wish* you had been given at birth, or a name you'd like to be known by just while you're writing. Think about it and come up with a name.

- Smile at a baby this week.

PLANETARY REENTRY: INTERSECTION

Here we are at your second intersection. All you need to do here is:

1. *Sign Time.* Choose one of the three road signs, *Doubt, Reassurance,* or *Decision,* before you enter the next state. Review the sections on the *Icon Box* and *Intersections* to remind you about gathering the totems and contemplating the signs. Take a few minutes to write down your thoughts as you make your choices.

- Doubt Sign
    "I think I'm going the wrong way."
    "I'm not even sure where this road goes."
    "Why did I begin this trip in the first place?"
    "I hope it's not too late to turn back."
- Reassurance Sign
    "I think I'm almost there."
    "This looks familiar—I've passed this way before."
    "I'm sure this is the right way."
    "I think it's going to be okay."

- Decision Sign

"I think I've gone far enough."

"I like it here. I think I'll stay."

"I'm going to go straight ahead and not make any turns."

2. *Name That Tune.* Pick out a song for *Planetary Reentry.* How about "Baby, It's Cold Outside," "I'm Coming Out," or "Reach Out and Touch"?

3. *Totem Time.* Pick a word and an object that reflects one or some of your encounters. Put them into your *Icon Box,* and crawl down the road to the next state.

Pioneers at Play: Toddler and Childhood

There is a story about a child who didn't talk at all. His parents were worried about him, but he seemed to be pretty healthy, so they just let him be. But months and years went by and he still did not utter a word. Finally one day when he was nine, he was sitting at the dinner table and said, "Pass the salt, please."

His startled parents stared at him in total amazement. "You can talk?" they asked.

"Sure, I can talk," he answered.

"Well then, why haven't you said anything before?"

"Everything's been all right up to now," he replied.

I was a quiet and very shy middle child who didn't talk much. Sandwiched between a beautiful and popular older sister, and a gregarious younger sister, I felt like an outsider in my own family. I grew up on the outskirts of New York City's Chinatown, in a Lower East Side development that would be called multicultural in today's language.

Immigrant populations settled into what was then known as a melting pot. In addition to African-American residents, there were Italian and Jewish, Irish and Polish, Asian and Latino ones as well.

At the time I had no idea how unique it was to live in a low-income housing project with people from all different cultures.

I grew up on my grandma Exia's put-up peaches in Mason jars, pecans from Uncle Lonnie's tree, slices of bacon cut from thick slabs fried into crisp-edged pieces, and dark salted hams Uncle Leroy would stuff next to dark sods of black walnuts on his drive back from Davisboro, Georgia. I also grew up on zeppole and Italian ices with real chunks of fruit, egg foo yung and pork fried rice, hamantaschen, noshes, and overstuffed pastrami sandwiches from Katz's Delicatessen.

Throughout my childhood, the Lower East Side was flavored by relics of the past. There was the knish man, who wheeled a silver cart containing trays of pillow-shaped potato knishes that he sprinkled with salt from a dented aluminum shaker. There was the junkman, who drove a horse-drawn wagon with bells strong across the back. These bells rang out his presence, and invited people to give him broken toasters and other things that no longer worked.

There was an organ grinder with a little monkey in a tiny red jacket and fez, who jumped and danced and delighted us on our way home from P.S. 1. The iceman kept huge blocks of ice sweating under burlap wraps, and vendors still sold their wares from pushcarts on Orchard Street.

The images and experiences that were indelibly etched into my childhood memories have filled the canvas of my adult years. Those early years begin creating a sense of how and who and what you are in the world. As a toddler, you fall down, get up, look around to see if anyone saw you, and decide if you're going to cry or not. You learn whether or not someone will pick you up, brush you off, and tell you everything is going to be all right. The lessons learned about being rescued may establish a pattern of need tht can be fed by anything from images of a mythical prince on a white horse coming to your aid to Fontella Bass singing "Rescue Me."

Toddlers are pioneers at play with new worlds to conquer and territories to explore. The call of the new and dangerous can be almost irresistible. There are ashtrays to taste, hot stoves to touch, and parents to test for consistency. You enter into a world of limitations where you are told what not to do, and you learn who wants you not to do it. You perfect the art of crying for manipulation and self-expression.

The toddler state can manifest itself during the adult years in many ways. Men leave their wives for the new territory of a younger woman; women start their own businesses, where they have to answer to no one; protesters act up, knowing the squeaky wheel gets oiled; lobbyists, diplomats, fund-raisers, gold diggers, and prostitutes apply the James Brown philosophy, "You got to use what you got to get what you want."

Toddlerhood is also a season of firsts—first words, first teeth, first steps. A friend of mind didn't take her first steps until her father held out a dollar bill and she walked across the room to get it. When making choices, you may decide to go with your first instinct or regret that you didn't.

If you never get a second chance to make a first impression, then the first words out of your mouth and the first moves you make in any given situation can have a lasting impact. The first actions taken by a nurse can save a life. The first words in your novel may determine whether or not someone will want to read it. I'll never forget the day I patted the rounded belly of a woman I hadn't seen for a while. I uttered the words "So when is the baby due?" only to have her respond, "I'm not pregnant."

Think about those first words on a page, the first strokes of a brush, the first frame of a film, the first note of a song. How you go about starting your work? When do you feel you can sink your teeth into what you are creating? What first steps you need to take to get a new idea off the ground? How do you go about conquering the world of a new job, a new marriage, or a new town you have just moved to?

As you move further into childhood you become more fluent in the language of the land. You start seeing yourself through the eyes of others. You begin looking for where you belong. In my elementary school, I did not see myself reflected in images of blond Dick, Jane, or Sally. Instead, the curriculum offered me a humiliating character, Little Black Sambo. Sambo was a spindly, charcoal-black creature with huge white lips—an embarrassing caricature of a black child. This book was required reading. I can still remember my face burning with shame as I and the other Black children in the class were forced to read aloud from its pages.

Shame and guilt begin to show their faces in childhood. Can you remember when you first felt guilty about or ashamed of something? Was bedwetting the earliest shame? Guilt about the divorce of your parents, feeling responsible for a parent's drinking problems, abuse and incest—the colors of life take on different hues, some of which hurt the eyes when looked at too closely. The increasing awareness and growing vocabulary of childhood gives rise to new experiences to communicate about, react to, grow from.

There may be a lot of truth in the sentiment expressed by one writer that everything a person writes about is based on what happened to him or her before the age of sixteen years. When you think about your life and your writing, does that statement hold true for you? I was down south and nine years old when I read the sign on the shiny chrome water fountain marked WHITE and the one on the yellowed and cracked porcelain sink that read COLORED.

I remember the dilapidated colored waiting room we had to go to at the back of the stationhouse. I remember getting on a train called Nancy Hanks and having to go to the left because we were black, while all the white people were seated in cars to the right. When we arrived in Washington, D.C., we had passed the Mason-Dixon line. We changed trains and then could sit anywhere we wanted.

I can still see the chain gang that stopped in front of my grandmother's house to ask for water. The men sweated and glistened as they worked on the red clay roads, their chains clinking like glasses being toasted. A long shotgun was nestled in the arms of one of the foremen as another went to the back of the house and pumped water into a zinc bucket. He ladled it out to the thirsty men, who gulped it down, letting streams of liquid fall across their heated chests. I stood there on the porch staring at the black faces, the red dust, and the thick anklets of iron, thinking about slavery.

PIONEERS AT PLAY: JOURNEYS

I hope you are discovering new pieces of music to play while you write and how evocative they can be. Some other musical selections I have enjoyed with my writing are:

Adrienne Torf's *Brooklyn from the Roof*
Richard Warner's *Quiet Heart*
Eberhard Weber's *Orchestra*
Mozart's piano sonatas played by Mitsuko Uchida
Haydn piano sonatas played by Alfred Brendel
Rick Kuethe's *Nebraska Suite* and *The Child Within*

As you look at the next journeys and prepare to do your five-minute freewrite, close your eyes for a few seconds and try to see the images and the words in your mind. I have always heard it said that hindsight is twenty-twenty. I happen to know that the same is true of inner sight as well. Take a look for yourself if you don't believe me.

• What is your earliest memory of your childhood? Describe it fully.

• Write about a time in your life when you fell down (whatever that means to you) and either got up again or were helped up.

• Think about some of your favorite things to do as a child. What did you like to do, where did you go, and who did you like to do these activities with?

- Imagine how one of your parents may have abused you physically, sexually, or emotionally when you were a child. Pick one incident and describe what was in your mind and what was in your heart. Next, describe what you feel was in the heart and mind of the parent. If you have never experienced this kind of abuse, write about someone you know who has. Close your eyes and try to look into the heart and mind of the parent and the abused child.

- Yogi Berra said, "You can have anything you want as long as you don't want it bad enough." When you were a child, was there something you wanted really badly? Write about what that was and whether or not you got it.

PIONEERS AT PLAY: SEASONAL SURRENDERS

- Go outside and play! Do something you think you're too old to do. Run, kick leaves, throw a ball, roll down a hill, skip, jump rope, eat spaghetti with your fingers. Play, and celebrate the way it makes you feel.

- Look for a very shy or quiet child. Let the child know that she or he is beautiful or special or loved.

- "If I asked for what I wanted. . . ." Write down five different endings for this sentence.

- Locate a photograph of you as a baby or as a child. Take it out and hold it next to your face in the mirror. How much of yourself can you see in that picture? Keep the photo around as you write about your childhood.

PIONEER AT PLAY: INTERSECTION

Here we are at your third intersection. All you need to do here is:

1. *Sign Time*. Make your choice and write down your thoughts. If you need to, go back and look at the examples at the first intersection.

- Doubt sign
    "I think I'm going the wrong way."
    "I'm not even sure where this road goes."
    "Why did I begin this trip in the first place?"
    "I hope it's not too late to turn back."
- Reassurance Sign
    "I think I'm almost there."
    "This looks familiar—I've passed this way before."
    "I'm sure this is the right way."
    "I think it's going to be okay."
- Decision Sign
    "I think I've gone far enough."
    "I like it here. I think I'll stay."
    "I'm going to go straight ahead and not make any turns."

2. *Name That Tune*. Pick out a song for Pioneer at Play. How about "You Got Me Runnin', You Got Me Hidin'" or "God Bless the Child That's Got Its Own"?

3. *Totem Time*. Pick a word and an object that reflects one or some of your encounters. Put them into your Icon Box, and toddle on down the road to the next state.

Blood, Sweat, and Tears: Adolescence

When I was 17, my mother finally asked me if there was anything I wanted to know about the birds and the bees. I answered, "No, thank you," and that was the extent of our mother-daughter talk about sex. Janis Ian sang, "I learned the truth at seventeen." I was not to be so lucky. Between huddled talks in the school bathroom, tales of a girl in the projects named Janice who let boys "do it" to her, whispered conversations during lights-out at sleep-away camp, and pamphlets from my junior high school hygiene class, I was sure I already knew everything there was to know about boys, sex, and where babies came from.

It is during the age of adolescence that we are forced to let go of our personal myths. We discover the uncomfortable spaces of silence within our parents, their lack of perfection, and the limits of their knowledge. We run headfirst into the extent of their unwillingness to let go of their children and their entrenched ideas. We also learn that bears do not really hibernate all winter, oceans are not blue, and that birds eat like pigs.

In my teen years I looked at life as it appeared in *Seventeen* Magazine, Archie and Veronica comic books and the sugar-coated TV shows of *Father Knows Best* and *Ozzie and Harriet*. Today's adolescents grapple with the dichotomy between their own lives and the sexually provocative images in music videos. They wrestle with the possibility of AIDS, date rape, teen alcoholism, girl gangs, 9-year-old drug dealers, and drive-by shootings.

Joseph Campbell, one of the world's foremost authorities on mythology, warned, "If you want to find out what it means to have a society without any rituals, read *The New York Times*." In other countries, many societies have special rites of passage, ceremonies that signal the end of childhood, special tools and teachings to prepare for adulthood.

Fifteenth-birthday parties of Puerto Rican females, recent African-American rites of passage, and bar mitzvahs may create some of these rituals for a small segment of the population, but what about the rest? What is there to guide young girls through the troubled passageways of their teenage years? When you think about your teenage years—the questions, the confusion—who and what was there to help you sort things out?

Our mothers may have warned, "Girl, you're getting too grown!" but did we really know what that meant? In Shay Youngblood's *Big Mama Stories* (Firebrand Books), a wise older woman tells a teen, "When a girlchile get her first blood, her mama or one

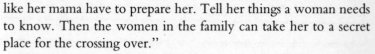

like her mama have to prepare her. Tell her things a woman needs to know. Then the women in the family can take her to a secret place for the crossing over."

When that young girl begins her first menstruation, a group of older women take her down to the river for a very special initiation into womanhood. In your life, who made time to talk with you about peer pressure, sex abuse, bodily changes, primal urges, teen pregnancy, date rape, or contraception? Did someone talk at you or with you?

Where do we learn who we really are? I remember how we felt sorry for the children who had to attend "Chinese school" after our regular school day had ended. In my adult years I realized how valuable it was for those children to have a place where they could go to learn their heritage, their language, and their culture. As an African-American whose language and culture were stripped away when my ancestors were brought here, I had only to look around me to see the devastating effects of not knowing where we came from or how to speak our own language.

When I was in junior high school, all the continents other than Africa on our classroom map were in pastel colors and were clearly broken down in countries and territories. In our textbooks and on this map, Africa was officially called the Dark Continent. It was totally black except for a small pale-yellow chink on the upper right-hand corner called Egypt, a place they insisted was not in Africa. We were taught that the only thing Africa had given to the world was Tarzan.

Think about who your idols were and who you might have modeled yourself after. I always wanted to be the beautiful African-American movie star Dorothy Dandridge. Did you find yourself wanting to be somebody else? As your new body and attitude began to form, who were you becoming, where did you belong, and how did you fit in?

Adolescence brings a whole other series of firsts: first body hair, first dance, first kiss, first period, first sexual act, first love, first heartbreak, and the first bra, called a training bra (though I never quite understood what it was training breasts to do!). What were those firsts like for you?

In *Zami: A New Spelling of My Name* (The Crossing Press), as poet-activist Audre Lorde experiences her first period, she writes: "My body felt new and special and unfamiliar and suspect all at the same time. . . . I felt the slight rubbing bulge of the cotton pad between my legs and I smelled the delicate breadfruit smell rising up from the front of my print blouse that was my own womansmell, warm, shameful, but secretly utterly delicious."

I heard one mother refer to teens as "hormonally challenged." With sexual energies as rampant as flowers in the spring, adolescents run smack into a new set of taboos, myths, and limitations. When a boy named Charlie got me in a back stairwell of the projects and began kissing me and pressing his hard body against mine I had a hard time sorting through the feelings of confusion, pleasure, fear, and passion that inhabited my body at the same time.

Later, while I was working in the Hell's Kitchen neighborhood in New York City, two Greek girls became greatly agitated as I sat in a chair just vacated by a male teacher. In a loud whisper, they shouted, "Get up, Miss Dorothy! Quick, get up!" and pulled me out of the chair. They explained to me that if I sat in the chair while it was still warm from the man's body, I would get pregnant.

As an adolescent, I had all the insistent urgings that came with puberty, but was just too busy being a "good girl" to do anything about them. I had to settle for a dance called the grind until the real thing came along. My poem "We Was Grindin" begins:

Saturday night
A basement in the projects
127th and St. Nick
Red lights in the ceiling
Black girls on the walls
It was hot
And we was grindin
A slow dance to a blue sound
A ritual chant played dark and close

Boys in leather
Trading sweat for style

We was grindin
And I was somewhere else
Transfixed between sensate landscapes
And tropical madness
Moving like ocean waters

Undulating black sand dunes
Hula hoops of rhythm
Encircling the minds
Of hips that moved without us
Sweet sixteen and never been loved
This as close as I could get
With my clothes on
And the lights out
And my mother waiting up for me at home

We was grindin
And Smokey's music
Moved between us
My blouse a toaster oven
Baking my nipples a crisp hard black
Persistent volcanoes
Pushing through circle-stitched bra
Reaching like fingers
Stroking his knit shirt
His pelvis turning my soft triangle
To ground round

Smokey's voice
Licked sweat off my thighs
Unlocked the gates
That held my juices captive
My cotton panties
Sopping them up like gravy . . .

As an adult, have you ever felt like a teenager again? Have you ever felt as if you were doing something for the first time even if you have done it many times before? Your first day at a new job, the first time you fit into a much smaller size, or your first date after being divorced or widowed can all evoke adolescent energies as well as anxieties. All the thrills and tortures of the teen years, all of the things you ever said, felt, and did, these are all sitting in the classroom of your Heartland, raising their hands and waiting to be called on.

As the teenage years question the childhood years and disavow the adult years, I think about the woman who used the words of James Barrie, who responded to her arrogant teenage daughter by saying, "I'm not young enough to know everything."

BLOOD, SWEAT, AND TEARS: JOURNEY

Don't forget to start each journey with a five-minute freewrite and music. (Actually, I don't see how that could slip your mind when I remind you every chance I get.) At the halfway mark of our journey through the *United States of Life,* I'm sure you know what to do by now.

- First blood, first sweat, or first tears. Write about one of these firsts in your adolescent years.

- You are writing a letter to a young girl who is about to enter puberty. She can be a former self of yours, a future self of yours, someone you know, or someone you wish you knew. What wisdoms, warnings, and wishes do you want to share with her?

- Sexual disasters, dreams, and disappointments. Write about one, two, or all of them.

- Choose a favorite song from your teenage years and play it. As you listen, close your eyes and think about where you

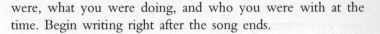

were, what you were doing, and who you were with at the time. Begin writing right after the song ends.

• Who and what and how did you want to be when you grew up? How close did you get?

BLOOD, SWEAT, AND TEARS: SEASONAL SURRENDERS

• Have a pajama party, chew bubble gum, giggle and act silly with a good friend, go to the movies in the afternoon, do something that makes you feel like a teenager again.

• Create a rite of passage for yourself. The next time there is an important change in your life, one that involves a change of either mind or heart, body or spirit, put together a ritual for yourself. You can ask friends to help you, witness or reflect for you.

• Make time to talk with or listen to a teenager.

BLOOD, SWEAT, AND TEARS: INTERSECTION

Here we are at your fourth intersection. Make a pit stop here at the halfway mark on your journey and then proceed. All you need to do is:

1. _Sign Time_. Choose one of the three road signs to take you to the next state. Review the sections on the _Icon Box_ and _Intersections_ if you want to refresh your memory about the totems and the signs. Write down your thoughts as you make your choices.
   • Doubt Sign
     "I think I'm going the wrong way."
     "I'm not even sure where this road goes."
     "Why did I begin this trip in the first place?"
     "I hope it's not too late to turn back."
   • Reassurance Sign
     "I think I'm almost there."
     "This looks familiar—I've passed this way before."

"I'm sure this is the right way."

"I think it's going to be okay."

• Decision sign

"I think I've gone far enough."

"I like it here. I think I'll stay."

"I'm going to go straight ahead and not make any turns."

2. *Name That Tune.* Pick out a song for Blood, Sweat, and Tears. How about "At Seventeen," "Why Must I Be a Teenager In Love" or "Let's Wait Awhile"?

3. *Totem Time.* Pick a word and an object that reflects one or some of your encounters. Put them into your Icon Box and dance on down the road to the next state.

The Age of Consent: Adulthood

"My mother only told me one thing about marriage," a woman confessed to me. "She said, 'When a man wants you to iron his shirts, you go get his best shirt and burn a hole in it. Then he won't *never* ask you again.' "

Adulthood brings its own lessons and languages—words to live by, codes of behavior. What words of wisdom were you given as you set out on the road to adulthood? What did it mean to be an adult? For some of us, it meant having our own apartments, getting married, or having a child. For others, it was getting our first full-time job and having our own money.

Some of us looked like women before our emotional and mental bodies were fully developed. Some were told that when we started bleeding, we became women. Then there are those of us who were forced to grow up early, as, for example, when the oldest child in a large family has to function as a second mother to her siblings.

Many of us had our visions of adulthood defined for us. Our parents may have expected us to become doctors or teachers, marry, have children, or follow in the family business. My mother, the eldest of nine, was able to go only as far as the sixth grade. She had to sneak across the farm fields to go to school because my grandfather didn't believe in education for girls. He believed that since they were just going to go get married and have babies, education would be wasted on them. Years later in Red Hook, Brooklyn, I met an elderly Puerto Rican woman who had never learned how to read. She told me her father had felt the same as my grandfather.

One of my early efforts to act like a grown-up had an impact on my life that lasts to this day. When I was in college, I lied to my mother about where I was going and snuck off to Cape Cod for a stolen weekend with an older man who was married but separated at the time, or so he told me.

My life up to that point had been plagued with chronic car sickness. On our car trips to Rockaway Beach, my uncle Leroy would inevitably have to stop and let me out so I could relieve my stomach by the side of the road. So as I was sitting beside this married man, dressed in my black lace blouse and trying for all the world to look older, I knew that getting sick on this trip would blow the adult image I was desperately trying to maintain. I willed myself to stay well for the entire 6½-hour drive to the Cape and have never been carsick again.

Shirley Temple says that there are three stages in a man's life: "He believes in Santa Claus, he doesn't believe in Santa Claus, he is Santa Claus." Sometimes there is still that Santa Claus place inside that you want to hold on to when you are an adult. I have seen grown-ups playing with toys more than their children do.

Have you ever witnessed the adult fascination with toys that sometimes manifests itself in train sets and doll collections? I hadn't even realized I was collecting Mickey Mouse souvenirs until I began seeing him all over the house, on my calculator, a radio, drinking straws, pins, puppets, and several postcards, including a risqué one with him and Marilyn Monroe.

I still have several toys I thought I had bought for children.

Among them are Duck Duck Goose, a wooden duck with wheels attached to webbed rubber feet that slap against the floor when I walk him; an alligator whose mouth flaps open and shut as he is pushed; wind-up toys; silly straws; marbles; and a music box that plays a theme from *Fantasia* when you turn its handle. They say it's never too late to have a happy childhood. Do you remember your favorite toys?

In a bio for the anthology *Gaptooth Girlfriends: The Third Act,* I wrote: "I began as a child and decided some years later to always maintain some essence of that all too-brief period of my life. Adulthood intruded as regularly as menstruation, its sanguinary shadows staining the underpinnings of my emotions." Think for a moment: What is *arrested development*? Are there development police who arrest you for failing to develop properly, for failing to live up to standards determined by others?

Perhaps as adults we suffer from lack of mystery and too much knowing, too many answers, not enough questions, and no time to play. At what age must we tell ourselves we're too old for our imaginings, for the dreams we still keep under our pillows and in the private spaces of our hearts? Perhaps it is the dreamers who write science fiction, the ones who never had toys who make a living inventing them, and those whose early years were unhappy who write stories about the glories of childhood.

We take our children to the circus because we never got to go and live out our parents' dreams because they never got to live them. We bend under the anchor of responsibility, pay our own bills, buy houses, settle down, settle for, get permanent jobs, watch *Oprah,* fall in and out of love, worry about finding and keeping love, decide whether to have a child or be a child, live together or live at all.

And in the midst of all of this adult becoming is a space where we begin to feel the power of our bodies, our words, and our actions. The words of wisdom we may have rejected when we were younger actually start to make sense. We see the choices among the chances, whether we make them or not. We can

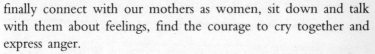

finally connect with our mothers as women, sit down and talk with them about feelings, find the courage to cry together and express anger.

At one age we are given permission to drink, at another to drive, and at still another to vote. We sign permission slips for our children's school trips and secure special permits for parking, vending, selling alcohol, giving block parties, making films, and fixing buildings. The Age of Consent has as many layers of permission as there are definitions of adulthood.

Miss Webster defines *consent* as "compliance in or approval of what is done or proposed by another; agreement as to action or opinion." *Permission,* on the other hand is defined as "something that is sanctioned by one who is in authority."

Looking at the critical distinction between agreement and authority can give us another sense of the rights and boundaries of adulthood. If, for example, there are two consenting adults who are acting in compliance with each other's wishes, how can anyone have the authority to tell them what they can and cannot do in the privacy of their own bedroom?

If permission is tied to authority, then authority is connected with power. Who have you ever handed your power over to: a husband or significant other, a boss, a parent, or even your children? How many of us have relationships by permission but not by consent? For many women, the mission is to transform power over to power to.

When you say you give yourself permission to do something, what you are doing is claiming your sacred authority. Think of permission as a precious gift you can give to yourself in all the arenas of your life. Give yourself your own stamp of approval as you walk through the halls of the *Age of Consent.*

THE AGE OF CONSENT: JOURNEYS

• Write about a time when you did not give consent or when you refused to comply.

- What do you think your mother wanted to give herself permission to do? Your grandmother?

- What did becoming an adult mean to you? What did you do more of? What did you do less of? What do you wish you didn't have to do?

- What aspect of your childhood have you kept or wished you could keep with you in adulthood?

- You have three children, an indifferent husband or life partner, and a frustrating job. An attractive, endearing person you know and trust falls in love with you. What do you do?

THE AGE OF CONSENT: SEASONAL SURRENDERS

- For each of these aspects in your life, write down at least one thing you would like to give yourself permission to do:

  1. my writing

  2. my home

  3. my job

  4. my spirit

  5. my relationship

- If you have a regular adult routine, find a creative way to break it—eat dinner with your family in an evening gown, play hookey from work and go to the beach, curl up on the sofa and read your favorite book in the nude while sipping wine and eating something forbidden. Do something your friends, your children, or others close to you would never expect you to do.

- Celebrate your feminine energy. Put on a beautiful piece of music, something that makes you feel romantic or sensuous.

Wear a dress, shirt, or scarf in the color that makes you feel the most beautiful. Smile at yourself as you listen and move to the music while you stand in front of a mirror.

Say this affirmation aloud three times: "I am a beautiful person in body, mind and spirit." Then close your eyes and feel the words travel throughout your entire being. Gently stroke your cheek three times and continue to move with your eyes closed until the music ends. Know that you are beautiful.

THE AGE OF CONSENT: INTERSECTION

Here we are at your fifth intersection. You know what to do here.

1. *Sign Time.* Choose one of the three road signs to take you to the next state. Write your thoughts as you make your choices.

- Doubt Sign

    "I think I'm going the wrong way."

    "I'm not even sure where this road goes."

    "Why did I begin this trip in the first place?"

    "I hope it's not too late to turn back."

- Reassurance Sign

    "I think I'm almost there."

    "This looks familiar—I've passed this way before."

    "I'm sure this is the right way."

    "I think it's going to be okay."

- Decision Sign

    "I think I've gone far enough."

    "I like it here. I think I'll stay."

    "I'm going to go straight ahead and not make any turns."

2. *Name That Tune.* Pick out a song for *Age of Consent?* How about "Games People Play" or "I Am Woman."

3. *Totem Time.* Pick a word and an object that reflect one or some of your encounters. Put them into your *Icon Box* and walk responsibly down the road to the next state.

The Middle Passage: Middle Age

During the Middle Passage of the 1700s and 1800s, African slaves were forced into a journey that forever changed their lives and the course of history. In what is known as the African Holocaust, millions died and were tossed overboard. Others jumped of their own accord. In this *Middle Passage* of our lives, some of us will not make it through to a new land. Others of us will be tossed overboard by our loved ones or jump the ship of relationships on our own accord. Some of us may have more than our names and identities taken from us.

In the cycle of seasons, autumn was considered to be a time to begin new learning, as well as time to learn to embrace the darkness within so that we could see our light more clearly. In the autumn of our own lives, as our bodies and beings change significantly, we begin the search for new ways of learning about who and what we are becoming and about what that looks like in the light of day. As with the trees during this season, our foliage may change color and fall off, and the bareness of our outer lives may not fully reflect the spirit that continues within.

When a woman asked her middle-aged aunt how she managed to have so many men in her life, she answered, "I find out just what they like and give them just a little bit. That way they have to keep coming back for more."

At this *State of Life,* experience has handed us many of her lessons and some of her favorite questions. Are you applying those lessons, or are you thinking perhaps you haven't learned them well enough yet? If your children have grown, have you let go enough to let them live their own lives? Are they letting you live yours? Should you keep the job you have worked at for over twenty years, take an early retirement package, or risk being replaced by a person half your age making half your salary?

In the *Middle Passage* you might dye your hair, diet again, wear sensible shoes, gain weight, get a face-lift, speak your mind, hold your peace, get divorced from a person or from reality, or experience the "change of life." You may be enjoying a new sense of self, holding on to old clothes waiting for them to come back in style, caring for a parent with a life-threatening illness, feeling you have more to lose or everything to gain, finally focusing more on doing for yourself than for others, or raising grandchildren because your daughter died of AIDS or breast cancer or at the hands of a disgruntled husband.

Sometimes mirrors don't accurately reflect what we should be seeing when we look at ourselves. In one of my short stories, "Sidona Lee," middle-aged Sidona Lee and her young lover C.J. have lived together for four years when her estranged daughter Ola Mae suddenly decides to pay a visit. Sidona, threatened by her daughter's overt attentions to C.J., begins to complain that her grey hair and wrinkles have made her feel less desirable. C.J. listens for a while, then says,

> "You talk about grey hair? Well, that's accordin' to how you see it. You know at night when the moon come creepin' in the window and sit on the bed, sometimes I be just laying there watchin' you sleep. Thinkin' bout how pretty all that silver look just shinin' like new fence wire.
>
> "An when I wake up in the mornin', it make me smile to see the moon still be shinin' in your hair. Grey? Baby, that's somethin' sad and lonely in a corner someplace the sun can't get to. But silver is a treasure you want treat kind of special, and hold on to through good times and bad.
>
> "And when I'm with you, I feel like I done traveled. Your face reminds me of places I came from and where I want to stay. I don't see no wrinkles, just roads tellin' me where you been."

In the Middle Passage you take a look at where your choices have brought you. It is here that you may get the fullest sense of who you are, what you really want or don't want. In the middle years you have the opportunity to become an experienced beginner, to begin new careers or relationships while savoring the lessons of the old ones. As the yearning for fulfillment and freedom becomes stronger, you may become more cautious and decide not to take the kind of chances youth afforded you or you may grab opportunities missed due to the ignorance of your younger days.

This is a Sankofa time, a place of being symbolized by the African bird whose body faces forward while his head looks back. It means that we must look to where we came from in order to move forward. If you want your life to move into a different state, you must first look to see how you have lived it in the *States* you have already traveled through.

At any time in your life, the *Middle Passage* may arrive on your doorstep. It may come with a shopping bag full of questions and a suitcase big enough for an indefinite stay. Think about the transitional times in your life, how you moved through them or how they moved through you. Think about what it was like to begin again, to change your looks or your life, or to face a crisis and survive. As you translate life into art and art into life, begin to see every problem as a possibility in disguise, every question as a call to clarity, and every change a step in the right direction.

MIDDLE PASSAGE: JOURNEYS

How are you doing with the musical selections you use to write with? Is it time to try some new ones? The *Middle Passage* is a great time for change. If you have been using the same one or two tapes of music, pick out two others and see how the difference affects the flow of words during your five-minute freewrites.

- You have just experienced the death of either a parent, a husband, a lifemate, or a marriage. Pick one, close your eyes and see the situation, then write about it.

- Your husband or lifemate leaves you for a younger woman or man. Describe the worst-case scenario. Write about how you feel at your best, then write about how you feel at your worst.

- You have been given six months to live. What do you start or stop doing? How do you change your life, if at all?

- In a marriage or committed relationship, if you had to choose between secure contentment with affection or passionate uncertainty with love, which would you choose and why?

THE MIDDLE PASSAGE: SEASONAL SURRENDERS

- Take inventory at each of your birthdays by making three lists for yourself:

    1. What I Have Learned This Year

    2. What I Still Want, Need, or Have to Learn in the Coming Year.

    3. How I Have Given This Year

    You might want to pick another date besides your birthday for making these lists—New Year's Day or the first day of spring, for example.

- Celebrate your age by eating something forbidden. Allow one bite for each year of your life. Before each fork or spoonful say, "This is for the ____ [first, second, third, etc.] year of my life," close your eyes, and savor the taste.

- When you look in the mirror, pick out one thing that you like about what you see, and thank that part of your body for being there.

THE MIDDLE PASSAGE: INTERSECTION

As you arrive at your sixth intersection, you will probably be able to take the next steps blindfolded.

1. *Sign Time*. Choose one of the three road signs to take you to the next state. Write down your thoughts.

- Doubt Sign
  "I think I'm going the wrong way."
  "I'm not even sure where this road goes."
  "Why did I begin this trip in the first place?"
  "I hope it's not too late to turn back."
- Reassurance Sign
  "I think I'm almost there."
  "This looks familiar—I've passed this way before."
  "I'm sure this is the right way."
  "I think it's going to be okay."
- Decision Sign:
  "I think I've gone far enough."
  "I like it here. I think I'll stay."
  "I'm going to go straight ahead and not make any turns."

2. *Name That Tune*. Pick out a song for *Middle Passage*. How about "For All We Know" or "Respect."

3. *Totem Time*. Pick a word and an object that reflects one or some of your encounters during the *Middle Passage*. Put them into your *Icon Box* and walk cautiously or courageously down the road to the next state.

The Silver Time: Senior Years

"Every time an old person dies, it's like a small museum burned down." I think about Alex Haley's words when I recall a journey I took to my grandmother's house in the furrowed farmlands of tiny Davisboro, Georgia, years ago. In a piece entitled, "Southern Chronicles, Grandma Exia," I wrote:

Grandma knows everybody's business and minds it. Says they call her house "headquarters." I listen to endless items about the townspeople, cousins and assorted relatives. I sit and watch her big smooth face, loving her and hoping my skin will treat me as well when I'm her age. And it occurs to me that love is the difference between passing time and spending time.

I take out my tape recorder and ask her to tell me some stories. Though she's been talking all evening, she now says she doesn't know what to say.

"What you call that thing?" I explain that it's a stereo cassette recorder with an AM/FM radio.

"And you want me to talk to it?"

She talks about her mother, Lizzie Kitchen, a full-blooded Indian who she says had, "hair all down her back" and nineteen children, thirteen of whom lived. Two of them had gone into fits when they were very young and they had tied garlic around their wrists to stop the spasms. She told us she married our grandfather because her mother was crazy about him. She had not been in love but wanted to get away from home. Later, she tells me she's always wanted to be a man.

"What? How long have you wanted to be a man, Grandma?"

"Ever since I was grown. If I could turn into a man right now, I would. I got a man's mind, you know." I am stunned into stuttering. My grandmother?

We finish the tape and I play it back to her. I wished I had another machine to record her talking back to the tape. On the recording she's naming all the chores she had to do on the farm. As her taped voice is saying, "I pulled fodder . . .," my grandmother comments, "That's right!" The tape continues, "I planted seeds . . .," "Did that too," she replies. And at the end of the listing of chores she says to the tape machine, "Yep, you got it all!"

She has never had her voice recorded before. She listens, fascinated, to her voice and mine asking questions. For the rest of the evening, whenever she talked, she'd ask, "Them two women ain't listenin' is they?" turning around to peek at the tape recorder. In the morning, lying in bed, Grandma looks over at the tape recorder, now silent.

"Them two women is still sleep," she whispered. "They ain't got up yet!"

Later as the tape cassette's radio plays, she looks at the blinking red light on the sound level and says, "Ever so often one of them women kinda winks at you with one eye!"

At 88 years old, my grandmother told me the names of almost two hundred and fifty relatives, stories about cousins and aunts, sang old gospel songs, and challenged me to a spelling bee. What with the bus from Atlanta, a two-hour wait in Milledgeville for the once-a-day bus that goes to Davisboro, then an additional ride of more than an hour, traveling to Grandma Exia's took up an entire day. Once there, you couldn't leave until the next day, when you had to stand in front of the only store in town and flag the bus down as it sped along the highway. If I hadn't taken the time to make that trip with tape recorder and legal pad in hand, I never would have known the museum she was. She passed away four months later.

The *Silver Time* is a time of silver hair and silver anniversaries. What is your vision of the senior years? In the American Indian tradition, the Spider Grandmother represents a person's biggest worries, greatest fears and frustrations, worst anxieties and disappointments. She is a goddess who points the way to the truth about ourselves and helps us to deepen and perfect our lives.

In African culture, age is the most important ingredient in attaining and wielding power. Elders are honored and highly respected. The white-bearded deity Obatala symbolizes maturity, great wisdom, purity of intention, and laughter.

In ancient European tradition and in present-day practices, an older woman is known as a *crone,* a word that means a powerful wise woman who has seen it all, a woman free from the sentiment and illusions of youth. The energies of both the maiden and the mother are within her. Crone energy represents your commitment to work on yourself and the reclaiming of power and wholeness at any stage of your life.

I have often heard a senior advise, "Don't get old," as if there were a viable alternative. "Old age is always fifteen years older than I am," Bernard M. Baruch's statement on his 85th birthday, could easily be applied to Eubie Blake, who at 100 quipped, "If I had known I was going to live this long, I would have taken better care of myself!" Even the Beatles mused about the senior years in their song "When I'm Sixty-Four." Camille Mayran was in her nineties when she wrote a novel and stated she saw no change in herself except for "a slight slowing down."

The Silver Time offers four mirrors for you to look into. These mirrors are called *shine, tarnish, melt,* and *polish.* Think about the definition of shine: something or someone conspicuous, distinguished, or eminent, having a bright or glowing appearance, emitting rays of light.

Is this your time to shine? Have you seen these aspects in any senior people you have known? I have. I saw jazz singer Alberta Hunter's brilliant performance at The Cookery, a cabaret in New York City's Greenwich Village. Her long, graceful hands punctuated the words she sang with seasoned resonance. She had come out of retirement to rekindle her singing career when she was in her seventies. At 81, she was playing to packed houses.

In New Mexico, I visited Santa Fe activist Mary Lou Cook, who in her seventies still drums, does calligraphy, designs, and performs weddings. One of the most fascinating women I have ever met is 84-year-old Elaine Pollard Lynn. A beautifully vibrant African-American and a former war correspondent, Elaine teaches college and still walks up twelve flights of stairs a day.

On his farm of several hundred acres in the woods of Vermont, Wilmer Brandt picked corn and potatoes from his fields to make our supper. At 76 he raises chickens, grows vegetables, tends bees, and makes elderberry jams.

In workshop sessions at an IWWG conference, I was thrilled by the acerbic wit of Ann Loring, a former screen actress and a star performer on the daily soap opera *Love of Life.* Vivacious at 83, Ann continues to write, teach, and guide the careers of aspiring screenwriters.

According to Miss Webster, the meaning of *tarnish* is "to dull or destroy the luster of; to detract from the good quality of." It also means to bring disgrace upon. When I met a woman who lost her 75-year-old mother to AIDS, she said, "I always thought my mother died of shame, not AIDS." Her mother's generation viewed the disease as something disgraceful that only homosexuals get. And when she looked at all the HIV/AIDS prevention ads, she saw only youthful people, not anyone that reflected her. For her, the stigma was doubled. Though the elderly make up 10 percent of the AIDS population, they are least likely to seek the help and support they need.

In Dianne Houston's brilliant Academy Award–nominated film, *Tuesday Morning Ride,* an elderly African-American couple dresses up in their best clothing and gets into their vintage car. They commit suicide on a final drive together rather than experience a decline in the quality of the life they had enjoyed.

Silver Time's third mirror, *melt,* is defined as "to disappear as if by dissolving; to become subdued or crushed; to lose outline or distinction." As an elderly person you might suffer from Alzheimer's disease or a terminal illness. You may watch your mind and body gradually dissolve, and distinct parental roles disappear as you become the child of your child. As a senior, you may be forced to alter your living situation and relinquish your independence by having to enter a nursing home.

You might be an old woman buying cat food for herself instead of her pet, or you might be desperately alone. One woman's grandson visited her twice a month. He would sit and talk with her for a while, then ask for money. Whenever he was told she didn't have enough, he would rough her up and take the money anyway. Once, when he got too rough, she landed in the hospital. When it was discovered that the grandson had been abusing her for years, the doctors asked why the woman had put up with it for so long. She replied, "Because he was the only one who came to see me."

Miss Webster tells us that *polish* means "to make smooth and glossy usually by friction; to smooth, soften, or refine in manners or condition." Often life can tumble you into a smooth stone. Well-known American artist Grandma Moses didn't start painting until she was in her sixties. Adult children may look on in amazement and resentment as their once-stern parent becomes a kind, permissive grandparent. And when that parent starts dating again and doing the macarena, they may go into shock.

In your later years, as you watch the younger generation, you may wonder whatever happened to things you thought were basic, like honor, manners, and respect for the elderly. In these years you find other freedoms—freedom from caring what other people think or say about you, the freedom to say whatever comes to mind without worrying about the consequences.

Perhaps novelist and poet May Sarton sums up the best of the *Silver Time* in the introduction to her book *At Seventy*. She writes,

> At seventy, I do not feel old at all, not as much a survivor as a person still on her way. I suppose real old age begins when one looks backward rather than forward, but I look forward with joy to the years ahead and especially to the surprises that any day may bring. . . .
>
> This is the best time of my life. I love being old . . . because I am more myself than I have ever been. There is less conflict. I am happier, more balanced, and more powerful. More able to use my powers. I am surer of what my life is all about, and have less self-doubt to conquer.

THE SILVER TIME: JOURNEYS

• If you are in your Silver Time, write about your biggest dream and what became of it. If you are passing through another stage of life, sit down with a *Silver Time* person you know and ask, "What was your biggest dream?"

Listen carefully. If the dream did not come true, rewrite the story with a different ending. If it did come true, write about something he or she might have done that would have resulted in a completely different outcome.

- Think about your grandmother, a great-aunt, or an elderly person you have been very close to. Of the four mirrors of the *Silver Time*—shine, tarnish, melt, and polish—which one have you seen manifested in her life? Describe how that reflection looked.

  Alternatively, you could cut a photograph of a *Silver Time* person from a magazine or newspaper or get one from a vintage shop. Study the image carefully, then close your eyes and imagine how one of the elements of the *Silver Time* might have manifested in his or her life. Write about it.

- When you think of things that can destroy your luster, what comes to your mind?

- Though your mother is becoming increasingly senile and unable to care for herself, she insists on living alone. Write a dialogue between you and your mother.

- Robert Browning wrote, "Grow old with me, the best is yet to be." Close your eyes with this thought in mind and see what comes. Then write about it.

THE SILVER TIME: SEASONAL SURRENDERS

- Make time to listen to an elderly man or woman not related to you, perhaps by visiting a senior citizen center or nursing home. Honor the museum that she is. Let him know you treasure his stories.

• Go dancing to music from a time in your life you most enjoyed. Do this at a dance hall, at home alone, or with friends.

• Surprise someone with a personal greeting from the president. If he or she is celebrating a birthday of eighty years or more or they are having an anniversary of more than fifty years of marriage, mail details four to six weeks in advance to The White House, Greetings Office, Room 39, Washington, DC 20500.

SILVER TIME: INTERSECTION

As you arrive at the seventh intersection, look back at all your silver encounters, and contemplations, then choose one of the three road signs.

1. *Sign Time.* One of these road signs—*Doubt, Reassurance, or Decision*—will take you to the next state, the final one. As you get older, these reflections take on a different perspective. Notice how these reflections may vary with age. Write down your thoughts as you make your choices.

   • Doubt Sign

      "Maybe I shouldn't have let someone else do all the driving."

      "I wonder if I should taken a different road?"

      "I hope it's not too late to go forward."

   • Reassurance Sign

      "I'm almost where I want to be."

      "I've passed this way before. This time I'll just move more slowly."

      "I'm sure I know what I'm doing by now."

   • Decision Sign

      "I think I've gone far enough."

      "I don't like it here. I'm not going to stay here another minute."

      "I'm going to go straight ahead, even if I am afraid."

2. *Name That Tune*. Pick out a song for Silver Time. How about "It Was a Very Good Year," "When I'm Sixty-Four," or "Sunrise, Sunset."

3. *Totem Time*. Pick a word and an object that reflects one or some of your encounters. Put them into your Icon Box; then pick up your cane and walk slowly down the road to the next state.

A Wake-up Call: Death

"It's not that I'm afraid to die. I just don't want to be there when it happens." Woody Allen's words mirror one facet of the diamond of death. In the thirties movie *Death Takes a Holiday*, death is named Mr. Jordan. Once an elderly Guy Standing traps him up a tree, no deaths can occur unless someone touches that particular tree. Only when Mr. Jordan convinces him of the necessity of completing life's natural cycle does Standing relent, allowing Death to climb down and claim him.

At death, Maat, the Egyptian or Khametic goddess of natural law and justice, uses a scale to weigh intentions and actions. While a feather represents what one intended to do in life, the heart shows what was actually accomplished. If the feather and the heart balance, it means you have done what you intended, learned all your lessons, and do not have to come back to earth. If they do not balance and the heart is heavier, the scale then represents what you still need to do, the lessons that are left to be learned, and the ways in which you will have to do things differently when you return to this dimension.

The Congolese cover a grave with the last objects touched or used by the deceased, believing that the strength of the dead person is still present within that object. This practice, still manifest in some African-American communities, may also involve spreading white shells on a grave site to keep a person's spirit from wandering. A Jewish person who dies has to be buried within twenty-four hours. During the period of mourning, friends and relatives sit *shiva,* a practice during which they sit on boxes and cover mirrors with black cloth.

Shakespeare asks, "Oh Death, where is thy sting?" On his deathbed, Sir Laurence Olivier was quoted as saying, "Dying is easy, comedy is hard." In Dante's *Inferno* the dead are required to make a boat trip across the River Styx. In *Bones and Ash,* Urban Bushwomen's dance performance of Jewelle Gomez's *Gilda Stories,* Jawole Willa Jo Zollar choreographed a joyous dance in which deceased relatives and friends hold their hands out to welcome a young girl who has just passed away.

Not long after that performance, the mother of a friend who accompanied me died suddenly. One of the things that helped comfort her, she told me, was the scene she had witnessed at this performance, and the image of a departed grandmother, cousins, and loved ones waiting on the other side to welcome her mother with open arms.

"Death is nature's way of telling you to slow down," one comedian quipped. "If this is dying," Lytton Strachey quietly remarked just before falling into unconsciousness, "then I don't think much of it." Upon arrival at *Wake-up Call,* the final *United State of Life,* you might hear things like "The operation was a success, but the patient died," or "Those who wait until the eleventh hour to see God usually die at ten-thirty."

Old southerners say that if a person dies with a smile on his face, it means he saw Jesus right before he passed. Think about your attitudes toward death. Do you greet it with fear or philosophy, dread or a desire to let go? The highway leading to this state can be filled with potholes of anxiety and pain or smooth stretches of acceptance and peace.

This highway can be a road of regrets. In my novel *Tamarindo,* Jacob McNeil visits a former lover, 69-year-old Oya Mae, for the first time in twenty years. After they laugh and talk about old times together, he says:

"I came here to ask your forgiveness, Miss Oya, to apologize for leaving without saying goodbye or nothing. My wife had two heart attacks. Said this thing with me and you was killing her. She turned my own son against me. I didn't know what to do when I saw hate making his eyes so narrow at me. I couldn't stand to see that look in your face too."

"That was twenty years ago. Why you just comin' to see me?"

"After Lureen died, it took me more than a year just to work up the nerve to come back to Cachita, and see if you was still here. I ain't had one day of peace since I left. Can you please forgive me for what I done?"

"You did what you had to do. What else you want from me, Jacob?"

He put his cap on, placing her cool fingers between the rough faces of his palms.

"Miss Oya, I know I'm a day late and a dollar short when it comes to you. Time done took some of the edge off me. Missin you's been like I had arthritis in my heart. All those years, I never stopped thinking about you. I heard you was living alone, and I been going over these words again and again in my mind. What I'm trying to ask you is, well, I wonder if you might consider taking me back—you know, marrying me? Maybe two lonely people can still make each other happy."

A chilling gust of wind blew through the mild winter air. Miss Oya took her hand back. "You come waltzin' in here after twenty years lookin like who-shot-John-last-night, with your roses and your memories and your bullshit story? You let somebody buy the dreams out your life, then come here offerin' me what's left over? You ain't even asked me nothin' about my life. Why the hell you think I want some piece of a man with no dreams and no guts?"

"Miss Oya, please . . ."

She turned her rocking chair around, lay the roses on the slatted porch, and faced him with a sharpened stare. "You think I been sittin' on my ass for twenty years just waitin for you to come back, don't you? Ain't that some shit! The night you slithered out of town, I was with another man! Always had one, always will. If you lonely, that's your cross to bear, not mine. Ain't never married 'cause I didn't need the worriation. Why you think I look so good now? Look what marriage done to you!"

As you look back on the highway of your life, how many regrets do you find paving the path? How often did you have to pull over to the side of the road to ask for forgiveness? In a moment of danger, when death appears imminent, it is said that your life flashes before your eyes. What does the movie of your life look like? Is it in color or black and white? Is it a melodrama, a romantic comedy, an action-packed adventure, or a horror story?

Thomas Wolfe wrote, *You Can't Go Home Again*. Have you ever tried to go back to someplace, something, or somebody you had not seen in a very long time? Did you get what you expected? Did you expect what you got?

"Nobody dies when Vera's on duty," a co-worker said about a nurse friend of mine who works in a hospital at night. She says she can usually tell when a patient is about to die. They often get restless and very anxious. Once she sits and talks with them for a while, they calm down and stay alive until she gets off work in the morning.

I had the honor of being with a friend as she lay dying in a hospital. Dellon had fought cancer for eight years. It had brought her close to death countless times, but on this day, only the respirator kept her alive. Her closest friend, Eve, agonized over the decision to honor the Do Not Resuscitate request. Dellon was tired of struggling to live, her mother had told us.

We all gathered to witness her final passage. Linda anointed her head and feet with fragrant oils and placed crystals around her bed. I held her feet, Ida held her hand. We circled the bed, praying and chanting, crying, kissing and talking to her, stroking her face, loving her into her last moments. As they unplugged the respirator, Dellon quietly crossed over to the other side. She was 37.

I once read, "Death is life postponed." When something is postponed, it does not disappear forever—it just gets rescheduled for a later date. Think about people having their bodies frozen until a cure is found for the disease they died of. Think about time being suspended and reincarnation as a lifting of that suspension.

Give some thought to concepts of life after life, near-death experiences, psychic abilities to communicate with the dead, angelic appearances, and ghostly visitations. What comes to mind when you think of these things? What are your experiences?

In the aftermath of death, grief can evoke unimaginable vulnerability, a sense of loss, outrage and anger. In Bill Holm's poem "The Dead Get By," he writes:

Who do the dead think they are!
Up and dying in the middle of the night
leaving themselves all over the house,
all over my books, all over my face?
How dare they sit in the front seat of my car,
invisible, not wearing their seat belts,
not holding up their end of the conversation,
as I drive down the highway
shaking my fist at the air all the way
to the office where they're not in.
The dead get by with everything.

When my mother died, I saw how easy it would be for someone to take advantage of a grieving person's vulnerability. I listened as the funeral director created a subtle parallel between how much I loved and respected my mother and how much I was willing to spend on a coffin. I was astounded at the prices charged for polished wood boxes lined with tufted pink satin. I put my grief aside for a moment and decided to turn the energy around.

The undertaker was taken aback when I asked him, "How much would it be without the satin? She can't feel it, and it's a sealed coffin anyway." After showing me even more costly models, he almost went into shock when I said, "I think it would be cheaper to bury my mother in a used car and roll the windows up!" What matters is how you treated a person when they were alive, how you honor their memory and live your life when they are no longer here, not how much you pay for a coffin to house a body empty of its spirit.

When writer Kate Millett's mother died, I helped plant a rose garden in her memory at Kate's artist colony. Often, people ask that a donation be made to a favorite charity instead of sending flowers. Others plant a tree or start a scholarship fund. Many of my friends and I have ancestor altars where photographs and flowers, candles, or favorite items sit on white cloths to honor loved ones who have passed away. It is there that we sit and talk with them, ask for guidance and blessings, cry, pray, and leave cards and letters.

One Mother's Day, I held a potluck dinner for friends who had lost their mothers. We each brought photographs, wrote down the names of our mothers and grandmothers, then put them next to plates of food we prepared for them. After saying their names and blessing the food, we ate dinner together and transformed a day of sadness into one of celebration. That night one friend's mother came to her in a dream and asked, "Why didn't you put more potato salad on my plate?"

When you are playing music and change the key a piece is in, it is called transposing. You are still playing the same song, but it sounds different. Perhaps death is the song of life transposed, a sound that lives in memory and mind, a song still heard in our hearts and in the things left behind. To some, it is a passageway to "a better home awaiting, in the sky, Lord, in the sky," as in the gospel song "Will the Circle Be Unbroken." To others it is a sudden, tragic, unexplained ending from which there is no recovery, no forgetting, and no respite.

However you view death, it can be always be seen as a wake-up call, a call for transformation of your thoughts, actions, or words. As it wakes you up, it can remind you to live life with a fierce reality, take better care of yourself, let people know you love them, love yourself, make time for joy, follow your dreams, take risks, laugh more often, forgive those who have caused you pain, forgive yourself.

Lily Tomlin began this chapter by telling us, "I always wanted to be somebody when I grew up. I guess I should have been more specific." In *Spirit of a Woman* you have been given a chance to grow up again, to travel through eight *States of Life* from conception to death, from wondering how you would enter this world to worrying about how you might leave it.

Everything you have ever experienced is waiting within you right now, waiting to be brought into the light of your words. Let these experiences shine on your creative spirit and your life. Let the spirit of any woman who has ever walked through your heart whisper words of love and courage to you as you write from your Heartland.

WAKE-UP CALL: JOURNEYS

These are your final journeys for this chapter. Remember, at any time you can go back and revisit the other journeys. You might arrive at completely different thoughts and writing. Let your writing surprise you.

• You are at a memorial service or funeral for yourself. Who is there? What are people saying? What do they remember most about you? If you had the chance to go back and say or do one thing in your life, what would that be?

Think about someone you know who is fighting or had fought against death. See them in your mind, then write about why they struggled so hard, what they are or were afraid of, what they might have done differently, and what they may be thinking now.

• Your spouse, life partner, or parent has a terminal illness and is in tremendous pain. He or she asks you to help him or her commit suicide. Write about why and how you would help or why you wouldn't.

• You are standing in front of Maat's scale of intentions and actions, where a feather represents what one intended to do in life and the heart shows what was actually accomplished. If the feather and the heart balance, it means you have done what you intended, learned all your lessons, and do not have to come back to earth.

If you died today, which part of the scale would be heavier? Think about intentions and actions in your life, then write what comes. Think about intentions and actions in the life of someone close to you and write what comes.

• Create two lists. Write down five of your greatest regrets and five things you would like to be forgiven for. Pick one of these things from each of your lists and use them as a seed for a freewrite.

WAKE-UP CALL: SEASONAL SURRENDERS

• Make a list of all the most difficult endings you managed to survive. Think about endings such as the end of a love affair, a pregnancy, a job, a parent's life, a friendship, a lawsuit, or an illness.

• Perform a random act of kindness for someone who is grieving whether you know them or not. Send a tape of a novel so the person can "read" with eyes closed, make a meal and deliver it, or send a note saying that you will be praying for him or her every day for a week or month at a particular time.

• Send light to someone you have loved and lost. To a quiet space bring some white flowers, a white candle encased in glass, and a photo of the person to be remembered. Write the person's name on the glass candle with a permanent marker. Place the flowers in a vase next to the candle, then fill a glass with cold water and place it near the flowers. Light the candle, and say the name of your loved one, adding, "I am sending light to you."

Now close your eyes and think of a pleasant time you spent with that person. Sit with the memory for a moment and smile. Then, open your eyes, and tap the glass with a spoon five times, saying "I love you," each time it rings. Slowly drink the water in communion with the remembrance. Take the white flower petals and sprinkle them out the window, along a sidewalk, or in a field as you walk in the moonlight. You can also try doing this for a part of yourself you feel you have loved and lost.

WAKE-UP CALL: INTERSECTION

Here you are at your eighth and final intersection. What a journey this has been. Dust yourself off, kick off your shoes, and relax. You deserve a rest. After you get something cold to drink, take a new look at the three road signs and think about what they could mean to you at this point.

At the *Doubt Sign,* "I think I'm going the wrong way" might now translate to "I think my life took some wrong turns." The *Reassurance Sign*'s reflection, "This looks familiar—I've passed this way before," may lead you to "And I know I'll pass this way again." At *Decision Sign*'s, "I'm going to go straight ahead and not make any turns," the reflection might become "I can't wait to see what the next incarnation will bring."

Take another look at the altered reflections in the *Silver Time*, and use them to shape your thoughts as well.

1. *Sign Time*.
- Doubt Sign
  "I think I'm going the wrong way."
  "I'm not even sure where this road goes."
  "Why did I begin this trip in the first place?"
  "I hope it's not too late to turn back."
- Reassurance Sign
  "I think I'm almost there."
  "This looks familiar—I've passed this way before."
  "I'm sure this is the right way."
- Decision Sign:
  "I think I've gone far enough."
  "I like it here. I think I'll stay."
  "I'm going to go straight ahead and not make any turns."

2. *Name That Tune*. Pick out a final song for Wake-up Call. How about "We've Come to the End of Our Road," or, "It's So Hard to Say Goodbye to Yesterday."

3. *Totem Time*. Now that you have experienced the fullness of your journey through the *United States of Life*, pick out your final word and object for your *Icon Box*. After you have done this, take a look at all of the words and all of the totems you have collected. The contents of your box symbolize the trips your life has taken, times that were treasured or traumatic, pivotal turning points, bygone days and ecstatic evenings, people and places that have carved themselves into your Heartland.

When you go on vacation or visit new places, you often bring back souvenirs to remind you of where you have been. Your *Icon Box* contains souvenirs of your past selves—priceless mirrors for you to reflect on, envision, create from, write about, and grow with. Visit with your box from time to time. Take out a word and totem for one of the States, hold them in your hands as you close your eyes, and see what other thoughts and memories come to mind.

Try asking an old, close friend what word and totem they might have chosen for you at one of your *States of Life*. You might also try sitting down with your mother or your daughter and asking them the same thing. Place the *Icon Box* in front of you when you meditate in the morning and see what images its energy plants in your consciousness. Your *Icon Box* gives you access to the power of all the selves you have ever been blessed with during this incarnation.

As you leave "Spirit of a Woman," keep with you the memory of Addie Mae Collins, Denise McNair, Carole Robertson, and Cynthia Wesley, and think about the parts of yourself that never had a chance to grow up. Take with you the words of William Penn as you move on to the next chapter: "I expect to pass through life but once. If therefore there be any kindness I can show, or any good thing I can do to any fellow being, let me do it now, and not deter or neglect it, as I shall not pass this way again."

chapter 6

·

SEASONS AND REASONS

·

Writing is one of the ways I participate in transformation—one of the ways I practice the commitment to explore bodies of knowledge for the usable wisdoms they yield....Writing is one of the ways I do my work in the world.

—Toni Cade Bambara

MEDITATION

In this season of my being
I stand beside the stream of my soul
watching night flow to day
and day watching the light
I know myself to be.

Spring's new voices
break through my trees.
Summer feeds me to my fullness.
Autumn paints life with
A palette of my own.
Winter warms me
With wisdom and waiting.

I am the circle of life
completing its journey
Giving birth to thoughts
That give birth to themselves

The Twenty-eight Faces of Dr. Change

When I was a teenager, the bathroom used to be one of my favorite places to read. In fact, it still is. No trip seemed complete unless I took a magazine or book with me. I would usually grab something from my stash of *Bronze Thrills, Jive, Seventeen, Mademoiselle, Family Circle,* or *Woman's Day* and head for the little room. There in the comfort of cell-like isolation, I would lose all track of time.

I was absorbed by stories of how other people lived, recipes with glistening pictures, articles on how to make Christmas gifts for under five dollars, photographs of beautiful homes in the country, floor plans to study so I could design my own. It's all good if you happen to live alone. But for my mother and two sisters it presented a bit of a problem. It's no wonder, then, that my mother would knock on the door and ask, "You in there for a reason, or you in there for a season?"

This chapter takes you to the realm of the seasons. One of my favorite songs begins, "Everything must change, nothing stays the same." Billie Holiday sings, "You've changed." Statistics show that three out of five women and one out of three men want to change the way they look. To change means to transform; to make or become different; to pass from one phase into another; to engage in giving something and receiving something in return.

You will be looking through the eyes of Dr. Change and exploring his twenty-eight faces, or different ways of seeing change. You are also going to receive something and give something in return. For each season I tore out a story from the thick pages of my life. I'd like you to create something for me in return. In other words, I'll show you mine if you'll show me yours.

Keep the seasons in mind and think about transformation, becoming different or wanting to be, about changes you have encountered or changes you are going through. You will have three Dr. Change faces to look at in each season. So let's make a deal. What kind of exchange would you like to make? Will it be poetry or a painting, fulfillment or a film? Will it be memoir, a monologue, or music; a shining spirit or a short story; a photograph, a novel, or a new lease on life? Or will it be what's behind door number two?

Seasoning the Spirit Sauce

We are all part of that universal manifestation of change. The humpback whale changes its song every year. Trees change the color of their leaves. After the female oyster lays a million eggs, she changes her sex. Who can blame her?

John Money works with hermaphrodite children at Johns Hopkins Medical Center. He tells us that they can change a child's sex through surgery up until the child is 18 months. After that, the male or female patterning is too established. What comes to mind when you hear the word *change*? Give that some thought as you walk through the spring, summer, fall, and winter of yourself.

In spring, the earth is a fertile woman giving birth in the grasses under our feet, on farmlands and fields, in leaves and branches bursting forth with new life. Our thoughts may turn to birth and renewal, starting over, spring cleaning, losing weight for the summer.

When summer visits the earth, we feel the fullness of its physical energy. The sun finds us craving the outdoors, tending gardens, camping, exercising, vacationing, painting and fixing things, and taking a break from mental pursuits. Teachers are witnesses to the lack of concentration and sheer restlessness of children during the last month of school. Summer theater is lighter fare, summer romances are not expected to last, and a summer cold is seen as a different breed from its winter sister. Summer tells us to do less, nourish ourselves more, and to tend to what we have already planted.

As leaves fall to the earth, autumn reminds us of the need to let go. We harvest ourselves, grieve the dying light of summer and the lighter side of our lives. We pull out heavier thoughts and clothing, consider courses to take, return to school, and bathe in the fleeting but glorious colors of the fall. Barren branches tell us of the inevitability of change and the need for thankfulness in this season of preparation. Without the leaves, we can clearly see the scalp of the hills and where the paths part them. We clear our minds of summer dreams and focus on intuition and inner contemplation.

In winter the earth is pregnant with the rich soil of the creative, the dark unknown, the deep realm of spirit. Some of the most sacred holidays take place during this season. We shop for gifts, ski across the snows, revel in family times and brightly colored decorations. The joys of Christmas, Chanukah, and the Latino holiday Three Kings Day can also connect us with the sorrows of the season, feelings of loss, and the cold winds blowing through our empty spaces.

The intensity of the earth's energy at this time can touch the darkest places in our souls. More people take their lives around the holiday season than any other time. For some, winter's diminished light may bring on the depression of Seasonal Affective Disorder (SAD).

At the turning of the year, new resolutions and a returning light point us toward the promise of spring again. Which seasons affect you the most? What season has brought you the most gifts or griefs?

Spring

> A seam has come undone in the quilt of my life.
>
> —MAYA ANGELOU

CHANGING THE COURSE OF HISTORY

"Martin Luther King is dead!" The words spread through City College's Finley Auditorium like a whispered wave. It just couldn't be true. We knew how rumor, smear tactics, and innuendo had already damaged political movements in these revolutionary days, These were Cointelpro (the FBI's Counter-Intelligence Program), Malcolm X, Black Panthers, Huey Newton, Eldridge Cleaver, Bobby Seale, and Fred Hampton days. These were Angela Davis and Kathleen Cleaver on posters, Stokely Carmichael married to Miriam Makeba days.

These were big afro, college takeover, protest, power to the people, fists in the air, riots in the cities, sit-in, be-in, love-in days. These were days of Gylan Kain, David Nelson, and Felipe Luciano starting the Last Poets, Imamu Baraka, and Don L. Lee. These were days of Jimi Hendrix, Richie Havens, Buddy Miles, the Chambers Brothers, the Blues Project, Janis Joplin, Fugs, and Slugs in the Far East. These were Charles Theater on Avenue B, the East, Big Black, folded arms, black clothing and dark sunglasses days. This was not the day to kill the Prince of Peace.

Onstage, a fleshy middle-aged Black woman in sequins kicked her legs high to a Scott Joplin tune. The ragtime band struck up a joyful fanfare and a Black man in a white beard and Uncle Sam costume cakewalked onto the stage waving an American flag and a piano grin.

Something acidic burned at the insides of my stomach. Anger grabbed my heart with red, familiar fists. I could feel its color in the people sittting next to me.

Finally, a shaken master of ceremonies came onstage to announce what some had not yet heard. "Ladies and gentlemen, I am very sorry to announce that Martin Luther King was shot and killed this evening. We are now going to continue the show in his honor."

The band resumed playing. The music had gone from merry to macabre. The Uncle Sam Black man began to dance again. Stunned faces, anguish, horror, and disbelief stared at the minstrel spectacle. A collective rage poured over the Black students like thick Alaga syrup. My entire body stiffened. A voice I did not recognize as my own stood up and yelled, "Stop the show! Stop the goddamn show!"

I had always been the proverbial good girl—passive, obedient, never swearing, never talking back to my mother, and always wearing clean underwear in case I got hit by a truck. Something else was burning inside of me now.

Something inside was breaking apart like ice floes. Another voice sounded, another awareness of what it meant to be Black in America. I felt another self stepping out of my self as if a Body Snatchers pod had been placed beside my chair. Dorothy Lovechild, as some had called me, the girl in pigtails with pressed hair and a daisy behind the ear and a V sign for "peace and love."

Dorothy, who believed passive resistance would liberate, that we could love our enemies into submission. Dorothy, who didn't walk down one flight of stairs to hear Malcolm X because she believed he preached hate and violence. Dorothy, who avoided sunglassed revolutionaries plotting the overthrow of a system they said would never give Black people what they were entitled to. I left that Dorothy lying in the pod and began to scream, "No, no!"

We broke. Students stood up shouting, crying, banging their chairs. We marched out of the auditorium and through the halls chanting the only mantra we knew: *"Martin Luther King! Martin Luther King! Martin Luther King!"* Dozens followed behind us. We threw open office doors and classroom doors and chanted as startled students and faculty watched the harmony of our fury. "Shut it down!"

The Black students needed no further words. They threw on their coats, grabbed their educations, and joined us. Salted anger rolled down the faces pouring out of campus buildings, bitterness on their tongues, fists punching the night air.

We gathered on one-way Convent Avenue and marched against the traffic. Cars backed up and got out of the way. *"Martin Luther King! Martin Luther King!"* The news spread on the drum. People peered out of windows at the hundreds of students massed on the avenue. They came running out of their buildings—women and men crying openly, coats and hasty scarves flying in the crisp spring air.

We moved downhill, downtown. We were sure our linked arms and collective pain were stronger than the barricade of flashing police cars stretched across the street ahead of us.

Police insisted we march across 126th instead of the main artery of 125th Street. We wanted to stomp our feet on the spinal cord of Harlem. We wanted to fill the wide boulevard with young voices grown older that night. The incensed crowd thickened its determination. "Off the pigs! Power to the people!"

The police braced themselves with bullhorns, billy clubs, and fingers poised on the triggers of their service revolvers. My heart pumped anticipation. I heard the good girl yelling, "Fuck you! You can't tell us what to do!" We tossed our defiant hymn like a hand grenade, and pushed past them shouting, *"Martin Luther King, Martin Luther King!"* The police parted like the Red Sea.

Harlem was Club Baron, Mister B's, Big Wilt's Smalls Paradise, Baby Grand, the Alhambra Theater, and Reclamation Site Number One protesting the state office building. It was Sonia Sanchez, Nikki Giovanni, Jayne Cortez, and Toni Cade Bambara reading poetry in back of Liberty House. It was the East Wind, Oscar Micheaux, Dr. Moore, Kanya and the Tree of Life, University on the Corner of Lenox Avenue called UCLA, National Black Theater, Barbara Ann Teer, La Famille, MJ Diner, and Wells chicken and waffles. But this night Harlem was on fire, and we were in the middle of a riot.

Storefront windows crashed to the sidewalk. Huge shards of glass fell like bombs. Smoke poured out of stores and onto people running on either side of us, arms filled with whatever they could grab. People screamed and sirens cried, garbage cans were tossed, alarms went off. Mayor Lindsay rose from the subway like a Greek god.

We continued to march, stepping over cracked glass and broken dreams. The streets were littered with rubble and rage. This was an anger ancient and rampant. This was a day for the death of illusion. This was the day I traded the flower behind my ear for an afro in my hair, and I have never been the same.

SPRING JOURNEYS

Remember your prep, meds, music, and five-minute freewrite. After that freewrite, take your writing anywhere it wants to go. Just don't mess with that freewrite after you do it. Leave it intact, like I've been telling you for five chapters already. Don't you think I forgot.

First Face of Dr. Change—
Changing the Course of History

One cataclysm can change lives, loves, and history forever. Think about where you were when John F. Kennedy was assassinated, Malcolm X was assassinated, the space shuttle crashed, a big hurricane struck, the San Francisco earthquake hit, the Midwest flooded, Philadelphia was bombed, the World Trade Center was bombed, or the Oklahoma Federal Building was blown up.

How did you react? How might you rewrite any of these disasters?

Second Face of Dr. Change—
A Change of Address

People tend to move in the spring. It's a great time to find a new apartment. Me, I hate to move. The mere thought of it fills me with dread. Maybe it's because of all these stacks of paper that sneak into my house at night while I'm sleeping. I had a friend who said she likes to move at least once a year. We're not close anymore.

Get a change of address card from your local post office. In the space for your former address, write, "Where I was." In the space for the new address write, "Where I went." Think about where you have moved from and where you have moved to, what it took to move, what you took when you moved, and what you left behind. Dr. Change wants to remind you that this doesn't have to apply to just a physical move. "Think it over," like the Supremes say.

Third Face of Dr. Change—
A Change of Clothing

In *The Accused,* Jodie Foster is blamed for her own brutal rape because of the provocative clothing she wore. Bette Davis in *Jezebel* was ostracized for wearing a red dress instead of the traditional white.

When did you feel you *had* to change your clothing because

of something or someone else? Another Dr. Change view—when did you *have* to keep a change of clothing with you?

SPRING SURRENDER

In many cultures, spring signals the beginning of the year, a time of renewal, of hope, creativity, health, and goodwill. It is a good time for making promises, vows, or resolutions. As spring begins, we experience a movement toward the balance of light and dark. We move toward our outer light, all the while honoring our inner dark. Jung says, "Without the darkness, we could not see the light of the candle flame." Spring is always an auspicious time for planting new seed thoughts. I always say that a promise is a seed we water with hope.

On a new moon day, think of five things you would like to have new in your life or five things you would like to renew. Make each of these things into sentences—for example, "I would like to be in a new relationship" or "I would like to renew my faith in my writing ability."

Write the sentences on a piece of paper. Take a glass of cool water and speak each sentence into the water. Your words will energize the water. Drink a little of this and feel the power of your words flowing through you.

Fold the piece of paper up as small as possible and bury it and a silver coin in the soil of a houseplant or beneath a tree or a bush. Pour the rest of the energized water over the soil, then let go. As the plant, tree, or bush begins to sprout new leaves and the moon becomes fuller, envision that your wishes are growing as well.

Keep in mind that the new moon is at its fullest point of power during the first three days.

Summer

> When you realize how powerful you are, you can change
> the world
>
> —BARBARA MARCINIAK

WON'T YOU CHANGE PARTNERS AND DANCE?

I was married at half court on a hot August day. That year
Ronald and I decided to get married instead of having our annual
party. I've always thought he married me just to find out my
age, info I guard with my life. When we first met and he asked
me for the umpteenth time how old I was, I sarcastically said,
"I'll tell you three days before we get married!" Well, two years
later, at 12:01 three days before our wedding, he cornered me.
"Okay, now tell me how old you are!" And I had to tell him.

We were casual people, eccentric, artistic. He was a superb
photographer. You know what I do. Neither of us had any
money. His mother lived in a housing development in the Bronx
called Hillside Homes, and his dad lived in a boardinghouse for
men. I had no parents to foot the bill. Our friends already knew
we were a bit strange, so it probably came as no surprise when
they received our mimeographed invitation tucked inside a
flowered note card telling them to come to a rooftop for a
wedding and to bring food.

We got our wedding bands from Gimbel's department store
because my sister worked there and could get us a discount. We
had to get a special permit from the judge because we had waited
until the Friday before our Sunday wedding to get our license. On
Saturday, Renee and Jan met to decorate the roof at Grosvenor
House, a community center on Manhattan's Upper West Side.
What could be nicer than an outdoor summer wedding overlook-
ing the city skyline? It was the day before the wedding. No one
was there to let them in. Something was rotten in the cotton.

Luna made a pot of rice and peas for fifty and had it delivered to the house. Anxiety set in and I began to eat. By the time Sunday morning rolled around, it was down to rice and peas for forty-eight and shrinking. It was the day of the wedding. No one was answering the phone at Grosvenor House. Renee, Ronald, and his brother left for the center.

At 1:45 in the afternoon, Ronald called, "Dot, we can't get in the building! I called my friend Richie and he said we could use his disco on Twenty-fourth Street. Call people and tell them to go there." The wedding was scheduled for 3:00. I was down to rice and peas for forty-five. I called my family before they left New Jersey and gave them the new address. I made some more calls. "What wedding?" Some had never received the invitation. Some had already left.

I called the storefront minister my mother had found for us. "Oh, I see, the wedding's been changed to A-hun-twenty-fourth Street?"

"No, it's on Twenty-fourth Street."

"That's what I said—A-hun-twenty-fourth Street."

"No, it's Twenty-fourth Street, 173 West 24th Street."

"Oooh, like A-hun-twenty-fifth Street's like a 1-2-5?"

"Yes."

"And like A-hun-twenty-third Street is like 1-2-3?"

"That's right."

"So, Twenty-fourth Street is like a 2 and a 4, right?"

"Yes, yes, that's right. 173 West 2-4 Street!"

"Okay, hold on and let me get a ink pen."

At 2:15, Ronald calls back, "Dot, we got the place open. Call everyone and tell them to come back!" I called my family. They had already left. Ronald sent his brother down to 2-4 Street with a sign redirecting people back uptown. Now it was down to rice and peas for forty-two.

The director of the center happened to be walking by and wondered what all these well-dressed Black people were doing standing on the sidewalks of Amsterdam Avenue carrying shopping bags and pots of food. He opened the door but didn't have a key to the elevator, so people had to walk up five flights of stairs in the ninety-degree weather. Once they got there, they had to sweep, set up chairs and tables, decorate, and throw away the sneakers, Spalding balls, and used condoms they found littering the roof.

Ronald called with updates: "You can come down here in about half an hour. We're almost ready!" It was getting later and later. I ate more rice and peas. A couple who had flown in from Boston for the wedding had to fly back home before I got there. By the time I walked in, people were already eating. "Oh, here comes the bride," they said, wiping chicken and potato salad from their lips.

Finally we were ready to start the wedding except for one thing—the minister never showed up. We picked out the person with the loudest voice, Ronald's high school principal, who sported a chartreuse jacket, white pants, and lavender suede shoes. We had people gather around us and hold hands in a circle of love. Errol played a mellow jazz riff on his upright bass as the words of Kahlil Gibran flowed from the ceremony I had written.

People were touched. Tears were still in their eyes as they hugged and congratulated us. An ex-boyfriend became so miserable about my getting married that his new girlfriend refused to speak to me. Then we heard a loud banging and a voice crying, "Help, help!" Ronald's brother Robert had gotten stuck inside the dumbwaiter while trying to get a watermelon. He missed the whole wedding.

We were scheduled to leave for our honeymoon in Jamaica on Tuesday. That was fine except for one thing—we weren't married yet. So Ronald, my friend Renee, and I walked into a civil office on the Bronx's Grand Concourse, only to have the desk clerk look us up and down and ask, "Is that native attire?" Ronald had on a burgundy dashiki and jeans; I wore a kurta, a thigh-length East Indian shirt, and some pants. When we said no, she told us. "I'm sorry, but the gentleman *must* wear a jacket and the lady *must* have on a skirt."

"Forget it!"

"Ronald, we have do this today. Everyone already thinks we're married!"

Renee was five feet ten and big boned. I'm five three and half. She had on a skirt. We went into the bathroom and exchanged clothing. My pants came up only as far as the bottom of her belly. Her skirt swam on me. She held the pants up with one hand and tugged her blouse down with the other. I pinched the excess fabric of the skirt's waistline and held on to it with my fist through the cotton top. They found a grey herringbone tweed jacket to put over Ronald's dashiki; it hung ten inches below the dashiki's hem. "Now," the clerk smiled. "That's better!"

Ronald had an attitude bigger than the Bronx. He sat scowling and indignant, his arms folded. His Sagittarian Jamaican St. Kitts patience had already been pushed to the limit. Renee was pissed. I thought the whole thing was hysterical and couldn't stop laughing. We sat next to a Latino couple all decked out in lace, sharkskin, patent leather, and Bristol Creme.

A red light went on with a bing. They got up and went into the room. Less than five minutes later, the light went bing again. It was our turn.

The darkened room was draped with purple curtains and looked like the inside of a coffin. There on the podium, ready to perform our ceremony, was the same clerk who had asked, "Is that native attire?" She was Emma Thompson with a side order of Rosanne as she read, "Dooo youuu, Ronald . . ." He kept his arms folded as he frowned and spat out, "Yeah!"

"And Dorothy, dooo youuuu . . ."

"Uh-hunh," I answered with my hand over my mouth to hold back the giggle.

"I now pronounce you man and wife." She stood there waiting for us to kiss. "I now pronounce you man and wife," she repeated.

"Is that it?" Ronald snarled.

"Yes, that's it," she said, smiling with anticipation.

"Well then, let's get the fuck out of here!" Ronald threw the jacket against the wall and stormed out of the door. Renee and I went back into the bathroom and changed our clothes again.

The next day we left for Jamaica, where I spent the first night of our honeymoon scratching, eaten alive by mosquitoes breeding in crab holes alongside the road. And so we were married, and I have never been the same.

SUMMER JOURNEYS

Fourth Face of Dr. Change—
"I Want to Change My Hair"

First Billy Joel sings, "Don't go changing, to try and please me." Then he has the nerve to tell you not to dye your hair, be clever, or get a new wardrobe because he wants you to be the "same old someone," he already knows. Have you really listened to that song? What kind of message is he sending out? I guess that's another book.

I was on the faculty of New York University when I used a vegetable dye to tint my hair pink. It gave my dark brown a deep magenta overtone in the sunlight and made the few gray hairs at my temples a lovely fuchsia.

It's summertime and you don't have to wear a hat unless it's straw and you want to. Have you ever changed the color of your hair or wanted to? What about a drastic change in its style? Write about how it did or would make you feel.

Fifth Face of Dr. Change—
A Change of Attitude

Maybe I should have called my actual wedding day "change clothing and stance." They say "If you can't change a situation, change your attitude about it."

Write about something that involved your changing your attitude or someone who changed their attitude toward you.

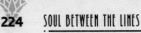

Sixth Face of Dr. Change—
A Change of Scenery

In the summertime we head for the great outdoors—camping, fishing, white-water rafting, concerts in the park. Attention spans shorten as the summer approaches. Even city offices shorten their hours. Maybe your mind is on something or is somewhere else. Maybe you need a change of scenery.

How would you change your scenery? Where would you go, what would you do, and how would you feel about coming back home?

SUMMER SURRENDER

Enjoy the heat and humidity of your own body by taking a Self Shower. Turn out the lights, light a red candle, put on some soft music. This exercise is best done with all your clothes off, but you can do whatever is comfortable for you.

Take a piece of red silk or some other very soft red cloth, cup it in your hands, and blow three long hot breaths into it. Then quickly close your eyes and hold the warmth of the cloth against your face. Softly speak into the cloth the words "I love myself." Feel the humidity of your words and the heat of your love.

Next, choose another place on your body, blow breaths into the cloth, say the words "I love you" into the fabric, then place the silk on the spot you have chosen. Repeat this exercise until you have done it a total of five times. Now lie in the love you have bathed yourself with, and smile.

Autumn

It is difficult to believe that we
even talked.
how did we spend the night

> while seasons passed
> in place of words . . .
>   —SONIA SANCHEZ, "Father and Daughter," from *Love Poems*

WOULD YOU LIKE TO TRADE FOR WHAT'S BEHIND DOOR #2?

I don't know many other New York City children who grew up with fog. We lived at the edge of the East River. At times when we looked out of our eighth-floor window, the fog was so thick we couldn't see the next building. It was absolutely magical, like living in the clouds. The rest of the world had ceased to exist.

When we walked through the fog to get to school, we were thrilled beyond words. Surely there were werewolves lurking out there by the playground just waiting to sink their fangs into us. If our classmates were more than twenty feet away, we couldn't see them at all. "Hellooooooo," we'd call as if we were somewhere on a mountaintop. "Is anyone out theeeeeere?"

The fog I was in a year and a half ago had a different flavor to it. I had changed with the season. I shed my job. Now I felt as naked as the autumn trees outside my window. I no longer had a title, a position on letterhead stationery, people to report to me, proposals to write, artists to hire, children to plan classes for, a community to serve. Now I was at home, a community of one, in between the inbetween. Saying I was a writer but not yet putting the pedal to the metal.

If this was my dream, why had I awakened? If this is what I had been wanting to do all these years, why wasn't I doing it? There was nothing in my way now, no one to blame, no time thieves stealing my moments. What I didn't know was, just because you leave a job doesn't mean the job leaves you. Maybe I needed a break, I told myself. Some downtime, perhaps. After all, I reasoned, the last month or so had not been easy.

For over a year I had been a part of Women and Environment, a working group of the UN Committee on the Status of Women. I helped edit and word resolutions to submit to the international forum and made plans to go to Beijing for the UN Fourth World Conference on Women. It was an exhilarating time.

I felt connected to a world community of women: Tibetan nuns in maroon and orange; French-speaking Africans who were astounded that I knew only one language; Dalit women from India blacker than I, who, inspired by the Black Is Beautiful movement of the sixties, had coined the phrase "Dalit Is Dignified!" I had even been commissioned to create an environmental poem to perform there at the conference.

A friend had arranged for me to do workshops with her Caribbean delegation to China. I was ecstatic about her government's providing the expensive travel and hotel arrangements. Then this friend disappeared, but not before telling me that a government official who had seized too much power was now under house arrest, that the phones were tapped and the capitol surrounded.

"I'll call you," she said, and that was the last I've heard from her to this day. I never got to Beijing. A month later, my fiancé told me, "I'm not there, I'm just not there," and broke off our engagement. Just a few weeks earlier we had talked about getting a big apartment together. The fog thickened.

Although my fiancé had warned me in advance, "It won't change anything. I never felt better!" we attended one counseling session. In the middle of the session, Mary, the therapist, turned to me and asked, "So what's happening with your writing?" I mumbled some foggy words.

"Are you doing your writing or not?" Now I felt pinned like a butterfly.

"Dorothy," she said, "all the successful writers I've read about say they have a schedule."

Schedule! The very word sent chills up my spine. You think I left a job so I could have a schedule? I write when the inspiration hits me. I write when it's raining because it helps the words flow. I collect seeds and notes in a little blue notebook I keep with me all the time. Why, just the other day, I picked up a chapter from the novel I started three years ago and actually went over it with my purple pen. Of course I'm doing my writing. Sure. I told myself a lot of things, none of which I repeated to her. I knew she'd see through the mist. All I could say was "Schedule?"

"Your life will never come out of chaos unless you do your writing. You're like a junkie or an alcoholic. Writing is in your blood. When you're not writing, you're off the wagon!" Well, that shook me up a quite a bit, especially the part about being off the wagon.

"So what's your schedule going to be, seven to ten? Eight to twelve?"

"Okay, okay, eight to twelve, I'll try eight to twelve, all right?" Truth pushed me up against the wall.

"When are you going to start?" Didn't she ever give up?

"Monday, I'll start Monday, okay?" What on earth did this have to do with my breakup anyway?

I peeled myself out of bed that Monday morning. I did my meditation with my eyes thankfully closed, then padded over to the computer. It was the longest four hours I have ever spent. The hands of the clock seemed to stay on the same numbers for at least ten minutes. I looked at some stuff I already had on file. That counts, doesn't it? I know, maybe I can organize my things. That's a part of writing, isn't it? Okay, Dorothy, get real. And I did.

Getting on a schedule was probably one of the hardest things I've ever tried to do. At first I was so tired I thought, *The hell with this! I'd rather clean an oven or lick ashtrays.* Then as the days went by and I forced myself to stay there, it got easier. I knew it took twenty-one days to establish a new habit. I gave myself time off for good behavior on the weekends. On top of my computer, I set up a writing altar inside a little red wagon just to remind me to stay on it.

Before long, the fog lifted. My body woke up automatically without an alarm clock. I turned on my computer precisely at eight. All kinds of writing ideas and sentences visited me during my meditation. I actually looked forward to getting up early and starting the writing. By noon I was finished. I had done my work for the day.

The feeling of accomplishment was intoxicating. I could go to a discount matinee. I could ride my bike through Prospect Park. I could finally drink in the precious sun I had avoided, feeling too guilty about not writing to take advantage of it. At two o'clock in the afternoon I biked to the park, lay down on a bench, and let the sun smile all over me. The fog was gone.

Being on the wagon helped me cope with the breakup and the part of me that felt lost along with it. When grief threatened to take over my body, I would tell myself, "You can't cry until after twelve. It's not in the schedule," and would force myself to keep on writing. Being on the wagon kept my self-sabotage devils at bay and erased the tapes from my childhood that said. "If you don't really try, you can't really fail."

When I left my job, I stepped out on a limb, trusting that the universe would support me. All I had to do was follow my dream and do my work. I started this book. I put a sign over my writing area, a quotation from Garth Fagan that read DISCIPLINE IS FREEDOM, and I have never been the same.

AUTUMN JOURNEYS

Seventh Face of Dr. Change— A Change of Heart

Autumn is considered to be a particularly powerful time for women, one that is likened to a period of gestation. Whether male or female, we have all gone through periods of gestation. We have all experienced labor pains of the mind, body, and spirit and had our lives changed by what we gave birth to. Sometimes we can even experience a sort of postpartum depression after completing a major project, important event, or troublesome relationship.

When have you had a change of heart about something you

labored over, wished for, thought about, or tried to get? What did you do, how did it feel, and was the operation a success?

Eighth Face of Dr. Change—
"Can I Exchange This for Something Else?"

Autumn is considered a time to begin new learning. It is a season of letting go and learning how to do it with grace and beauty, like the leaves that surround us. A changeling is a child who was secretly exchanged for another in infancy. In a recent case, two baby girls were mistakenly exchanged at birth. When one little girl lay dying and her father donated his blood to help save her, he was told that he couldn't possibly be her parent.

After some research, they learned about the mix-up that happened at the hospital ten years earlier. When the little girl died, the parents filed suit to have their *real* daughter returned to them after having been raised by a couple who thought *they* were her parents.

What would you do? Would you let go of the daughter if you were the parent who had raised her. Would you let go of a legal action to get your daughter back?

Ninth Face of Dr. Change—
A Change of Pace

More than the leaves change in autumn. Those Nat King Cole, "lazy, hazy, crazy days of summer" are over. We look at vacation photos longingly. Time to get busy. Autumn tells you to get serious, start school, make plans, begin projects. The pace quickens. October is known as the month of overwork. November brings cooking and overeating at family Thanksgiving gatherings. December finds you running around shopping for presents and overeating at holiday dinners.

When you need a change of pace, what do you do? How do you find that place in your spirit where it is still summer?

AUTUMN SURRENDER

Look in your closets and cabinets, take out everything you have not used or worn in the past two years, and let it go. Give it away, sell it, throw it away—just let it go. As you do this, keep repeating the affirmation "There's always more."

Winter

> To everything there is a season, a time for every purpose under the sun: a time to be born, and a time to die: a time to plant, and a time to pluck up what is planted.
>
> —ECCLESIASTES 3:1

THE CHANGE OF LIFE

On the nine o'clock bus that December morning, my sister Juanita, my 6-year-old niece Dawn, and I had cracked pecans in the shell by squeezing them together hard in our palms. Scrambled eggs and biscuits from Burger King still sat heavily in my stomach. I watched the signs as we rode further into Georgia, past Avondale, Covington, Madison and Eatonton, Milledgeville, Sandersville, Winn Dixie, Big Star, Food Giant, and Piggly Wiggly.

Grandma Exia was waiting for us when the bus pulled into Sandersville. She needs two sticks to walk with now. A black scarf covers her salt-and-pepper wig. My happiness was tainted with sudden thoughts of death. Her large, round face looked almost swollen. I wished she hadn't worn black.

At 88, she was still beautiful, her skin smooth and unwrinkled. I hear my soul whisper, "This might be the last time you'll see her alive." I know how death can be a next-door neighbor. I put those thoughts back on the shelf and listened instead to her laughter, her jokes, and her spirit.

Night in Davisboro, Georgia. The temperature drops fifteen degrees. Grandma Exia insists that we stay at her house overnight instead of going up the road to Aunt Mattie Lou's, where there are gas heaters in every room. She keeps saying, "I'm so glad you children are here. Ol' Exia just rattlin' around by herself in this big ol' house."

She turns on the one gas floor heater, which had replaced the pot-bellied stove with the long black pipe that a bat once traveled down one summer night years ago. It flew around the room for an hour before Uncle Bob finally knocked him down with a broom. We pull our chairs around and sit and talk with Grandma. The room is filled with the warmth of the heater and the mischievous smile on her face as she tells us that her neighbor Marguerite is a prostitute.

"A prostitute?" I ask, not quite believing my ears. "You mean people pay her?"

"Yeah," she replies, "they pay her no mind."

Later, she tells me she's always wanted to be a man.

"What? How long have you wanted to be a man, Grandma?"

"Ever since I was grown. If I could turn into a man right now, I would. I got a man's mind, you know."

That evening I write down the names of all her brothers and sisters, their children and grandchildren. She remembers the names of almost two hundred and fifty. All except some of the ones that moved to Florida, or New York, where she says our men don't last long because they get "assassinated." I fall in love with the poetry and music of the old southern names, Lunelle, Ossie Mae, Alma Rita and Lily Jane, Charley Will, K.P., Picola, Reebee Lee and Valentine.

We take out photographs of aunts and cousins, my mother as a young woman, beautiful and slimmer than I had ever remembered. My grandfather in his overalls, scowling in the sun and carrying a rifle. I felt connected. Part of a whole family much greater than the sum of all its parts.

I looked at my grandmother and thought about the three generations of us sitting there, and the extended family—cousins and "grands up the road apiece." I could not help but wonder who is going to take care of me when I'm old, what baby pictures will I have to hang on my walls, and who will I have to call me grandma.

Grandma Exia talks about aches and pains, but she has outlived five of her nine children, including her oldest daughter and youngest son. She tells us that tongue and teeth fall out just like people do, and that if you peel an apple in one piece and throw that peeling over your shoulder, it will form the initial of the man you're going to marry. And I think, *Who will sit and listen to me when I'm 88?*

Grandma Exia has never worn a bra, taken vitamins, or eaten broccoli. And I think about how all the grits and white flour biscuits are making mucus in my system. She is sitting in a house she owns, but says she never tells the white folks that she doesn't pay rent.

The house and eighty-seven acres of land were paid for by two of her sons years ago when they installed the indoor bathroom. And I sit in my rented apartment wondering if I'll be ready when the light begins to grow dim in the daytime and old age is more foe than friend.

Grandma Exia, in her eighties, is filled with the love and photographs of her family. I, in the 1990s, create words but no children to be grandmother for. She died four months later. I listened to a tape I made of her singing old gospel songs, laughing and joking, and I was never the same.

WINTER JOURNEYS

Tenth Face of Dr. Change—
Change of Life

My grandmother shocked me when she talked about turning into a man. She said she felt like she could do more if she were a man. I don't even remember asking her what she meant by "a man's mind." How many of us spend time wishing we could be something or someone else?

If you could change into a ____ right now, how would you fill in that blank?

Eleventh Face of Dr. Change—
Change of Mind

I once heard a smart-aleck comment that was right up my alley. It went: "So you changed your mind. Does this one work better?"

Pick one of these and write about a change-mind situation: "I changed my mind," "She changed his mind," or "They changed my mind about . . ."

Twelfth Face of Dr. Change—
A Change of Climate

In Desert Palm Springs at a small, unassuming lodge called Miracle Manor, I melted into the warmth of a natural hot springs pool in the January moonlight of a California night. I salivate just thinking about it as I thaw out from this twenty-degree New York weather.

"I need a change of climate!" Dr. Change wants you to look at this statement in its fullest sense, emotionally, psychologically, physically, from every angle. See what comes up for you.

WINTER SURRENDER

In winter we celebrate the inner darkness of ourselves and the season. Try and practice inner listening. Be still. Sit in the dark for five minutes and listen to what the shadows inside you are saying. Do this at least once a day throughout the winter season.

DR. CHANGE BONUS ROUND

• _Change of venue_—what if O.J. Simpson had been tried in Brooklyn? Or Mississippi?

- *A changing of the guard*—out with the old, in with the new

- *Change trains at the next stop*

- *Change your vote* [after being lobbied or well paid]

- *Change places with me*

- *Change your daily routine*

- *Change the key*

- *Change the baby*

- *Change the tire*

- *Change the oil*

- *"I had a change of plans"*

- *"Can I change places with you?"*

- *"I need to change my diet"*

- *"Let's change seats!"*

- *"Here's your change, ma'am."*

- *"Money goes from hand to hand, but my baby goes from man to man."* (country and western song)

chapter 7

·

ANCESTORS AND ANGELS

·

I gathered up the historical and psychological threads
of the life my ancestors lived, and in the writing of it I
felt joy and strength, and my own continuity.

—ALICE WALKER

MEDITATION

The ancestors dwell inside my heart.
Their talk is in tongues
ancient and new.
Their thoughts are as time
looking back on itself.
I look through their eyes
and see the past of my present.

The Angel of Joy fans me with her promise.
She whispers to me in roses and dreams.
And I am in the breeze of her wings.

The Angel of Peace fans me with hope.
She sings from the soul
in the land of the doves.

The Angel of Truth
holds me deep
in the crest of her wings,
and the taste of her telling.
She speaks like water.
Her hand on my heart.

I am truth coming to know itself,
I am peace infinite in its days,
I am the joy of taking my time,
I am the dream of all those who came before me.

Ancestors Within

> My ancestors were Capricorn
> they broke the soil beside the house
> where I was born
> In the cool Georgia clay of winter
> —"SOUTHERN SONATA: MOVEMENT IN E FOR EMANUEL"

It was an early summer evening and I was having an anxiety attack. I was down to my last few dollars. A huge tight knot sat in my stomach and wouldn't budge. I had to remind myself to breathe. I felt like crying. I was all dressed and ready to go out for an evening—a celebration for two friends who had been happily married for twenty-seven years. Maybe that was enough to make me anxious. I wanted to be relaxed, share their happiness, eat food, and drink a loving toast to them. But this knot was too present for me to ignore.

"The world was too much with me," Wordsworth might have said. I sat down in front of my altar and prayed. Help me. Then something told me to get up and go outside. I ran out into the backyard and began digging without a shovel or gloves. I still had on the dress I was going to wear to the party. Somehow it didn't matter. I felt as if I *had* to touch the earth, had to seek its cool comfort.

And as I dug and sweated and prayed and sweated some more in the dying light of the sun, something happened. I smelled my grandfather's sweat. It was coming through the pores of my body. I kept digging. I hadn't seen him in over thirty years. But I remembered how he came in from the fields smelling like a hard day's work.

I remembered his overalls and plaid shirt, the ancient work-boots and felt hat. He would lift up that hat and mop the sweat from his brow and from his forehead with a red handkerchief. That scent had stayed in my mind since childhood. And now it was coming out of me.

Emanual Jordan. He had been a farmer all his life—up at sunrise, milking the cows, feeding the chickens, splitting wood, mending fences, driving mules, slaughtering hogs, drinking moonshine, growing corn and peas that floated in fatback on my grandmother's wood stove. I smelled him as I touched the same earth that provided for him and his family. This was his way of telling me not to worry. Everything's going to be all right.

Ancestors are citizens of the earth. They offer strength and guidance, wisdom and understanding to those who call on them. They send messages and comfort. They are the keepers of all the wisdom and knowledge that came before you. The underground universe of ancestors can ground and center you.

Did you ever lie down on a blanket outdoors? You may have found yourself shifting around a bit before settling into a position that felt comfortable. Every time you lie down on the earth, you are allowing the ancestors to realign your body. After a while, as they continue their work, you can feel your entire body breathing a sigh of relief and becoming totally relaxed.

Ancestors are honored in many ways. People in Africa, Japan, China and other countries maintain ancestor altars as an integral part of their households. In these places, venerated ancestors are still considered a part of the family. Their spirits are believed to have the power to intervene in the affairs of the living.

The African custom of pouring libations, offering water to the earth and calling the names of departed relatives, honors people who have helped to pave the way. Americans visit the earth that holds their ancestors' bodies and pour libations to them with tears as they stand by their graves. As part of my morning meditation, I pour libations and give thanks for the blessing of my being here and for the words I have been inspired to write.

I always talk about growing up on the Lower East Side. What I didn't know until recently was that the area was once called Little Africa. Hundreds of former slaves were buried under my elementary school, P.S. 1 on Henry Street. They attended Mariners Temple on Oliver Street and walked the same streets I walked on my way to Chinatown.

About five years ago in New York City workmen were digging the foundation for a new federal building on Reade Street. They unearthed a burial ground containing skeletons of African people who had lived there more than 150 years ago. Hundreds of African-Americans visited the site to pay homage. Drums were played in their honor, libations were poured, priests of African and Christian traditions chanted and prayed over the spirits that still lay buried in the earth. That site is now designated an official federal landmark. The ancestor bones are now at home in the hands of their descendants, specialists at an African-American institution, Howard University.

In Pittsburgh, a 70-year-old man discovered his grandfather was a Buffalo Soldier by reading old letters he found in his grandmother's attic after she died. Everyone kept saying, "Throw all that old stuff out," that those letters were just a firetrap. I told him to put them in a fireproof box.

Metaphysics and spirituality lecturer Marianne Williamson was deeply affected when she heard a charismatic Catholic priest say to non-Catholics, "If I or any of my people have ever done anything to offend you or your people, please forgive me and please forgive us."

She commented, "As a Jew, experiencing that request for forgiveness was one of the most profound experiences of my life—and I wasn't even consciously aware of my anger. I was thoroughly surprised by the tears that ran down my cheeks on receiving that apology for my people. I felt that I was literally standing in for my ancestors in that moment."

In one story, an American woman was laying flowers on her husband's grave when she looked next to her and saw a Chinese woman placing a bowl of rice in front of her husband's tombstone. The American could not contain herself at the sight of what she thought was such a strange custom. She leaned over and asked, "Why are you doing that? He can't eat rice!" The Chinese woman retorted, "He can't smell flowers either!"

As an adult, I came to recognize a way of honoring ancestor spirits that took place in my childhood. Though they would never have called it that, my parents had us take part in a special ritual when there was a thunderstorm. We had to unplug all the electrical appliances and turn out all the lights. My mother would make a pallet of blankets folded into a mat and lie down in the hallway. We were expected to stay totally silent until the thunder and lightning went away.

My sisters and I would balk at these old-timey southern ways, then do as we were told. My younger sister Juanita and I would crawl into my older sister Ruthie's bed, where we'd giggle, fart, and whisper in the dark. Sometimes I'd go to the window just to watch the streaks of lightning crack the sky.

The thunder excited and frightened me. While it raged outside, if we made noise enough for my father to hear, he'd yell, "Quiet, the Lord is speaking!" Juanita in her innocence once asked, "What's He saying, Daddy?"

Many native cultures erect elaborate shrines and perform intricate rituals in tribute to their ancestors. In the American system of ancestor worship, ancestors are considered so important that holidays are declared in their honor. Memorial Day, Veterans Day, and Washington's Birthday are all ancestor holidays. In honoring these ancestors, schools are closed, workers are given entire days off with pay, stores miraculously lower their prices, and incredible sales are offered in tribute.

On these holidays, soldiers put on native uniforms they haven't worn in forty years. Images of idols are erected in statues, carved into mountainsides. We call these images Mt. Rushmore, the Lincoln Memorial, Tomb of the Unknown Soldier and the like. Spectacular parade rituals and floats are filled with sacrificial prom queens and hopeful candidates. Even Wall Street, the National Shrine of the Almighty Dollar, shuts itself down.

There is a proverb that says, "No tree can flourish without

roots." What are *your* roots? How do you celebrate them? Many people of European ancestry adopt names and spiritual customs from American Indian, African, and East Indian cultures while ignoring their own. In doing this, they dishonor their grand-mothers and great-grandmothers, who carried history in their hearts and in their bellies. When you connect with the culture of your own ancestors, you will find that each has its own tradi-tion of ritual and magic, earth-honoring, and celebration of the living energy in all things animate and inanimate.

You can honor yourself and your ancestors by making a dis-tinction between the spirit of a culture and the practitioners of it, just as you can honor the spirit of a religion while bypassing the practitioners of it. Somewhere in each of our lineages is an ancestor that prayed to the skies for rain and to the earth for food. Somewhere in your background is an ancestor waiting to be remembered and acknowledged.

When you speak the names, reclaim the ritual, make the magic, touch the tradition, you give tribute to the lives of those who made it possible for you to be here reading these words. When you celebrate what is yours, you are fed with the food of all those who have eaten before you.

Angels About

Ancestor has been defined as "a person from whom one is de-scended" or "a manifestation of energy transformed." Let's take a look at another manifestation of transformed energy—angels. Angels have been called citizens of inner space, divine messen-gers, guardian spirits, and thoughts of God.

In *Field of Dreams*, Kevin Costner receives the divine message "If you build it, they will come." He is also visited by baseball ancestors Babe Ruth, Shoeless Joe, and his own father. Baseball angels made another appearance in *Angels in the Outfield.*

In *It's a Wonderful Life,* an angel gives Jimmy Stewart a glimpse of how life might have been without him. In *The Preacher's Wife,* angel Denzel Washington helps a minister restore his faith and renew his marriage. John Travolta plays an all-too-human angel in *Michael,* and Michael Landon took us all on the *Highway to Heaven.* While *Touched by an Angel* maintains a celestial presence on television, multitudes of books, tapes, movies, television programs, and specials feature angel stories and visitations.

Angels are masters of divine intervention. Like ancestors, they have the power and responsibility to intervene with the living. They are here to help us, keep watch over our lives, and guide our actions. The kachina is a guiding spirit among the Pueblo peoples, the pitarah is a protective guardian spirit in India, and the wajima is a spirit ancestor to the Australian aboriginal. The angel Michael is believed to have rescued Daniel from the lion's den and informed Mary of her imminent death.

According to Islamic beliefs, Gabriel is said to have dictated the Koran to Muhammad. In Jewish lore Gabriel helped part the Red Sea to assist the Hebrews in escaping Pharaoh's oppression. In his duty as a messenger, Gabriel also appeared to Joan of Arc and inspired her to assist the dauphin, the eldest son of the king of France. Raphael is the healing angel whose image appears in paintings by Botticelli and Rembrandt. Michelangelo said, "I saw an angel in the marble and chiseled until I set it free."

I was in the cafeteria at Skidmore College talking to Marilar Mayher, a minister who has worked with angels for many years. We were standing by the dessert bar and I was jealously guarding the last piece of cake. There was no one standing near us as she talked about how important angels had been in her life. When I went to reach for my dessert and continue the conversation, the cake was gone. The plate was still there, but the last slice had disappeared. "Oh, they just love to play tricks like that," Marilar said. It was angel food cake.

Marilar told me she works with angels so closely that she'd be surprised if they didn't give her what she asked for. She once asked the angels for a car, a red Chevrolet. When a friend gave her a gift, she got exactly what she asked for—a red Chevrolet model car ten inches long. "When you ask them for something, you have to be very specific."

One night a woman got into her car in a deserted indoor parking lot. The car wouldn't start. As the engine continued to stall, a strange man began banging on the window and threatening her with a tire iron. No one was around to help her. She began to pray and cry as the man shouted for her to get out of the car. Finally the car started and she was able to drive away.

She arrived home in a panic and told her husband what had happened. "You've got to check that battery. I was almost killed!" When he opened up the hood to take a look, the battery was gone. The would-be mugger had removed it to set her up for a robbery or worse. He hadn't counted on her prayers being answered or her getting home by angel power.

A young man fixing an old car in his garage propped its front end up on milk cartons and began working underneath. Suddenly the cartons collapsed, pinning him under the car. His brother was in an apartment more than two hundred feet away and could not hear his weak cries for help.

Soon he saw the legs of a man wearing sneakers and blue jeans. The man lifted the car and held it up just long enough for him to roll to safety. Then he slowly let the car down. The young man sat there trying to catch his breath for a while, then looked around for the man to thank him. There was no one there. The garage door was still locked from the inside.

Books abound with stories of angelic interventions, messages, and assistance. Angels have feelings, divine insight, intelligence, and a presence that operates on a different vibratory level than ours. Imagine the difference between a cheap AM transistor radio and an expensive full-sized model with AM/FM, shortwave, digital and international capabilities. One operates at a higher frequency, has access to more signals and sounds, and can receive and transmit a greater range of information.

You can't connect with the frequency of that hip-hop station in Borneo unless you have the right equipment. To that equipment add some heavenly juice and an ability to transform energy into an infinite variety of forms, and that gives you some idea of what angels are like.

The word *angel* comes from the Greek word *angelos,* which means messenger. Angel messages are designed to serve a definite purpose. In times of great changes and transitions in our lives, they appear to us. They enlighten our souls, remind us to trust in our spirit, and help us believe in ourselves. Angels encourage us to move in harmony with the world around us and to develop our capacity for compassion and forgiveness.

Whether you believe in them or not, I'm sure there's an angel reading over your shoulder right now saying, "You tell 'em, sistah!"

Are You Minding My Business?

Spirit interventions are not always laced with drama. When I'm coming home late at night and the streets in my Brooklyn neighborhood are deserted, I ask them to walk with me for protection. More than once, when I sensed someone walking behind me whose energy did not feel good, I called for help. When I looked around, the person was gone.

I was in Washington, D.C., doing a workshop at the Institute for Policy Research. On the last night of my visit, Brazilian artist Milton Nascimiento, a singer whose music I love, was performing. One of the workshop coordinators told me, "The concert is sold out! I'm sorry, we just couldn't get you an extra ticket." I went down to the concert hall anyway. I took my angels and ancestors with me.

When I got there, the lobby was jam-packed with people all

desperately trying to find someone with an extra ticket. There were two big signs on the box office window that read SOLD OUT. Then above the crowd and the noise and the chaos, I heard someone clearly say, "There's one ticket here at the box office." I thought I must have been hearing things since nobody else made a move toward the ticket window.

I excused myself all the way across the room, through the crowd, and to the box office. "Do you have a ticket here?" I was astonished when he replied, "Yes, I have just one." Much to the amazement of the people still waiting in the lobby, I walked right past and into the theater. Milton put on a great show.

I couldn't think of a better way to reward myself for all the hard work I did on this book than to hear one of my favorite performers, Toshi Reagon. At this special birthday concert, she was performing with her mother, Bernice Johnson Reagon from Sweet Honey in the Rock. The Great Hall at Cooper Union was built before the turn of the century and has huge support beams in its auditorium. If you don't get there early enough, you get stuck in a seat behind one of those poles.

I arrived fifteen minutes before the concert to find most of the seats filled. My spirit folks know I don't like sitting in the back and I don't like sitting on the sides. I'm a smack-dab-in-the-middle kind of woman. That's exactly where they put me, fourth row center, where there just happened to be an empty seat hidden under some coats. The concert was absolutely unforgettable.

Spirit interventions happen to me all the time, maybe because I ask for them. Don't they happen to you? Think about it for a moment. How many times have you heard, "There are no coincidences?" Think about every time you have said or thought, "What a coincidence!" Think about every time you found the right dress, apartment, job, or opportunity exactly when you needed it, either by stumbling across it or in some other unplanned way.

Think about the number of times you walk down a street you don't usually take and run into someone you haven't seen in fifteen years or someone you've been thinking about intensely and meant to call or someone you haven't been able to get in touch with. And suddenly there they are! Accident? Coincidence? No, my dear, these are spirit interventions.

This is the way angels and ancestors mind your business. They have been doing it for so long, and in so many subtle ways, you might not have even noticed. So now that I've put it that way, take another look and see if you can begin to recognize angel and ancestor interventions in *your* daily life.

Stretching the Spirit

Maggie Fox tells us, "Real writers understand the elasticity of experience." We talked about an ancestor being a person you are descended from, or a manifestation of energy transformed. Let's take that transformed energy and expand the elasticity of your experience. For the purposes of your creative spirit, let's expand the definition of ancestor.

Have you ever known someone who was *like* a mother to you or *like* a grandmother to you? Sometimes the energy from a blood relative becomes transformed and creates a strong bond between you and someone not related to you.

Have you ever said, "We're like sisters" or "He's been like a father to me"? When people feel like family to you, they *are* family. When someone feels like a mother to you, they *are* your mother in the spirit of that energy transformed. Perhaps you were related on another plane, in another time, in another galaxy—who knows? Spirit brought you together on this planet at this time. The angels and ancestors intervened and made manifest that divine coincidence. I say blood is thicker than water, but spirit is stronger than flesh.

Let's stretch the creative spirit even further. Is there someone famous you'd like to have as a mother or grandmother? Who might you pick if you had to choose a person of note to be an ancestor?

Have you ever said, "Boy, am I glad she's not my mother!" Well, what if she was? Whether you were talking about Joan Crawford or not, expanding the possibilities opens several doors for exploration.

What would your life have been like if Zora Neale Hurston had been your mother or Eleanor Roosevelt your grandmother? What about Frederick Douglass as a great-uncle or George Burns as your grandfather? What if you had Frida Kahlo, Ho Chi Minh, Picasso, Martin Luther King, or Mahatma Gandhi as an ancestor? How might things have been different for you? What would you have to tell us about their lives? How would you transform their energies and record them for all time?

The seeds have now been planted for any flight your creative spirit would like to take. Perhaps you'd like to construct a family tree, begin a historical novel, or take photographs of the oldest members of your family. You might want to set your grandfather's memories to music, put together a collection of coincidences, paint an angelic intervention, or make a film about the early days of your ancestors. You might tape interviews with your elders and use their lives and dreams to transform yours.

Exploring these ancestor and what-if questions gives you yet another realm of personal, creative, and spiritual fields to roam in. I use the names of my ancestors as names for the characters in my novel. Once I saw an old photo of an elderly Black woman in an antique shop. I decided to adopt her as an ancestor. When you go to a flea market, thrift shop, tag sale, or antique shop, always take a look at the old photographs. One of your ancestors might just be there waiting for you.

Healing Your Mother's Karma

Miss Webster, our ever-present dictionary diva, defines a descendant as "proceeding from an ancestor or source." Let's expand on the elasticity of experience. Let's say that you are your own source, or that each situation contains its own source. In other words, ten years ago, you were an ancestor of your present self. And the way you are now is a descendant of the way you were years ago.

Are you still with me? We are really doing some spirit stretching now, and it's good exercise. Using this perspective, we can ask, What was the ancestor of a situation or what is the ancestor of a particular relationship? What did it look like five or ten years ago? If this is the winter of our discontent, what happened in the summer?

Let's bring it home. A few chapters ago I mentioned Sankofa, an African bird symbol whose body faces forward while its head faces backwards. The literal translation of Sankofa is "Your future is behind you. Go back and pick it up."

We encounter this concept in our daily lives all the time. When you are going for therapy, you first have to go back to your past before you can move into a healed future. When trying to resolve conflicts at a job, between friends or partners, you start by examining what has already happened, then work on getting the relationship or situation to move forward.

Knowing about your past can alter the way you live your present and your future. I once watched a talk show that featured a black psychologist who studied the origin and reasons for the breakups of the marriages of not only her female clients but also their mothers and her grandmothers.

What she found was that daughter after daughter's marriage had broken up for the same reason that her parents' marriage came apart, even though each swore they would not repeat the sins of their parents. Each daughter manifested the same kind of relationship dynamics her mother did.

I thought of the journal I had written about my grandmother. I remembered her saying about my grandfather, "I didn't love that man. My mother was crazy about him." I remembered my mother being a dutiful wife and mother, but I never felt her being in love with my father. Then I looked at myself. There I was in a relationship with someone I really cared about but knew I wasn't in love with.

What the psychologist said really struck a chord. I didn't want to just settle for someone out of duty, convenience, or ancestral patterning. I decided then and there to heal my mother's karma by breaking the pattern. Whatever it took and however long, I decided that I'd wait for the passion and deep connection, the ebb and flow I like to feel when I'm in love.

Imagine going back into your mother's or grandmother's life and thinking about what it might have looked like if she had made different choices when she was younger. My 70-year-old Aunt Cora was the oldest of ten children. When she was growing up, that put her in the unenviable position of taking on a lot of the responsibility for her nine younger brothers and sisters.

One day she said to her mother, "Mama, I don't want to have any kids when I get married." Her mother looked her in the eye and replied, "Girl, you gonna have 'em all." My aunt went on to have five children with her first husband, and another five with her second. How might she have shaped her life differently if she had been childless?

I have an old photo of Aunt Cora looking very young, sexy, and carefree. I wonder what the thoughts of the woman in that photo were. Have seen photos of your parents or grandparents at a much younger age? Those photos are images of what they looked like when they were ancestors of themselves. What if you had known them then? What do you think you might have said to each other? What can you dream that they didn't dare to? What can you do now that they couldn't do then? Did they have silences that needed breaking? How might that have changed the way they raised you?

When you make a film or tell your children about the lives of ancestors who have gone before you, you are giving voice to the silence they might have had to embrace as their own. When you perform a monologue about your grandmother's struggles or write a story about your mother's sacrifices, you are giving direction to a pattern of broken dreams that had nowhere to go. When you take lessons from the well-worn pages of their lives, you are helping to change yours. Whether you are an artist or an accountant, a spiritual seeker or a salesman, a poet or musician, every time you do these things, you participate in an act of transformation.

When you decide to live a fuller life and to love yourself more than your mother felt entitled to, you are healing your mother's karma, and therefore yours. If there was something your grandmother always wanted to do, do it for her at least once in your lifetime. If your ancestors were afraid to dream, dream for them. If your mother was abusive and controlling, rewrite, repaint, replay her life. Try to uncover the ancestor of her bitterness and fear.

If your mother had nine children and didn't have much life of her own, live yours every chance you get. Rewrite her as a happy childless woman. Think about the way she used to be, and what you two might have enjoyed together when she was younger, thinner, less burdened, more joyful. There is still time to rescue her dreams.

The Present Past of the Future

You have experienced the power of expanding, transforming and intervening with ancestor energy, visions and dreams. Let us look to the past and pass through the present so we can move toward the future. To this same space of understanding, let us add the light of divine intervention and see what further insights we can bless ourselves with.

For this we call on three citizens of the inner self: the Angel of Joy, the Angel of Peace, and the Angel of Truth. Remember, angels appear to inform and encourage, enlighten and strengthen.

Each angel comes with its own Angel Food Cake from Inner Space, a series of journey questions and seed thoughts to write on, ponder, and otherwise ingest. If you do not know much about the lives of your mother or your grandmother, then invent truths about them. If you have a photo, use that as a way of connecting with their energy. Just look at the photo, ask it the question, and write the answers that come.

The Angel of Joy

Joy: "the emotion evoked by well-being, success, or good fortune or by the prospect of possessing what one desires."

ANGEL OF JOY JOURNEYS

- Pick out two occasions when the Angel of Joy visited you as a child and write about them.

- How would you have changed your mother's or your grand-mother's life to make it a happier one?

- What joys do both you and your mother or grandmother share?

- What kind of happiness or dreams did your ancestors envision for themselves? For you?

- If you won ten thousand dollars in the lottery, what would you do with it? And your mother, what would she do? Your grandmother?

- Create a sexual fantasy for your grandmother that would make her happy.

- If you could send your grandmother to any state or any country in the world, which would she be happiest in? What would she want to do there? What kind of setting would she most like to be near: tropical forest, mountaintop, or waterside?

• If your joy could be poured into a cup, how would it measure?

ANGEL OF JOY SURRENDER

• Begin to keep a *Joy Journal*. Write down all the things that make you smile, laugh, feel good, cared for, loved, honored, and thought about—a letter from an old friend, a day off, the first bud in springtime, a baby holding your finger, dreaming about Hawaii, remembering a childhood game. Create headings:

> *Joy in the Morning.* The first smile or pleasant thought of the day; also a place to plant seeds for what you would like to experience that day.
> *Joy in the Evening.* Any joyful happening that takes place during your day.
> *Fossil Joy.* Remembered joys from your distant past, recent past, or a past life.
> *Wish Upon a Star Joy.* Fantasies, wishes, dreams, hopes, vacation plans, prayers for peace.
> *Unadulterated Joy.* All the things that don't fit under any other heading.

ANGEL FOOD CAKE FROM INNER SPACE

• *Joy*

• *Joyless*

• *Yearning for happiness*

• *Things a person does to find joy*

• *What a person thinks will make them happy*

- *What happens when they get these things and joy still eludes them*

- *The threat of losing a source of joy*

- *The search for the source of joy*

- *Finding joy in the smallest things*

The Angel of Peace

Peace: "A state of tranquillity or quiet; freedom from disquieting or oppressive thoughts or emotions; end of hostilities, freedom from disturbances."

ANGEL OF PEACE JOURNEYS

- Choose a situation from your life in which there was a conflict. Ask your own Angel of Peace take a look at it. Choose a different ending or outcome and write about it.

- What got on your grandmother's nerves? Your mother's?

- What did your mother or your grandmother argue or fuss about?

- Would your ancestors think that you are a peaceful person?

- What conflicts did your mother or your grandmother leave unresolved?

- How would you have changed your mother's life to make it a more peaceful one? Your grandmother's?

- How did you bring peace to your spirit five years ago? Ten years ago?

THE ANGEL OF PEACE SURRENDER

Make peace with someone or something in your life. If you have been in conflict about anything, try to resolve it before the end of a new moon cycle. If you are not sure how to do this, ask for guidance.

Write a question about the circumstances on a piece of paper and put it under your pillow. Ask clearly and simply what you should do. See what comes to you when you put the question to the ears of the angel.

ANGEL FOOD CAKE FROM INNER SPACE

- *Peace of mind*—what brings it

- *When can you stop worrying*

- *Avoidance of conflict*

- *What we do to stay out of harm's way*

- *What does it do to us when we move away from conflict or when we take it on or confront it*

- *How do we create peace? How are other people affected?*

- *Destruction of peace*

- *Inner and outer conflict*

- *What color is peace?*

- *Settings of peace, indoors and outdoors*

- *Peaceful sit-in, the art of inaction*

The Angel of Truth

Truth: "sincerity in action, character, and utterance."

ANGEL OF TRUTH JOURNEYS

- There is a truth you have held on to for a long time that needs to be told. There could be some words stuck in your throat or in your spirit, something you've been meaning to say to a person who is either still with you, a physical or emotional distance away, or no longer alive. Write him or her a letter about it.

- What happened when you knocked over a rock and the truth slithered out from underneath?

- "We hold these truths to be self-evident": what truths are these?

- What truths would you like to learn from your ancestors?

- What were your mother or grandmother's *true* feelings about something or someone, despite what she told you?

- Name five truths about yourself, your mother, and your grandmother.

- How would you have changed your mother's life to make it a more truthful one? Your grandmother's life? Your ancestors' lives?

- What is true for your mother that is not true for you?

- When was the truth not told, either by you or by your mother?

- When were you injured by a truth that hurt?

- Of absolute truth, creative truth, or fantasy truth, which one

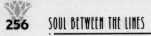
best fits the communications between you and your mother? You and your grandmother? You and the rest of the family?

- Pick one and write about it: denial, white lie, half-truth, believe me, sincerity, exaggeration, a big lie, infidelity, reality check, larger than life.

ANGEL OF TRUTH SURRENDER

Spend some time tonight with the ancestor of your past self. Think of how you used to be and the things you used to do. Pick five of these ways of being or doing and write them down. Get a glass of juice or wine and read the list out loud. After each item, drink a toast saying, "I celebrate the passing of my past self" and smile.

ANGEL FOOD CAKE FROM INNER SPACE

- *The elasticity of truth—how far does it stretch?*

- *Truth—historical, hysterical*

- *How far do you dig to unearth the truth? Are you ready for what you've brought to the surface?*

- *What happens when your reality check bounces?*

- *Faithfulness, faithless*

- *Which part of ourselves feels something is true or feels someone is not telling us the truth?*

- *Will anyone ever believe Joey Buttafuoco?*

- *Are your characters believable?*

- *Are the events in your stories believable?*

- *Are the events in your life believable?*

- *Are you believable?*

- *"I can't believe this is happening to me"*

- *"I know you won't believe this but . . ."*

- *Do your words ring true?*

- *Inventing the truth*

- *How many truths are there?*

- *How does your parent or sibling remember an incident you recall?*

- *How does their recollection differ from yours?*

- *How much truth do you tell; how much do you keep for yourself?*

- *Truth hurts*—does it wear spiked heels or sneakers?

- *Lies:* What is a little white lie? Why is it white? Why is it little?

- *Lies that hurt, lies that help*

- *Fantastical truth*—science fiction, realistic implausibilities

- *Exaggerations*

chapter 8

·

PLEIADES, GREEN CHEESE, AND BLUE SEAS

·

Shoot for the moon because even if you miss, you will
land among the stars.

—Les Brown

Cycle of the Spirit

Pack your spaceship, parachute, walking shoes, rubber raft, and scuba-diving equipment. Yes, it's time for another Heartland adventure. This time you will reach out and touch every realm of the universe that lives around you. You will explore an ancient cycle of life that takes you from the heights of the galaxy to the depths of the ocean.

First stop is the sky, then on to the stars. After a moon dance and a cloud chase, an earth walk, a river run, and a deep dive, the circle swings back home again. Each stop along the journey is a passageway to yet another creative experience that draws its strength from the heights of your creative spirit and the depths of your Heartland.

So put on your helmet, turn on that computer, load up your film, get out your paintbrushes, tune up the piano, and break out the stardust. The universe awaits on these next pages. Don't keep it waiting too long.

MEDITATION

In the spirit of the sky
I walk the path of wisdom and light.
The blue infinite surrounds me
Like celestial skin.
I am magic
and Milky Way.

I am the sky reaching for itself.
I am a star that knows
Its own shining,

And a moon of radiant wonder.
I am a cloud that feeds the horizon
And earth that spins beneath me.
I am fertile river water
Flowing deep within my heart,
Then heading home again
As I celebrate
The galaxy within me.

The Sky Above

I have a sky fetish. Every summer I teach a workshop at Skidmore for the International Women's Writing Guild's annual summer conference. What I truly love about the Skidmore campus is that the dormitory rooms are all designed with picture windows and cushioned window seats. One of my greatest pleasures is to curl up in that window seat and stare out at the vast expanse of sky spread before me.

I love to wake up to the sky's dawning, its subtle palette of light spilling onto the horizon. And when I go to sleep, I love seeing the sky draped across heaven like navy-blue velvet. I watch as tiny dots of light shine through the holes poked into its fabric.

Just so I get my proper dose of sky, I usually start to redecorate as soon as I check into my room. The student desk is pulled away from the wall. I then push the heavy twin bed clear across the carpet until it is aligned with the edge of the window seat. After I set up my altar and lay a colorful Indonesian scarf across the bed, I am ready for my beloved skygazing.

Why go through all of this? You see, I live on the ground floor of a brownstone in Prospect Heights. This area, near Grand

Army Plaza, is the highest point in all of Brooklyn. But from my vantage point, I can see only the small piece of sky. That piece is framed and scalloped by building tops, sycamore trees, and a church steeple.

I often wish I lived on the upper floors of one of the small apartment buildings in my neighborhood. Then I might command one of those astounding views of the downtown Brooklyn and Manhattan skylines and feast on the sky every day. But then, I reason, I wouldn't have access to my backyard, and the organic garden I have been meaning to plant each year.

When I was a child, we played a clapping game called Mary Mack. Mary loved to dress in black and had silver buttons all down her back. Then the rest of the chant goes:

She fly so high, high, high
Nearly reach the sky, sky, sky,
And she never came back, back, back,
'Til the fourth of July, ly, ly . . .

As an adult, I think about what I believe to be the African origins of that particular verse. African-American author Virginia Hamilton wrote a children's book entitled *The People Could Fly*. On its cover is a beautiful Leo and Diane Dillon illustration of a family actually flying toward the sky. The book was inspired by the belief among some African tribes that their people actually have the ability to fly. One of the old folktales from the days of slavery tells of slaves who were able to fly away to freedom.

Several American Indian as well as African tribes trace the origin of their people to the sky. Some Indians refer to heaven as the Great Sky. We think of heaven as that final resting place somewhere in the sky. Images of this celestial address abound throughout religious texts, in literature, songs, and movies. Angels are always flying down from it, cast out of it, or being sent on a mission from it.

Our good friend Miss Webster of dictionary fame says that

heaven is "the expanse of space that seems to be over the earth like a dome; the dwelling place of the Deity and the joyful abode of the blessed dead; a place or condition of utmost happiness." When you are lying on the beach of some tropical island, closing your lips around a perfectly sumptuous dessert or getting a much-needed massage, you may have felt transported to that place of utmost happiness and found yourself saying, "Oh, this is heaven!"

It has been said, "Heaven is right here on earth." Distinguished historian Dr. Yosef Ben Jochannan says, "Heaven is between a woman's thighs." An inscription placed on the office wall of the eleventh-century official in China read:

> Heaven is my father and earth my mother and even such a small creature as I finds an intimate place in its midst. That which extends throughout the universe, I regard as my body, that which directs the universe, I regard as my nature. All people are my brothers and sisters and all things are my companion.

When a pilgrim asked about the essence of his teachings, the Buddha held up a flower. In *Creative Meditation and Multi-Dimensional Consciousness* Lama Anagarika Govinda writes:

> The flower, which opens itself to the light of heaven, while yet being rooted in the earth, belongs to the deepest symbols of the East. The darkness of the earth and the light of heaven: the powers of the depth, in which the experiences of an infinite past . . . are united in the blossom of spiritual unfoldment in conscious form.

One day St. Peter needed a break as he guarded the pearly gates of heaven. He asked Jesus if he would do him a favor and watch the gate for a moment. Jesus said, "Sure." After a while an old man came wandering by looking as if he were lost. "Can I help you?" asked Jesus.

"Yes," answered the old man, "I'm looking for my son."

"What does he look like?"

"Well, he has holes in his hands and holes in his feet and a wooden cross on his back," the old man replied.

Jesus looked closely at the old man, then said, "Father?" The old man looked back at him and asked, "Pinocchio?"

What were some of your childhood connections with the sky? I know that there is an utterly explainable technique involved, but I still like to think of skywriting as something magical. As a child I remember staring at the sky, totally transfixed as a plane inscribed its mysterious message into the air. What a thrill it was to watch words hang in the sky like clouds. My sisters and I loved to recite this little ditty:

Little birdie in the sky,
Why you do that in my eye?
I good girl,
I no cry.
Whew, it's good thing cows don't fly!

My love affair with the sky has continued throughout my adult life. When a friend who lived upstate invited me to her country home for the weekend, I thought for once in my life I would get to bed early and sleep soundly surrounded by the peaceful woods of Esopus, New York.

What I didn't know was that when she and her partner remodeled their cozy home, they had installed a skylight over the bed in each room. I thought I had died and gone to heaven! I kept my eyes open all night long, just so I could watch the sky go by. At the end of my restful weekend in the country, I was ecstatic but thoroughly exhausted.

Give some thought to your own personal experiences with the sky. During World War II, air wardens were assigned to watch the skies for enemy planes. Bird watchers look to the skies for the joy of observing the variety of winged species in flight.

Thousands of people have reported spotting UFOs flying across the sky.

One of the ways of looking at the sky is to see it as a reflection of character, mood, or emotional climate. A bright sunny day seems an unlikely setting for horror. Yet, situating an extraordinary or frightening event in that very setting can make the unexpected seem even more terrifying. A dark, stormy sky can signal a shift in mood or emotional foreboding.

Think about the use of sky in writing, in paintings, or in movies you may have seen. One of the most memorable scenes in *The Ten Commandments* is the one in which the plague comes creeping down from an ominous sky. In the movie *The Good Earth,* based on Pearl S. Buck's classic novel about life in China, the sky became darkened with a plague of locusts that ate everything in their path. See how many ways you can find to let the sky hover over your creative spirit. Remember, the sky's the limit!

THE SKY ABOVE: JOURNEY

You know the drill—music, meditation, preparation, and concentration. In the Heartland, when I say, "Give me five," I'm talking about your five-minute freewrite.

- When something landed on his head, Chicken Little went into a panic and ran around telling everyone, "The sky is falling, the sky is falling!" You might even say that he ran around like a chicken with his head cut off, but that's another story. Anyway, write about an incident that made you feel as if the whole world were falling down on you.

- The Fifth Dimension sang about flying, "up in the sky in my beautiful balloon." Would you like to fly? How?

- There is a seaman's credo that says, "Red sky at dawning, sailor take warning." Write about a warning that you didn't listen to.

THE SKY ABOVE: FOOD FOR THOUGHT

- *"Look, up in the sky, it's a bird, it's a plane, it's superman!"*

- *Skycaps*

- *Skyline*

- *The Skyliners,* a doo-wop group that sang, *"Since I Don't Have You"*

- *The sky's the limit*

- *Sky Masterson*

- *Sky blue*

- *Forties song* "Blue skies following me, nothing but blue skies do I see"

- *Skydiving*

- *Sky-high*

- *Skyway*

- *Skyjacker*

- *Sky marshals,* federal plainclothes officers who are assigned to prevent skyjackings

- *Skyscraper*

- *Skyward*

- *Sky King,* an old television show about a law officer who patrolled his territory in an airplane.

- *Lucy in the Sky with Diamonds,* Beatles song rumored to be a thinly disguised promotional for LSD

- *Skylark,* forties song and Buick car model

- *The Sky Above, the Mud Below* film

- *Tanabata,* known as the beautiful Japanese princess of heaven

- *Heaven-sent*

- *Heaven on earth*

- *"There's a better home awaiting, in the sky, lord, in the sky,"* line from gospel song

- *"Swing Low, Sweet Chariot"*: "If you get to heaven before I do . . . tell all my friends I'll be there too, comin' for to carry me home."

- *Fred Astaire singing,* "Heaven, I'm in heaven," in "Cheek to Cheek"

- *Fly now, pay later*!

THE SKY ABOVE: SURRENDERS

- Sometimes we are so busy looking ahead that we forget to look up. Before we know it, we are suffering from sky deprivation. Don't let that happen to you. Take time to see the world from a different angle. Every day the sky watches over you. Why not return the favor? Do some skywatching for at least five minutes each day.

- It's time to play! See how many lyrics, poems, or quotations you can name that contain the word *sky*.

- In Western movies, a classic phrase bandits use is, "Reach for the sky!" During your writing time, try taking a *Sky Break*. Inhale, and as you raise your arms, stretch your body and reach for the sky. Then exhale and let your arms drop. Try and look at the sky while you are taking your *Sky Break*. Do this exercise five times, then go back to your writing. You will feel a heavenly difference.

When You Wish Upon a Star

As children, my sister and I would eagerly scan the sky for the first star. Once we spotted its singular glow, we would chant:

Star light, star bright
First star I see tonight
I wish I may, I wish I might
Have the wish I wish tonight

Then we would put our hands over our hearts, close our eyes tight, and make the most earnest wish imaginable, fully believing in the magic contained in that moment. When we watched television's *Walt Disney Presents,* Jiminy Cricket would end every program with "When You Wish Upon a Star," a song whose lyrics still hold a lot of meaning for me. The song also promised, "Fate steps in and sees you through."

Do you remember any of the wishes you made as a child? I always wished I was rich. One of my favorite cartoon characters was Uncle Scrooge, not because he was cheap, but because he had an entire room filled with money. How I dreamed of having a room like that in my own home.

On one of those rare occasions when I had a decent bank account, I fantasized about withdrawing it all in dollar bills, spreading them out on my bed, then rolling around on the money completely naked. After this orgasmic experience, I would then get dressed, stack the bills together, and take them back to the bank before the interest was lost.

Perhaps I can blame my mixing practicality with fantasy on the stars and planets of my astrological makeup. For thousands of years, people have used the stars and planets to help guide their lives, plan their crops, and foretell the future. In India, an astrological chart is drawn up at a child's birth so the parents can help their child achieve its destiny.

I don't do charts or anything, but over the years I have observed patterns of behavior that I can consistently relate to people of particular signs. As much respect as I have for the science of astrology, I sometimes cannot help but respond to the clichéd getting-to-know-you question "What's your sign?" with either "Wet Paint," "Slow Curves Ahead," or "Slippery When Wet."

I have been told that my astrological blend of planets in Capricorn and Libra—three of each, in fact—gives me great power and influence. If that means it helps me reason with and talk people into things, the astrologers just may be right. When I was an associate field manager for the University of Chicago's social research organization, I was designated a *refusal converter*.

In one nationwide study, for example, we had to interview adolescents between the ages of sixteen and twenty-one once a year for a period of five years. Each person in the study reflected hundreds of lives. Statistically, we were not allowed to just pick someone else if we couldn't interview the person selected by the computer. Imagine, then, what a monkey wrench it threw into the works when the teens refused to participate, would relocate, disappear, or have parents that refused for them. These were the cases they gave to me.

My astrological and other skills were really tested when, in another study, I was assigned to visit the apartment of a woman who had twice refused to participate. I talked to the husband while we stood in the doorway. I saw his wife glaring at me in the background. The smell of alcohol hung in the air like a heavy cloud.

Suddenly I looked over his shoulder and saw his wife coming at me with an eight-inch butcher knife, yelling, "I'll kill that fuckin' bitch, I'll kill her!" He caught her hand in midair and threatened her, saying she had better act right so they could get some rum with the token fee the study paid. Then he asked for the money in advance and left me in the apartment with his sullen wife.

It took us almost four hours to get through an hour-and-a-half interview. I got her to relax. Rum had wiped the beauty from her face. She told me about the child she lost when the hospital she had taken him to sent him home saying nothing was wrong. He died the next day. One evening she and her much older husband were out for a night on the town. As they came back from the movies on Forty-second Street, the cops thought he was a pimp and beat him so badly, he lost an eye and his confidence as a man.

Their second child was taken away by the welfare department when they were both thrown in jail, he for resisting arrest and she for a prostitution charge the police later dropped for lack of evidence. When her husband came back with the rum, she sent him away. "Come back later, baby. We talkin' woman talk!" By the time I left their apartment, she told her husband that I was her best friend. She made me promise that if I ever had a baby, I would let her watch it for me. I wonder what her wishes are tonight.

The Pleiades are a tiny patch of stars often known as the Seven Sisters. The difficulty in seeing more than six of these stars gave rise to the myth of the Lost Pleiade. Among the Nez Perce Indians it is said that the seventh sister was so ashamed of falling in love with a mortal that she hid herself form view.

In classical mythology, the Pleiades were daughters of Atlas. When he was condemned to carry the weight of the world on his back, Jupiter took pity on the grieving daughters and changed them into stars.

According to an Australian aboriginal myth, the sisters were reunited in the sky after two escaped the clutches of a hunter who had abducted them. Aztecs believed that when the sacred and secular calendars coincided and the Pleiades reached their highest point in the sky at midnight, the world would come to an end. Although this happened every fifty-two years, they were usually able to avert disaster with a human sacrifice.

In Africa, the Dahomey believe their people descended from the star Sirius. In China the Milky Way is known as the River in Heaven. The Big Dipper is one of the most easily recognized constellations. It is visible every night of the year. Blackfoot Indians used it like a clock and were able to tell the time of night by marking its position.

To Harriet Tubman and the slaves on the Underground Railroad, the Big Dipper was also known as the Drinking Gourd. She used the bright North Star at the end of the Little Drinking Gourd, or the Little Dipper, to guide slaves to freedom. Frederick Douglass saw the North Star as a symbol of freedom and used it to name his anti-slavery newsletter. African nationalist Marcus Garvey dreamed of freedom from oppression for his people when he named his shipping company the North Star Line.

When Sarah Vaughan sings, "So many stars," I can almost see them. The Three Wise Men saw the Star of Bethlehem and used it to guide them to the baby Jesus.

I once said to a lover as we stepped into my boudoir, "Baby, when we make love, you'll see stars." When we turned out the lights, my entire ceiling became the midnight sky, filled with glued-on glow-in-the-dark constellations, planets and stars that helped me fulfill my promise. Star-crossed lovers are promised an ill-fated destiny, and a star witness can actually seal someone's destiny.

In the Florida of the seventies, mannerly jewel thief Murph the Surf staged a daring heist of a priceless star sapphire and became a folk hero. When someone steals your heart, you become starry-eyed. In Hollywood, either your star is rising or it might be slowly sinking below the horizon, as with fading star Norma Desmond in *Sunset Boulevard*.

In Mexico years ago, our touring group included a star-struck woman who dragged a huge hood hair dryer with her on our small tour bus just so she could do her hair every day and look like Elizabeth Taylor. "Oh," she'd say in great excitement, "I got two Elizabeth Taylors today!" meaning two people had told her she looked like the movie star.

On a Saratoga Springs evening one summer, I lay in an open field on a blanket with Bari, Chiquita, and Beverly, three friends I call my Hoochienas. We watched the August sky, laughing and searching for shooting stars, feeling the warmth, the sisterhood, and the dreams of each other. In the movie *Car Wash,* Rose Royce sang about wishing on a star.

What does it take to make dreams come true? You can also think of wishing on a star as a way of exploring the extent to which a person's or character's dreams are fulfilled. Think about the proverbial gold stars of life, the signs of approval, the acknowledgment of qualities that are outstanding, the reward for a job well done. What happens when these things are ignored? What are the dreams of the unsung heroes, the selfless worker who never takes enough credit and the person fed disapproval on a daily basis?

WHEN YOU WISH UPON A STAR: JOURNEYS

- The lyrics of a song ask, "Would you like to swing on a star?" For some, a star might symbolize the pursuit of something unattainable. Write about when you have witnessed or experienced that pursuit, even if you didn't know it was unattainable when you began.

- Write about a time when fate stepped in and saw you through.

- Two years ago, a well-known star received an Academy Award and called to tell her historically disapproving mother the good news. "Mom, I won an Oscar!" "Yes," her mother relied, "and after everyone else worked so hard." Write about a disapproval that caused you to shine a little less.

WHEN YOU WISH UPON A STAR: FOOD FOR THOUGHT

- *"The fault, dear Brutus, lies not in our stars but in ourselves"*—Shakespeare

- *Star apple*

- *Starfish*

- *Starchild*

- *Stargazer*

- *Star grass*

- *Stardust*

- *Star of David*

- *Stars and Stripes,* flag of the United States

- *Stars and Bars,* the first flag of the Confederate States of America

- *"The Star-Spangled Banner"*

- *Star-Spangled Girl,* movie

- *Star-studded occasion,* an event covered with stars or studs or any combination of the two

- *Shooting Star Review,* African-American literary publication

- *Shining star*

- *Starry, Starry Night,* Don McLean sang

- *Stardom*

- *Star chamber:* fifteenth-century English secret court that was often irresponsibly arbitrary and oppressive; also a movie starring Michael Douglas

- *Ornament or medal worn as a badge of honor, authority, or rank, as in five-star general or a sheriff*

- *Four stars,* highest rating for a movie

- *A star:* highly publicized or outstandingly talented performer, or a person who stands out among his peers

WHEN YOU WISH UPON A STAR: SURRENDERS

- A wish is a dream with wings. Make three wishes: one from your past, one from the present, and a third one from the future. Write each wish down on a separate piece of paper, then fold them very small.

  Take a balloon, place the folded wishes inside, and blow up the balloon. If you can get helium for your balloon, all the better. Take the balloon outside at night, look up at the stars, say your three wishes aloud, and let the wings of the wind take your wishes to their destination.

- Stars are often used to place something on a scale of value, like a four-star restaurant. How many stars would you give to each of the following aspects of your life?

  job
  love life
  finances
  creativity
  home environment
  joy
  things settled for but not satisfied with
  friendships
  family
  other relationships
  daily diet
  spirit feeding
  quality time spent with self
  quality time spent with others

Moon Dance

When I was director of a day-care center, I used to wonder how the children could be rambunctious, irritable, and quarrelsome one day and attentively quiet the next. Ethel was one of my student aides, a middle-aged woman who had returned to school to complete her college education. One day she took me aside and said, "It's the moon."

"What about the moon?" I asked in amazement.

"Whenever you see children acting up like that, check out the moon and see if it's full."

Soon I noticed that the children's behavior was directly related to the moon. I started scheduling more active physical activities around the full-moon days so that their energy could be channeled in a positive, constructive direction. I have been checking the moon ever since.

In fact, I always check my astrological calendar, whether I'm looking for the best times to have events, sales, or a heart-to-heart talk. I know the new moon is a great time to start new projects. If I am planning a party, I look to see when the moon is in Sagittarius or Leo so we can all have a good time.

When I am facing a painstaking job I've been dreading, like tackling mountains of paperwork or cleaning an oven, I'll wait until the moon is in Virgo. If I find myself eating more than usual, I'll know the moon is probably in Cancer.

I once gave a potluck brunch and thought there would be enough food left over to avoid cooking for a week. By the end of the brunch, everything had been eaten except for a box of crackers. The moon was in Cancer.

If I want to raise a touchy subject and avoid a sharp exchange of words, I'll stay away from a moon in Scorpio and wait until it reaches a more humanitarian place in Aquarius. If friends seem to be particularly weepy or moody for no apparent reason, I look to see if the moon is in Pisces and let them know they'll feel better in a day or two.

It was the moon goddess Artemis who placed Orion among the stars after the angry earth goddess Gaia sent a scorpion to kill him. When members of the International Women's Writing Guild started an African-American, Caribbean, and Latina cluster group, we named ourselves Full Moon Sistahs and began meeting on the first full moon of each season.

When Ralph Kramden got frustrated with his wife, he would always threaten, "To the moon, Alice!" Cher and Nicolas Cage hid their own frustrations in the movie *Moonstruck*. Van Morrison sang, "It's a marvelous night for a moondance." Michael Jackson created a movement and called it the Moon Walk.

When I returned to Davisboro, Georgia, as a teenager, I was finally allowed to go to the local juke joint. One naked red bulb hung from the smoky ceiling of the run-down one-room, one-story building. The women hugged the walls in tight polyester dresses with stripes and flowers circling their hips. Men gathered in their best overalls to shuffle across the rough wooden floors to a low-down funky blues beat dripping from a jukebox lit up like a Christmas tree.

The liquor they drank had no label. After each turn of the bottle or tilt of a glass, there was a loud "Ahhnngh," a face that looked as if it had just swallowed acid, and a wipe of the mouth with the back of the hand as the glass was slapped back onto the counter. I asked my cousin what they were drinking that seemed to cause them to make such ugly faces. She answered, "Moonshine."

Around the time of the full moon there are more homicides, suicides, and violent crimes. It is a medical fact that patients bleed more during operations performed when the moon is full. High tides and higher emotionalism usually prevail. Planting and fishing are done by the cycles of the moon. It is said that if you want your hair to grow faster, you cut it around the new moon. If you want to slow down its growth, then cut it after the full moon, when it is in its waning period.

Have you ever heard yourself say, "Easter is early this year"? Most people never stop to ask why Easter takes place in March one year and in April the next. All of the other holidays have predictable dates; why not Easter? You need only look to the moon for an answer. Easter is determined by the arrival of the first full moon after the vernal equinox, or the first day of spring.

The moon is also the determining factor for Passover, Ramadan, the Chinese New Year, and many other sacred celebrations throughout the world.

Knowledge of the moon's importance was frequently suppressed in European cultures. For centuries people had lived and planned their lives in accordance with the cycles of the moon. The Celtic tree calendar assigned a different tree to each of the thirteen moons in a given year, each with its own energy and meaning.

The first moon of the year, the one after the winter solstice, was the *beth* or birch moon, which signified death and knowing, new goals, prosperity, and focus. The *muin* or vine moon was in the sky from the mid-September to mid-October. It was a time of joy, richness, exhilaration, wrath, poetry, and imagination.

The lunar calendar was outlawed in 45 BCE by Julius Caesar. In the fifth century AD the concept of its cyclical process was declared heretical by the Council of Constantinople. The solar calendar we use now completely ignores the lunar cycle that women's bodies have never forgotten.

In most cultures, the moon has traditionally had a special significance for women. The cycles of the moon correspond to the cycles of menstruation in a woman's body. These cycles also reflect a consciousness that operates in harmony with the sacred energy that flows around us. This kind of consciousness tells us to focus on the ideas of acceptance, reflection, and waiting for the right time to take the right action.

The lunar cycle reminds us that our outer realities are reflections of our inner conditions. And at the same time, our inner world is constantly shaping the outer world in which we live, work, eat, and make love. Think about the quote from South African president Nelson Mandela: "As we let our own light shine, we unconsciously give other people permission to do the same. As we are liberated from our fear, our presence automatically liberates others."

Let's take another look at the full moon, the new moon, and other phases of its being. Try gauging the emotional content of a story, film, or someone's life in terms of the moon. Think of a person's desire for fullness, fear of fullness, or attempts to gain that fullness. Think about people not seeing the whole picture or thinking the part they do see *is* the whole picture. In the Japanese movie classic *Rashomon,* the same incident is portrayed four completely different ways based on the testimony of four people who witnessed it.

In many cultures, the moon also represents sexuality and psychic powers, gardens, animals, and insights. In writing, for example, think about the sexual nature of your characters, the insights they inhabit, the animals that people their lives, the gardens that flower or fail, and the psychic abilities that move them into action when, for example, they "just know something is wrong."

When we talk about the dark side of the moon, we are looking at the shadow self, the other side of midnight, the evil twin, Dr. Jekyll and Mr. Hyde, the self that may not have been aware of its power to kill, hate, or destroy.

The Shadow, an old radio mystery program, always began with an announcer saying, "Who knows what evil lurks in the hearts and minds of men? The Shadow does!" When you look at your own shadow, what do you see? When you stop "looking on the brighter side of things," what becomes apparent to you?

Think about the phases of the moon as a metaphor for your life. Is there someone or something standing in your light so that the fullness of your shining cannot be seen? Does it appear as if you are only half full because you are standing in the shadow of your own doubts or fears?

Are you blocking your light so that someone else can shine? Again I quote from Nelson Mandela: "We ask ourselves, 'Who am I to be brilliant, gorgeous, talented, and fabulous?' Actually, who are you not to be? You are a child of God. Your playing small does not serve the world. There is nothing enlightened about shrinking so that other people will not feel insecure around you. We are all meant to shine as children do. We were born to make manifest the glory of God that is within us—it is within everyone."

MOON DANCE: JOURNEYS

- A line from a song goes, "Blue Moon, you saw me standing alone." Write about a time when you were left standing alone, or felt that you were.

- Think about an emotional incident or an event from the past year. What did the dark side look like? What did the light side look like? See what your five-minute freewrite looks like when you shine a different light on your experience.

- I wasn't aware that I was operating with moon consciousness when I recorded an outgoing message on my answering machine that asked the caller to "do the right thing at the right time." Is there a situation in which you are waiting for the right time to take the right action? See what comes up for you around that situation when you bathe it in the glow of your five-minute freewrite.

MOON DANCE: FOOD FOR THOUGHT

- *"Fly me to the moon, and let me sing among the stars."*

- *First man on the moon*

- *Once in a blue moon*

- *Moon glow*

- *The Moonglows,* a doo-wop group

- *"If they can send one man to the moon, why can't they send them all!"*—feminist button

- *Moonie,* follower of the Rev. Sun Myung Moon

- *Mooning*—making an ass of yourself and showing it

- *Man in the moon*

- *Moon shadow*

- *Moonbeam*

- *Moon madness*

- *Lunatics*

- *The Harvest Moon Ball*

- *"Shine On, Harvest Moon"*

- *"By the Light of the Silvery Moon"*

- *"Moon Over Miami"*

- *"Yellow Moon"*

MOON DANCE: SURRENDERS

- Go dance in the moonlight. Pay no attention to whoever may be watching. If they don't pay your rent or your salary, what does it matter what they think?

- Celebrate the things that are full in your life or the things that bring fullness to your life. Make a list of them, beginning each item with "I celebrate the fullness of my . . ." Hold the list in front of you as you stand in your window or outside in the moonlight.

  Put a marble, rubber ball, orange, crystal ball, or other round object in your left hand. Have your favorite celebration beverage in a glass nearby. Read that list aloud. Then smile and drink a toast to the full moon as it reflects on your fullness.

• Take a moon bath. Get a group of people together or take one by yourself. You can do this in the park, in the woods, in the backyard, or in any room where the moon shines in through the window. Bring a battery-operated tape cassette player and a nice soft piece of silk, cotton, or other natural fiber fabric to spread the moon all over your body with.

Select a beautiful, soothing, calming, or softly empowering piece of music to play. As the music plays, feel the moon bathing your body with its light. Move to music of its rays. Use the soft cloth to wash away the shadows from your body and from your life. When you have finished, look up at the moon and howl.

Chase the Clouds Away

There we were, driving through the incredible beauty of Joshua Tree National Monument in California—Hannelore, Eleanor, and me on our way to an International Women's Writing Guild conference in San Diego by way of Desert Palm Springs. We passed a jackrabbit, a coyote skulking behind a sparse shrub, and huge towering rocks, smooth monuments to the wind and sand that had shaped them into Noguchi sculptures.

As we climbed higher and higher along the mountain road, the air became filled with a mist that dampened the windows. Had we run into some fog? I wondered. No, came the explanation, we were up so high that we were passing through a cloud. "Stop the car!" I rolled down the window and took a deep breath. I had never inhaled a cloud before. I wanted to hold on to it and this moment forever.

In Chuck Mangione's "Chase the Clouds Away," Esther Satterfield sings, "You must be the sun . . . only you can chase the clouds away." In the Lambert, Hendricks, and Ross jazz classic

"Cloudburst," they sang about a person who "found my love and that's when the old gray cloud burst." When the Temptations rocked us with "Cloud Nine," they sang about a place where "You can be what you want to be . . . You ain't got no responsibility."

According to Dante's concept of paradise, cloud nine is the ninth and highest heaven. Its inhabitants are most blissful because they are nearest to God. Have you ever felt as if you were on cloud nine?

Whenever I fly, on a plane that is, I always take a window seat and watch the clouds. It is one of the ways in which I get as close to heaven as I can. Sometimes the clouds seem so solid, I feel like stepping out of the plane and walking on them.

When I fly back home from a visit somewhere, I usually end a roll of film by taking photographs of clouds from the window. If the sun happens to be setting, I am absolutely ecstatic. When I see those clouds clothed in a kaleidoscopic radiance that transforms right before my eyes, I feel as if I actually *am* in heaven.

Once as I was talking with my friend Bari on the Skidmore campus lawn, she suddenly interrupted the conversation, pointing to the sky and saying "Look, a *rainbow*!" There had been no rain. The sky was Windex blue and the clouds were in a clear white cumulus formation. Yet, sure enough, there was a brilliant rainbow whose wispy colors danced among clouds tossed by the wind.

We were spellbound by its magic as it changed shape, flew across the sky, then disappeared just as quickly as it had arrived. I have never seen anything like it before or since. Perhaps what we saw that day was a *cloudbow,* and this was heaven's way of letting us know that it was watching too.

Whenever I hear the gospel song "Will the Circle Be Unbroken," I think of my mother. As the singer stands by the window "on a cold and cloudy day," he sees the "hearse come rollin', come to carry my mother 'way." It takes me back to the dark cloud I was under when I went back to the projects I had grown up in. I had returned this time to clear out the belongings of my mother, who had been found dead in a pool of blood on the kitchen floor.

My grandmother's patchwork quilt had been thrown over the spot in front of the stove where the body lay for three days before it was found. My cousin and I worked for a week going through dresser drawers, closets, and trunks trying to put thirty years of her life into cardboard boxes. The police said the cause of death was a heart attack, but they couldn't explain the blood. My grandmother asked God to show her how her oldest daughter had died. That night she had a dream my mother had been murdered.

Think of clouds as the obscured truth, the unclear meaning, the idea that "there's more to this than meets the eye." Think of clouds as the link between confusion and clarity, being and nothingness, as ominous endeavors or solid intangibles. Clouds are also a reflection of the mysterious, the "now you see it now you don't" and "I can't quite put my finger on it" aspects of life.

Look closely at what you are creating and what you are living. What kind of clouds do you find when you examine your emotional and psychological skies? Are they clear or overcast? Is it about to rain? Check your inner weather, then see what the forecast is for the next five days, five years, or five lifetimes.

CHASE THE CLOUDS AWAY: JOURNEYS

- "I watched her face cloud up"
  "I get misty and too much in love."
  "My head was in the clouds."
  Choose one, two, or all three of these for your five-minute freewrite.

- Pick an incident from the past year of your life that was characterized by confusion or a lack of clarity. Write about what clouded the issue and how it became clear again, if it ever did.

- "He worked under a cloud of secrecy." Close your eyes and

think about what this person was hiding, why he was hiding it, and what he might do if he were found out.

CHASE THE CLOUDS AWAY: FOOD FOR THOUGHT

- *Cloud formations*—cirrus, cumulus, stratus
- *"With a cloud of dust and a hearty hi-ho, Silver, it's the Lone Ranger!"*
- *"As Clouds Roll By,"* song
- *White Cloud*
- *A cloud of mosquitoes*
- *Clouds of another war loomed over the horizon*
- *Its meaning was cloudy*
- *There was not a cloud in the sky*
- *These shoes made me feel like I'm walking on a cloud*
- *I don't want to cloud the situation*
- *Pigpen,* the *Peanuts* character with a dust cloud constantly around him
- *Fog, mist, haze*
- *"A Foggy Day in London Town"*

CHASE THE CLOUDS AWAY: SURRENDER

- Use the new moon energy to chase the clouds away. Make a list of five things in your life that you would like to have moved from cloudy to clarity. First read the list to the clouds, then read it to the new moon. Do this for three days and nights, then put it under your pillow.

- What kind of things make you feel as if you were walking on a cloud? Make sure you do one of them this week.

- Take time do some cloud watching, and see how many people, animals or other objects you can find in the formations. So far Elvis and Mother Teresa have been spotted. Who would you like to find up there?

Earth Angel

I was scrambling for my footing as I scaled the grey boulders and sharp black stones beside the river in the tiny fishing village of Bardur, Iceland. Hundreds of gray and white puffins dotted every plane of a huge rock jutting from the water in front of me. The cerulean sky was untouched by clouds. A sod house nearby seemed to grow right out of the earth.

For days we had toured the countryside, sleeping in schools that let their children vacation in the scant months of Icelandic sun. With fourteen women writers in a minivan, we traveled across the strangest terrain I have ever witnessed. This was a land devoid of trees, plants, or bushes. Orange, brown, green, and white moss and lichen coated the ground like a close haircut. Rocks and more rocks covered almost every inch of the land.

We never passed another car during the entire time we spent on the road. Yet it took less than a day to become enchanted by the beauty in this strangeness, the spirits in the rocks, and the magic in the earth.

The others were walking somewhere along the shore or visiting the rustic concession stand. I felt drawn to this hill of massive rocks off the beaten path, so I strayed from the group and headed towards them. As I began to climb, I looked around and there was our guide, Sunneva, a psychic and Icelandic native, and her colleague Helka right behind me. They exchanged a knowing look. Then one said, "Go ahead, the spirits sent you to the right place."

We climbed to the top and sat there in silence, bathed by the breeze, the warm sun, and the sacredness of the space we all shared. Suddenly my ear cuff jumped off my ear, tumbled down the rocky crags, and disappeared into a deep crevice. Again they looked at each other and smiled. "The Owner of The Earth wanted your earring," Sunneva told me. "Now you get to ask a question and make a wish."

We visited with many of the earth connections in the "Sowing the Sacred Soil" section of Chapter 4. Let's explore some more of these connections and also take a look at things that fall to the earth. In the movies, aliens who land on this planet stereotypically introduce themselves by saying, "Greetings, earthlings." On New York City subways there is always an assortment of people who panhandle, sell knickknacks, solicit funds, and entertain.

One of the more interesting characters I've seen was a musician who dressed in a Mylar spacesuit, cape, and silver helmet with two antennae. He would hop onto the subway car, start playing a loud, wildly annoying, high-pitched saxophone riff with no apparent tune or rhythm, then announce, "Greetings, earthlings. I am in need of earthly funds to repair my spaceship. If I do not receive these funds immediately, I will continue to play!"

Lou Rawls sings, "Down Here on the Ground." An adolescent who misbehaves and a pilot who is incompetent or insubordinate both receive the same punishment—they are grounded. When hostages or natives are returned to their lands after a long absence, or when a plane lands after being in imminent danger of crashing, you might hear them say, "I kissed the ground!" When we say, "He kisses the ground she walks on," are we paying a compliment, making a complaint, or hiding contempt?

I was very excited when a new romantic prospect whose phone had not yet been installed called me the day after we met. As I remembered how powerful our initial attraction was, I thought to ask where the call was coming from. I was amused and flattered by the reply: "I'm lying on the floor in my neighbor's apartment. After meeting you, I could hardly sleep. I just needed to get grounded!"

I'm convinced that 90 percent of the health food stores in this country have green awnings and the word *land* or *earth* in their names. When I'm writing a check to pay for my organic goodies, I am constantly confusing Park Slope's Back to the Land with Soho's Down to Earth. Or is it the other way around?

In their book *Earth Prayers,* Elizabeth Roberts and Elias Amidon state, "Today the ability of the Earth to support life is being deeply eroded. . . . Within the animal and plant kingdoms we are witnessing the greatest holocaust in history. . . . Every aspect of life on the planet is profoundly altered by the way our culture has organized the business of its existence."

When you listen to "Home on the Range," you realize you can still locate deer, but you might have to go to San Francisco's Golden Gate Park to find where the buffalo roam.

When you hear the words of Woody Guthrie's "This land is your land, this land is my land," think about them for a minute. What were they singing when the American army invaded the tiny island of Grenada or when they killed dozens of Panamanian people and destroyed homes and property just to capture General Noriega?

What does that song mean to disfranchised Hawaiian nationals whose land was seized by a consortium of American business interests when U.S. Marine troops forced reigning Queen Liliuokalani from her throne? From her prison cell, she wrote her own song, a beautiful tune we have all come to identify with the islands of Hawaii, "Aloha Oe."

The folk song also echoes a sentiment reflected in populations throughout the world. Its words are in the hearts of Arabs and Israelis, Greeks and Turks, and Tibetans whose culture, religion, and identity are systematically being erased by Chinese forces occupying their land.

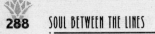

David Bowie starred in the movie *The Man Who Fell to Earth*. Baby Superman was catapulted through space and fell to earth in a farmer's field. *The Brother from Another Planet,* Arnold Schwarzenegger in *The Terminator,* the pods in *Invasion of the Body Snatchers,* and any number of science fiction characters all arrived in much the same way.

Rain, snow, fog, and hot and cold weather also fall on the earth. How many scenes have you read or witnessed in which rain featured prominently? Joan Crawford plays a woman of easy virtue in the vintage movie *Rain.* Tea Cake and Janie get swept away when a rainstorm causes a disastrous flood in Zora Neale Hurston's classic novel *Their Eyes Were Watching God.*

Let's look at two forms of weather and make some creative connections. Think of all the ways that cold, for example, can be used to express the nuances of emotion: "He was very cold to her" indicates emotional distance, a "cold fury" signifies intense anger, and "in cold blood" tells of premeditation. "Out in the cold" conveys deprivation, while "he was turned away cold" represents utter finality.

Cold-blooded characters add excitement to your monologues, films, musicals, and novels—to everything, in fact, except your personal life. A conniving bitch or a son of a bitch with ice water in his veins can heat up any drama—witness Alexis Carrington, J.R., Erica, or Bette Davis in half her films. How do you or your characters warm up the situation when either of you encounters a chilly reception or an icy stare, hears the cold facts or gets cold feet?

At the other end of the thermometer, you can use hot weather to make your creative connections. That kind of weather can take you from the anger of a hot temper to a rapidly selling hot item, from the sexual proficiency of "hot in bed" to old blues singers who are known as the last of the red hot mamas. In a dangerous neighborhood that is a hotbed of crime, you will often find the raging conflict of a hot battle. When children play Treasure Hunt, the closer you got to that hidden object, the more excitedly they say, "You're getting hotter." I imagine that same thing can be said to someone engaged in foreplay, a menopausal woman, or Joan of Arc. Have you ever been hot and bothered or tired and hot, or been involved in a hot scandal? What is the emotional climate where you live or work?

Give some thought to other weather conditions and the various forms of precipitation that fall on, flow on, or hover over the earth around you. After a downpour, do you think about the song "I can see clearly now, the rain has gone"? Have you ever tried saving for a rainy day, or been the victim of a snow job?

Storms can suggest arguments or powerful emotions, while *thunder* signifies something full of sound and fury, and *lightning* flashes us with sudden realizations. *Fog* can stand for bewilderment—"I haven't the foggiest"—or illusion—"I don't know, I just don't know." *Floods* indicate too much of a good thing, and *hurricanes* tell us "it blew me away" or "I was swept off my feet."

After I nearly drowned in the Atlantic Ocean, I fell to my knees when the water brought me back to dry land again. In Mexico City, devout Catholics may show their devotion by walking to the National Cathedral on their knees, carrying flowers for the Virgin Mary.

I was in midtown Manhattan one day, running myself ragged as usual, when I decided to go to St. Patrick's Cathedral to sit for a while and breathe in some spirit. There was a mass going on, so I sat with the rest of the parishioners. Just as I had settled into my seat and started to relax, everyone stood up. So I stood up. After that part of the service was over, everyone kneeled down. So I kneeled down. Within a few minutes everyone was sitting again, so I followed suit. Then we stood, and then we kneeled again.

I was raised in an Episcopalian church, so I was used to Anglican aerobics. But I had forgotten about the Catholic practices. For the rest of the service I stayed on my knees with my head bowed and my hands devoutly clasped in prayer just so I could get some rest.

In King Arthur's court a noble warrior kneels to be knighted. In a vivid scene from the movie *The Nun's Story*, supplicants in white robes lay facedown on the ground in total humility. In African religious practices, followers kneel to salute their spirits, priests, and elders.

When there is a national strike, political catastrophe, or economic disaster, we say that it "brought the country to its knees." If something can affect a whole country in that way, imagine how personal tragedy can devastate an individual. When did something in your life bring you to your knees? How were you able to stand on solid ground again?

As you think about what you are going to create next, give some thought to people you know or may have read about who have been brought to their knees. People who have been humbled either through their own doing or because of circumstances that caused their undoing.

Think about hotel queen Leona Helmsley, evangelist Jim Bakker, and former president Richard Nixon and the actions they took to cause their own unraveling. How would you rewrite their lives?

Former Miss America and New York City commissioner Bess Myerson got caught in the shadows of boyfriend Andy Capasso's illegal doings. Geraldine Ferraro's bid for office was damaged by the shady operations of her husband. Think about people who got caught in the wrong place at the wrong time or with the wrong people. No matter what happens in your life, on your page, or on the stage, always ask this question: What are the lessons and what are the blessings?

EARTH ANGEL: JOURNEYS

- "There is no earthly reason for this behavior!" Have you ever said or thought these words, or had them said to you? Write about that behavior and the environment around it.

- When situations are uncertain, or you feel you have no one backing you up, you might say that you are "standing on shaky ground." I remember a rhythm and blues song whose next line was "ever since you put me down." Aside from an earthquake, describe a shaky situation, or one that shook the ground under your feet.

- Dr. John the Night Tripper sings the lyrics "I was in the right place, but it must have been the wrong time." Write about a time when you those words were true for you.

- James Brown sings, "I break out in a cold sweat." When have you shared that reaction with Jimmy?

EARTH ANGEL: FOOD FOR THOUGHT

- *As above, so below*

- *Earth Mother*

- *Roots*

- *Ancestors*

- *Earthy*

- *I felt like someone pulled the ground out from under me*

- *Back to the land*

- *Landfill*

- *Landslide*

- *Coming in for a landing*

- *Things that fall to the earth*: a shooting star, hail, meteor, wounded bodies

- *"Catch a falling star and put it in your pocket, save it for a rainy day"*

- *"I can see clearly now, the rain has gone"*
- *"Listen to the falling rain, listen to it pour"*
- *"Raindrops keep falling on my head"*
- *"So many raindrops falling from my eyes"*
- *"Baby, It's Cold Outside"*
- *"Who'll Stop the Rain"*
- *"I Can't Stand the Rain"*
- *"My blood ran cold"*
- *A cold act of aggression*
- *Knocked out cold*
- *The actors had their lines cold a week before opening night*
- *A cold trail*
- *Cold news*
- *Cold-blooded*
- *Cold cash*
- *Cold comfort*
- *Cold cream*
- *Cold cuts*
- *Cold duck*
- *Cold fish*
- *Cold front*
- *Coldhearted*
- *Cold shoulder*

- *A cold call*

- *Cold sore*

- *Cold storage*

- *Cold turkey*

- *Cold war*

- *Cold-water flat*

- *Hot off the press*

- *Hot colors*

- *Hot-wired*

- *Hothead*

- *Hot line*

- *Hot plate*

- *Hot potato*

- *Hot seat*

- *Hot shot*

- *Hot water*

- *Hot air*

- *Global warming,* the greenhouse effect

- *Effects of too much heat and not enough water*—drought and famine, dehydration

- *Heat prostration*

- *Prickly heat*

See "Sowing Sacred Soil" in Chapter 4 for more earth food.

EARTH ANGEL: SURRENDERS

- "This land is your land, this land is my land." Go back and pay a visit to the land where you were born. Visit the country, city, neighborhood, street, block, hospital, or house where you first entered the earth. When you do, just stand there and take in all that you can see and feel, smell, touch, and taste.

   If this is difficult, impossible, or inconvenient, use old photographs or talk to someone who knew you then or grew up with you, or someone who knew the neighborhood. Ask him or her what it was like and visit with the images.

- "I'm on my knees" can be a plea for help, "I fell down on my knees" can be a child's lament, and "I got down on my knees" can be a prayer of thankfulness. Get a piece of paper and place it horizontally so you can make three lists side by side. Above the first list write *Help*; the second, *Regrets*; and the third, *Thanks*. Starting with the first list, write down five things you need help with; next, five things you regret; and finally five things you are thankful for.

- Bring a rose and some spring water to a quiet place outdoors. Think about people you know that have gone home to Mother Earth. If there is something you would like to say to one or to a few, speak your words into the water. Call out the names of those you wish to remember. Drop rose petals on the ground to sweeten their day. Now pour water onto the earth to connect you with the flow of life from them to you and beyond. Know that they have been blessed.

By the Rivers of Babylon

It was a New York summer—hot and humid, thick with the hum of air conditioners, music played through open windows,

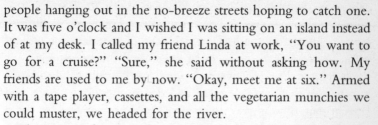

people hanging out in the no-breeze streets hoping to catch one. It was five o'clock and I wished I was sitting on an island instead of at my desk. I called my friend Linda at work, "You want to go for a cruise?" "Sure," she said without asking how. My friends are used to me by now. "Okay, meet me at six." Armed with a tape player, cassettes, and all the vegetarian munchies we could muster, we headed for the river.

The twenty-five cent fare bought us a priceless breeze and a full moon on the Staten Island ferry. Aaron Neville serenaded the air with my theme song: "Earth angel, earth angel, will you be mine." As we sat there in our yellow and green clothing, we thought about beloved Oshun, African goddess of the river, queen of dance and music.

We got up and began to twirl around the deck, dancing in the moonlight, savoring the air made sweeter by music and magic and the sounds of the river. Soon other passengers began to dance as well. One man liked the music so much, he came over and gave us a five-dollar bill. Ten minutes later he came back. "You won't believe this! I was just sitting there and a five-dollar bill dropped into my lap! Can you believe it?" Oshun's number is five, and we were on her turf. We looked at each other and smiled. Of course we believed him. After all, this was New York.

I grew up right across the street from the East River. From the eighth floor of my window in the Smith Projects, I could see the Brooklyn Bridge, FDR Drive, the Brooklyn shoreline, and in the distance, the Statue of Liberty. For hours I would sit in my window and watch the parade of tugboats, passenger ships, Circle Line boats, and freighters go by.

In the evening, the lights made a diamond necklace of the bridge and the sunsets painted the sky with more colors than my imagination. Sometimes we'd go for walks along the water's edge, past the old Domino Sugar factory, where they'd give us free samples, past the Fulton Fish Market, on up to the Staten Island ferry terminal.

In those days, blue laws forbid stores and businesses from operating on Sundays. So on that day the entire Wall Street area, with its narrow streets and towering office buildings, would become a ghost town. Blocks and blocks of abandoned buildings were sandwiched between our projects and their prosperity.

Under the bridge's overpass were huge, vaulted, abandoned warehouses that were deserted and dangerous. If my sisters and I went out of our way to get to the Tribune Theater for a double feature and ten cartoons, we could pass through these streets forbidden to us by our mother. Scared to death, loving the echo of our footsteps and our fears, we traveled the route we called the Spooky Way and swore we'd never tell.

After Tina Turner went "Rollin' on the river," Marvin Gaye and Tammi Terrell gave us, "Ain't no mountain high enough, ain't no river wide enough," and Bob Marley sang, "By the rivers of Babylon." The world was enchanted by "Moon River" and Audrey Hepburn in *Breakfast at Tiffany's.*

Composer Stephen Foster changed the American Indian name Suwanee for the convenience of writing "Way down upon the Swanee River." A person sentenced to prison is sent up the river.

In one definition of the word *ocean*, it is called a river that encircles the earth. Think of your bloodstream as a river encircles your body—a river that overflows its banks in time of injury or menstruation.

The entire chain of Hawaiian islands was formed when rivers of lava spilled over the banks of its volcanoes and solidified into a lush, tropical paradise, one of the most beautiful places I have ever seen. Waterfalls spill from fertile mountains and cascade three hundred feet into valleys resplendent with fragrant plumeria and pikake, anthurium and orchid.

My friend Clover and I paid homage to Hawaiian deities Pele and Halema'uma'u by drumming and chanting atop the blackened crests of Kilauea, the massive volcano whose continuous eruptions cover six thousand square miles of land. We drove to the end of the Kalapana Trail.

Four years earlier, an eruption had buried part of the road and most of Kalapana, leaving cars, appliances, and bits of houses sticking out of the solidified lava.

As I stood there on the sands of Pali Uli, I had one of the greatest thrills of my life. As night fell, I watch the molten blood of Hawaii flow down the slopes of Kilauea, past the crimson sky, and into the sea.

What happens when a person blows his or her top and over-flows? Do you cool him off with water or let her drown in it? If someone's anger has been smoldering for years, what would it take to make them erupt? What do they do to dam their own waters? The work you create, does it bleed words, tears, blood, or fears? Does it dance on the river, or does it sit in the window and watch it? In my novel *Tamarindo,* the river flows through an erotic love scene between an elderly couple.

The river's current drew his finger inside her. Again and again it dove beneath the waters, swimming to the surface with muscular strokes, only to plunge deeper into the abyss. Miss Cicero arched her back and let a slow moan fly toward the ceiling.

A tremor ran through her body and dropped into the stock-ings rolled beneath her knees. She leaned forward to rip open his buttons. His steel passion molded itself to the curve of her hand. She pulled its column to her navel, then pushed it back to its roots.

Mr. Thackeray's groans caught the rhythm of her fingers. He felt for the smell of her breast and drew it into his mouth. With tongue and his heart wrapped around her nipple, he sucked fifty years of guilt for having loved his best friend's wife.

"Oh yes! Oh Jesus, yes!" She dug into the curve of his back.

The dam began to weaken. Pieces of the river spilled over its edge and trickled down Mr. Thackeray's arm. It mingled with perspiration and yearning seeping from his pores and took him to the place of his dreams.

Laughter and screams danced at the back of her throat. The reins slipped thorough her hands. She felt her walls being sucked through her skin. They breathed each other into their lungs. He let her breasts fall behind his neck as he lay his cheek on her stomach, tightened the circle around her hips, and pressed into her with a new fever.

"Let it rain, sweet darlin. Please, let it rain!"

Laughter and screams leapt to the front of her mouth, and fell into the river, breaking free. The torrent raged through the cracked dam, pulling chunks of concrete, loneliness, and fear of death in its path. Her knees softened. Her bones cried for release. The river rained afterbirth, sweet wine, and butter-milk down her leg.

In the United States, and in other countries with African an-cestral populations, an Ifa, or African spiritual reading, is tradi-tionally held at the beginning of every year. A few years ago it was divined that female deities Yemaya and Oshun were coming to claim their lands and that floods would predominate. The ocean is Yemaya's domain, while Oshun rules river and fresh water.

That year floods ate up the Florida coastline during one of the worst hurricanes ever recorded. They tore away beaches and houses at Coney Island, Fire Island, and other northeastern areas. An incalculable amount of devastation was caused by flooding in several midwestern states. Small streams swelled into huge, unrecog-nizable rivers. The water rose so quickly that people became trapped on the upper floors of their houses in a matter of minutes.

I spoke to one woman who had volunteered to help with the rescue efforts. As their boat passed a large round dome sticking five feet out of the water, she asked what it was. Someone an-swered, "That's the top of a silo."

Many had already seen the ocean toss boats around and beat her angry fists against the shore. But no one was prepared for the fury with which calm streams and peaceful rivers suddenly raged across the land, consuming everything in their paths. "Don't push the river" is one of my favorite sayings.

Water is a symbol of feminine energy, the life force, the flow of eternity. Think about the river as a female entity, pushed around, dumped into, dammed up, held back and willfully diverted, told where to and where not to flow. Think of the river as an abused woman finally standing up, getting ahold of her power and fighting back.

What kind of connections have you had with rivers? Did you ever fish, swim in, boat on, clean out, dam up, drink from, or wash in one? Think of the river as a symbol of the water of life flowing in and around you. When you think about your life, is it a smooth lake, a stagnant lagoon, or a stream running swiftly to its destination? Do you have molten memories of being in the flow of things? What makes your creative juices flow? What causes them to stop flowing? Is your spirit taking a birdbath, drowning in truth, or floating with fierceness? Are you?

BY THE RIVERS OF BABYLON: JOURNEYS

- "The river is deep and the river is wide, milk and honey on the other side. Keep your eye on the prize, oh Lord." These are words to an old gospel song. What kind of prize have you had your eye on? What river did you have to cross in order to get it? When were you promised that there would be "milk and honey on the other side"? What did you find when you got there?

- "I feel like I'm going under." Write about a time when you felt like this?

- In the late eighteenth century, riverboat gamblers plied their trade as they floated down the Mississippi River. If you had the nerve, the time, or the money, what would you like to take a gamble on?

BY THE RIVERS OF BABYLON: FOOD FOR THOUGHT

- Miss Webster says: *river*—"a natural stream of water of usually considerable volume"

- *River god*—a diety believed to rule a river as its principal divinity

- *Riverboat queen*

- *"They dragged the river"*

- *Riverside Drive*—a place of being, state of mind, John Coltrane composition

- *River*—overwhelming quantities, as in "I drank rivers of coffee"

- *"Up a lazy river by the old mill run"*

- *Riverbed*

- *River horse,* or hippopotamus

- *"I'm gonna lay down my burden, down by the riverside"*

- *"The shipwreck sent its passengers to a watery grave"*

- *"He held me underwater"*

- *"I feel like I'm drowning"*

- *"Drowning in a sea of love"*

- *"Her water broke!"*

- *"Boil some water!"*—classic movie line when a woman is about to give birth

- *"I have reached my boiling point"*

- *"Her eyes were watery"*

- *Still water runs deep*

- *To water down*—reduce effectiveness

- *Waterspout*—"the itsy bitsy spider went up the . . ."

- *Watertight alibi*

- *Water Wagon,* an alcoholic's downfall if she/he tumbles off.

- *Things that swim in or float on or live under water:*
    a rubber duck
    Sophia Loren in *Houseboat*
    Tom Sawyer on a raft
    Ivory Soap
    The Creature from the Black Lagoon
    dead bodies
    boats
    sea life
    wreckage of an airplane crash
    toxic waste
    the San Andreas Fault
    the Bermuda Triangle
    bones of slaves from the Middle Passage

There is a lot more water and plenty to "sea" in the "Water of Life" section of Chapter 4.

BY THE RIVERS OF BABYLON: SURRENDERS

- Give a gift to the river, and show her your appreciation for providing you with food, transportation, and water, the sustenance of life. Bring her some flowers and drop them in one by one, saying "Thank you" each time the petals touch the water.

- Take a *River Rest*. Pick out a piece of music that sounds like water or rivers, or makes you think of those things. With your hands, take some fresh water, wipe it all over your face, and leave it there to dry. Lie down on something soft and comfortable with your face pointed to the ceiling or to the sky. Now put the music on, close your eyes, and rest there. Float on.

20,000 Leagues Under the Sea

There I was at two o'clock in the morning, heading to the bombed-out, desolate Bushwick section of Brooklyn, dressed in white and carrying a coconut. My husband thought I was either crazy or having an affair. I was neither. I was on my way to be initiated.

A week earlier I had met a guru, Swami Shivom Tirth, a Siddha yoga master who traveled back to the States with my friend Cliff. "Talk to him. Ask him if he'll initiate you." I didn't know guru from hoodoo. What was I supposed to say to a bearded man who sat cross-legged on a rug wearing an orange sheet? "Hi," I said, and not too much else. In less than five minutes I was out of there.

Something had happened. As soon as I came near this man, I felt like crying. There was no rhyme or reason to it. Just this strange ball of tears that rolled around in the pit of my stomach.

I was shocked to learn I was one of the few people he had chosen to initiate. I used to overhear bearded brothers in knit kufis as I volunteered to wait tables at Aquarius House, an African-American spiritual center in Harlem. Those esoteric conversations went way over my head. And I couldn't relate to all the Hindu terminology in the book Cliff gave me to read.

Why was I doing this, anyway? My apprehension deepened as initiation day got closer. I was afraid my life would never be the same again. I didn't know how true that was.

About twenty of us assembled in a large room at Khalil and Susan Sayyed's Piling Street brownstone. People had come from as far away as Texas and California for the ceremony. An altar with fruit and flowers, incense and candles was set up in front of the room. The guru taught us a chant and talked about kunda-lini yoga. "Allow yourself to let go."

At precisely four in the morning, the lights were turned out and we began to meditate. The guru's body shook from side to side. Within fifteen minutes, a tall hairy man began to growl like a bear, and the woman in back of me made operatic noises. One guy did cartwheels in the next room. Somewhere in the dark a woman laughed aloud, while others just shook or sat still. Now I was *sure* this was all a mistake. I had to get away from these crazy people before I went nuts.

Then from somewhere deep in the bowels of my soul, there came a whisper that turned to a shout that grew into a storm. I felt that ball inside my stomach again. It was growing larger, pushing against my insides, against every organ it could find. It moved up through my chest and into my throat.

The candlelight danced to the strange sounds. I stopped thinking about what was happening around me and began to worry about what was going on inside me.

"Let go," I told myself. "Let go!" Suddenly that ball broke open like a water balloon on a concrete street. Tears ran up to my eyes, nose, and mouth, eager for escape they had plotted for years. A monsoon rolled out of my heart and down my face. I found myself pounding the floor. The guru placed his hand on top of my head. My body trembled. Orange and violet circles appeared when I closed my eyes. A streak of lightning moved up my spine. I couldn't stop crying.

When we stopped exactly at six, dawn was peeking in the window, wondering. I was lying down on one of the blankets. Gradually people got up and went downstairs to eat. I was one of the last ones in the room. When I tried to stand up, my legs felt like water. I fell back onto the blanket. I was totally intoxicated and couldn't walk for another twenty minutes. After three mornings of these ceremonies, the initiation was complete.

The sounds I heard, the movements I witnessed, the tears I cried, these were all called *kriyas*. They were signs that the kundalini, or divine power, had been awakened. It is written that the kundalini acts as "a spiritual guide who directs, controls, governs, and leads the aspirants on a spiritual path like a living, conscious, divine help-mate." That was twenty-five years ago, and my life has never been the same.

The divine spirit that still guides my life is at the same inner core your spirit spins upon. It is the stuff your Heartland is made of. It is the hub of the wheel your story revolves around. A core is defined as the central part of the earth or the essential, enduring part of an individual, class or entity.

This is the part Barry White talks about when he sings, "I want to know all the deepest secrets in your garden." To singer Tina Marie it is "behind the groove, there's another side inside of me." Diana Ross has "this burning burning, yearning feeling inside me, ooh deep inside me." This is the part you refer to when you say, "In my heart of hearts."

A core group is the most enduring part of an organization. If a person is rotten to the core, they are totally beyond redemption. If you are discussing core issues, you are getting to the heart of the matter. The word *inner* refers to something relating to the mind or spirit. If you are thinking about inner dialogue, you may ask, "What is the character saying to herself?" or "What's on his mind?" When there is an inner conflict, you want to see how it manifests itself on the outside.

A person who is inner directed may ignore external norms and his or her own scale of values to direct their thoughts and actions. In Quaker doctrine, *inner light* is a divine presence that is said to enlighten and guide the soul. What divine presence guides your soul?

An African spirit known as Olokun is called the Keeper of Secrets. He is associated with the unknowable, the unreachable, the skeletons in the closet. He dwells at the bottom of the ocean amidst the untold riches of shipwrecks and precious ores and metals that have yet to be discovered. Scientists have learned that at the bottom of the ocean no erosion occurs. Fully preserved artifacts have been found there.

During the Middle Passage, when slaves jumped, or were pushed overboard, it was Olokun's arms they fell into. Eleven million descendents of those slaves do not know what their real family names are, what tribes they come from, whether they were commoner or king, or which African country their ancestors are buried in. Those secrets lie with Olokun, and he has no voice.

Olokun is the deity of psychology, ruler of the unnamed unknown. Take a good look at the psychological dimensions of what you are painting, writing, composing, filming, and living. What are the fears and phobias of the friends, relatives, strangers, characters, and objects that people your work? How are they manifested? How are they hidden? Who knows about them? Who is threatening to reveal them?

Lady Macbeth's constant handwashing spoke volumes about her inner conflicts. In the court-martial scene of the movie *The Caine Mutiny,* when Captain Queeg rolled those steel balls in his hand, it told more about him than his testimony did. In *The Bad Seed,* little Rhoda's too-perfect looks and behavior made her crimes seem that much more heinous. What psychological fingerprints did your childhood leave on your life? What telltale spots are you trying to wipe away? What do you do that reveals who you are?

In Jules Verne's *20,000 Leagues Under the Sea* and again in *Journey to the Center of the Earth,* he took us to the inner core of two different worlds. If we took a journey to the center of your soul, what would we find there? What are the places inside your spirit that have no voice? What secrets are buried in your family closets, crypts, and condominiums? What treasures lay undiscovered at the bottom of your world? And when was the last time you gave yourself over to something, knowing that you might never be the same?

20,000 LEAGUES UNDER THE SEA: JOURNEYS

• In a Marx Brothers movie, one of the characters responds to a question by condescendingly saying, "It is beyond me and beneath me!" Write about something you have encountered that fits that description.

- Unconscious motivations are at home in the inner core. Pick one or both of these sentences for your usual five-minute freewrite.

    "I don't know why I did that"
    "He went crazy! He just went crazy"

- Start with the phrase "In my heart of hearts," then close your eyes for a moment and inhale deeply. When you open them again, write what comes to you.

20,000 LEAGUES UNDER THE SEA: FOOD FOR THOUGHT

- *Apple core*

- *Inner voice*

- *Inner city*

- *Inner City Mother Goose,* book by Eve Merriam

- *Fantastic Voyage,* movie in which people are reduced to micro- scopic proportions in order to travel inside a person's body

- *Meditation,* inner travel inside your own body

- *Inner sanctum*

- *The inner circle*

- *Your innermost thoughts*

- *Inner space,* space at or near the earth's surface and especially the bottom of the sea

- *"Let's get to the bottom of this"*

- *Underwater origin of volcanoes and earthquakes*

- *Bermuda Triangle*

- *Inner sole*

- *Inner tube*

- *Inner ear*

- *Inner bark*

- *"I'm in with the in crowd,"* song

- *Psychic power*

- *Instinct and sixth sense*

- *"I had a funny feeling"*

- *"I kept feeling you all day"*

- *"I could feel it in my bones"*

- *"I knew I'd run into you"*

20,000 LEAGUES UNDER THE SEA: SURRENDERS

- Describe your inner core in five words.

- Take five minutes at the end of the day and devote them to your innermost thoughts. Sit with them, write them down, acknowledge them, and distinguish them from your everyday thoughts and worries.

- Make a list, beginning each sentence with "I am afraid of." Take a look at your fears and think about how they manifest themselves in your life.

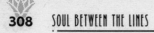

Will the Circle Be Unbroken

It was four days before Christmas, and the Cultural Crossroads potluck dinner had filled me with more than just visions of sugarplums. I did not let being full stop me from having another piece of apple pie. There's nothing that makes me overeat more than seeing a table loaded with food that I didn't have to cook. Besides, I was eating for two—I had a bird at home.

Janice Russell and Mike Weatherly's Fort Greene brownstone was warm with their spirit and the laughter of Lafayette Avenue Presbyterian Church members who gathered there. We had eaten as much food as we could, and wrapped the rest up in aluminum foil to take with us. We all sang Christmas songs as Mike played the guitar. Janice and Oliver Williams, the choir director, sang a duet that went straight to our hearts.

This is the way I always thought the holiday season should be—good friends and good food, good people gathering together to have a good time. We knew it was getting late, but no one made a definitive move toward the door. That is, until Oliver uttered the classic line "You ain't got to go home, but you got to get up from outta here!"

So, children of the universe, you have been on yet another long journey. This one has taken you from the sky to the stars and the moon, from the clouds to the earth and the river, and finally to the depths of the inner core. Now it's time to go home. What does that mean? We can't ask Lassie or Bill Bailey, so we'll go to Miss Webster. She says that home is "a congenial environment; a familiar or usual setting; the focus of one's domestic attentions.

Think about which place you might like to call home. Will you have blue skies following you, sing among the stars, or eat green cheese from the moon? Will you have your head up in the clouds and your feet on the ground? Will you go rollin' on the river or diving in the depths? Which one do you think is your place of origin? In which place would you find the most congenial environment?

One of my all-time favorite movies is *Harold and Maude*. In it, Maude says, "The earth is my body. My head is in the stars." In *The Wiz*, Diana Ross begins a beautiful song with, "When I think of home I think of a place." How would you complete that thought?

Thomas Wolfe says you can never go home, baseball asks you to "root, root, root for the home team," and J. California Cooper serves up some *Homemade Love* in her wonderful book.

You can come down the home stretch, slide into home plate, and hang with your home boys. So I'll ask you again, of the sky, stars, moon, clouds, earth, river, and inner core, where's home for you? Close your eyes and try to see the place in your mind. Then click your heels three times, and say to yourself, "There's no place like home, there's no place like home." Trust me, Dorothy knows about these things.

We will end with a few beautiful lines that seemed to speak to our journey. They are from a much longer poem entitled "Uprising" by G. Winston James.

I want us to shatter the windows of heaven
With diamonds
To assemble before the throne of God
Dressed in the stars
And holding the planets in our hands
Asking the angels simply:
Are we not beautiful . . .

chapter 9

·

I CAN'T BELIEVE I WROTE THE WHOLE THING

If I just work when the spirit moves me, the spirit will ignore me.

—Anaïs Nin

I Can't Believe I Wrote the Whole Thing

But I did. That's how I know you can do whatever it is you really want to do. If someone had told me that I could turn in an almost 500-page manuscript, I would have had thought they were absolutely out of their minds. In college, I winced at the thought of a 5-page term paper. But that's what this book is all about, isn't it? Belief in your spirit, in your creative abilities, in your power to transform, to do what needs doing.

Soul Between the Lines has been a test of everything I believe in. I have passed that test with flying colors. Now that this book has been completed, I am going to resume work on my novel *Tamarindo*. It's been great to have you as a traveling companion on these many journeys.

Remember, be sure to do your preparation ritual, and give yourself at least five minutes a day for your freewriting, if you do nothing else. Think of ways to use your time creatively— between returned phone calls, sitting on a subway, waiting in the line at a bank, having lunch at your desk, right before you go to sleep, right after you wake up, sitting in the bathroom, or standing in the shower (think about writing).

Take a piece of paper and pen wherever you go. Write down your thoughts, dreams, poems, fragments of life, images you want to capture, sketches of sounds that have no home yet. Surround yourself with people who believe in you, people who will kick you back onto the wagon when you fall off.

Dedicate each day to your craft, to your spirit, to your ability to heal yourself as sharpen your skills. Let this be the year your dreams come true. I want to leave you with this quote until the next time I peek at you again from the pages of my heart: "When distractions overcome desires, dreams are shattered. If you let your desires overcome your distractions, then your dreams will come true."